Grandmothering

FAMILIUS

Familius books are available at special discounts for bulk purchases, whether for sales promotions or for family or corporate use. For more information, contact Familius Sales at 559-876-2170 or email orders@familius.com.

Library of Congress Cataloging-in-Publication Data
2017959531

Print ISBN 9781945547904
Ebook ISBN 9781641700467

Printed in the United States of America

Edited by Leah Welker
Cover design by David Miles
Book design by Brooke Jorden

10 9 8 7 6 5 4 3 2 1

First Edition

Grandmothering

The Secrets to Making a Difference While Having the Time of Your Life

NEW YORK TIMES #1 BESTSELLING AUTHOR

LINDA EYRE

To my mother, Hazel Jacobson, who is my beloved hero . . .

To my mother-in-law, Ruth Eyre, who gave me my extraordinary husband . . .

To my daughters and daughters-in-law, whose expert help kept me sane . . .

To my favorite (and only) sister, whose genes I share and who embraces adversity . . .

To all my grandmothers, who passed me their "molten gold" . . .

To my treasured friends, who have contributed their stellar ideas to this book . . .

To Inklings, who initiate, calculate, and stimulate . . .

To my grandchildren, for their delightful deliveries of love . . .

. . . this book is for you.

Contents

Chapter 4: The Importance of a Strong Family Culture | 87

Chapter 5: Adding In-Laws and Babies | 115

Chapter 6: When Things Go Wrong | 143

Having the Time of Your Life!

N o one can fully describe the exhilaration of holding that first grandbaby in your arms! The baby of your baby, fresh from heaven. There lies joy and rapture, anticipation and wonder, along with some worry about what the future will hold for that precious bundle! But for grandmothers, the inevitable ups and downs are all wrapped up in a big beautiful sphere of adventure called "having the time of your life."

It is said that "parenting is an investment and grandparenting is the return on the investment." Taking that one step further, how much time and thought and effort we invest in grandmothering can eventually produce substantial returns. Maybe we don't start out thinking about leaving a legacy to these beautiful little people who bring so much light to our lives. As time goes on, though, we realize that the legacy that we leave to our grand-children probably won't end with a monument built of brick or stone or even a bronze plaque dedicated in our honor. What we leave will be invisible. It will be a monument of love and under-standing and integrity and courage inside their minds and hearts that will stand forever.

I have recently realized that most of us are going to be grand-mothers much longer than we were mothers with children in our homes. Hover over your life as a grandmother for a moment. Look down from above and, as you see yourself with your pres-ent and future grandchildren, ask yourself these questions: *How do I maximize my time with my grandchildren? Do they know how much I love them? Am I teaching them about our family narrative? Do I spend quality one-on-one time with them if they live near me, or do I communicate frequently enough even if they live far away? Am I thinking about actively teaching them, or am I just tending them? What will they remember about me? How do I become a champion for each one? Am I remembering to have fun? What leg-acy do I want to leave that will help light the path ahead of them in this jarring but joyful world?* These are sobering questions that we'll ponder together as you read on.

I've learned that, try as I might, I can't find one grandchild who is exactly like another one, even our identical twin grandsons. When all our children were home and people asked me about our family, I would I say, "We have nine children . . . one of every kind!" Little did I know that there were many, many more "kinds" which would later show up in our grandchildren. The diversity that comes with these little people is divine! At the moment of this writing, we have thirty-one precious grandchildren. Each has unique gifts and unique problems. Some grandchildren are dreamy and artistic, some are balls of fire, some are quiet and reflective, and the others are about everything in between. All have gorgeous gifts and sometimes intense issues. And each one is dearly loved. As Anne Morrow Lindbergh said, "Only love can be divided endlessly and still not be diminished."

Grandmotherhood is a time of ripening. I love this quote as it applies to grandmothers:

"The thing you are ripening toward is the fruit of your life. It will make you bright inside, no matter what you are outside. It is a shining thing."—Stewart Edward White

The grandmothers' learning curve is slow and mellow, unlike the refiners' fire that we felt as young mothers. We are getting better, and even though we're a bit "wrinkled up," we can shine!

The nice thing is that we are usually no longer responsible for the nitty-gritty, everyday discipline and character building of these children. But the secret is that we are still able to teach them the values we hold dear. They may not snatch it right up and say thanks, but they will remember more than we realize if we make deliberate efforts to teach them about the meaningful and magical things of life. And looking to the far distant future, our example of love and care and encouragement will almost surely make *them* better grandparents.

Sadly, just when we think we deserve to relax and enjoy life, we may be thinking more about aching backs and creaky knees than we'd like to. Even though we sometimes can't remember what we just came up the stairs for and our sight may be getting fuzzy, we can more clearly see solutions to problems with wisdom beyond what we could have imagined when we were young. In fact, we sometimes feel that we have the solution to many of our granchildren's problems if someone were to ask, right?

Being a grandmother is no walk in the park! Life and relationships become complicated. We may be dealing with a nasty divorce of one of our children, a grandchild with serious medical or emotional issues, or even a grandchild that seems to be lost to drugs. But surviving those sometimes-grueling trials elevates us and makes us stronger in ways that only come with age. Like it or not, those experiences produce a plentiful supply of wisdom and understanding, even "beauty for ashes" (Isaiah 63:1 KJV).

No matter what our circumstances are with our grandchildren, we can make a difference in their lives! Whether we live next door or halfway around the world, we can be an influence for good in the lives of our grandchildren in ways that they sometimes won't get until we are gone.

We can love them unconditionally and with abandon. As the clever Erma Bombeck said, "A grandmother loves you from when you are a bald baby until you are a bald father and all the hair in between." One of the best secrets about grandmothering is that the love we give to our grandchildren they so freely give back to us—love that is filled with delight! Our daughter Saydi transcribed this message straight from the mouth of her three-year-old, who was too young to write and send it to me: "Dear Grammie, I like your face. I like your cheeks. I like to kiss and cuddle them. Love, Emmeline."

I am grateful for the many brilliant, creative mothers and grandmothers, friends, and family members who have added their own secrets as well as their unique depth and breadth of experiences (and recipes) to this book! Hopefully these ideas will add to the unique plans you already have and cheer you on to your joyful journey of creating a legacy and making a difference while having the time of your life!

Note: What a joy it is to write books in a time when I can not only describe ideas and events but also show them to you in living color through the wonders of the internet. Simplified web addresses are available throughout this book!

CHAPTER 1

Our Journey

Luckily, We Are All Different

To be honest, writing this book was pretty daunting! There are so many stellar grandmothers out there who are better and more knowledgeable than I am! Some are farther down the grandmothering path and have creative ideas far beyond mine, while others are just starting their journey. Writing books to mothers who are scrambling for good ideas is one thing. Writing to grandmothers who already have years of experience is different.

I have been a grandmother for twenty years, and my grandchildren live all over creation, from Utah to Zurich, from Boston to New York City, from California to Arizona, and from London to Hawaii. Our oldest grandson lives in Taiwan. Others of you may have all your children on the same cul-de-sac! As a result,

Let's start our journey together through this book with the understanding that every grandmother's life and situation is unique.

some of the stories and ideas you will find in this book may sound a little bit crazy to you. My family does have a lot of bodies. There will be fifty-one at our annual reunion this year. Still, I am only about halfway down my path of grandmothering. Some of our older friends have astounding numbers in their progeny, including lots of great-grandchildren. For others, their first grandchild just arrived!

Let's start our journey together through this book with the understanding that every grandmother's life and situation is unique. Even our titles are different. Just in our own extended family, we have a plethora of "Grandmas," attached to their first or last name, but we also have one "Nana" and one "Luvy." For some of you, your name is the result of the first thing that came out of your first grandchild's mouth; for others, the chosen name is something totally unrelated to the word *grandma* but is a name your grandchildren cherish. In our family, I am called "Grammie."

For those of you who are just starting your journey. I heard a young grandmother say, "It's amazing how grandparents seem so young—once you become one." Some of you don't have the luxury of a grandfather at your side because of a divorce or a death and are "going it alone." If you are living with a spouse, your spouse will be different too! Sometimes very different! Ha! Some of you are married for the second time and are juggling new grandchildren in an effort to blend both sides of the family. And what about you grandmothers who are helping your children with their adopted or foster children, or who are keeping grandchildren grounded after a divorce? Many of you grandmothers still have part- or full-time jobs. Some of you probably have single kids still at home, along with the ones who have flown the nest. And of course, there are lots of your kids who have flown the nest and come back to roost for a while, which may mean that you have grandchildren living in your home.

In addition, a growing group of women are pining for any grandchildren at all, or at least a few more of that precious commodity, as our society puts less and less emphasis on bringing children into the world. Other women are overwhelmed with a multitude of grandchildren. Some spend many hours every day caring for grandchildren while mothers and fathers work, or the grandmothers may even have legal guardianship over the grandkids and are doing their best to raise them as a parent would. And let's not forget those wonderful aunts who don't have genetic children but love and nurture children as though they are their own. Even if they aren't related by blood, sometimes a child needs a "grandparent figure" in their lives to give them love and security in an difficult world.

Other issues are also vastly different! Some have abundant financial resources to share, while others have been widows for a long time or are barely able provide for themselves. Some grandmas have all their grandchildren living within walking distance and see them almost every day, while others have grandchildren halfway across the world and are lucky if they get to see them once a year. Some glory in every minute they are together with their grandchildren, and others feel really happy to see the taillights of the family car after several days together. (And most of us feel some of both.) Some had fabulous grandmothers of their own and are replicating their example, while others may never or have barely known their grandmothers. One friend told me that her grandmother was "downright mean!"

One of my dearest friends claims that she doesn't feel that she is a really great grandma right now. She and her husband are on a full-time church mission with an enormous responsibility to care for those who are most needy, and she is at a place in life where she can't spend a lot of time with her grandchildren. She, of course, is beloved by her grandchildren, and she has what Stephen Covey calls "an emotional bank account," which means that she has previously deposited a huge amount of time and love into her grandchildren, a wealth they can draw on until she has more time to spend with them.

As grandmothers, we also have varying levels of faith and devotion to religion. I felt as though this book would not be complete or as personal as I wish it to be without references to my own faith. I am a devoted Christian, and many of our family traditions and certainly much of our family narrative relate to our faith, as is the case with so many of you who will read this book. Still, I have tried to write in a way that will relate to all grandmothers, regardless of your beliefs.

Yes, we are all different, but we are also all in the same boat. We all have a common thread. We all have grandchildren of some sort, and we are on a journey to do our best to love them, guide them, nurture them, and cheer them on. Because of that common bond, I feel that I am talking to friends. No matter how different our lives are, we are all on this journey together. As you read on, I hope this feels more like a letter to a friend than a book!

I will be throwing out many thoughts and ideas from my perspective. Get ready for a

No matter how different our lives are, we are all on this journey together. As you read on, I hope this feels more like a letter to a friend than a book!

smorgasbord of ideas. But please don't feel guilty if you can't "eat it all." Some of them might work for you. Some of them will seem preposterous. Others will be things that you've already thought of and done more successfully than I have. Sometimes you'll think, *I could teach her a thing or two!* But in any case, just sit back and relax and pick and choose ideas that sound delicious to you.

Since I can't get feedback from you directly and every grandmother's life is different, I solicited ideas from a wonderful group of friends who are terrific grandmas. They represent different views, different thoughts, different trials, and different passions but all have stimulating ideas as we think together about how to be more deliberate grandmothers.

To add value to what you will read, at the end of most sections in the book, there is a **Thoughts?** prompt that will hopefully stimulate your own ideas about what has been said. Since you are the only expert on your own particular situation as a grandmother, there is a space for you to jot down your thoughts and ideas as you ponder the questions or challenges at the end of each section. Fill the space however you wish. You might want to include symbols or illustrations that remind you of your thoughts. Hopefully you will use your thoughts as a "journal" to record your present grandmothering life. Here is the first example.

Thoughts?

- What makes your circumstances as a grandmother unique?
- How can you make those differences your strengths?

The Joys of Growing Older

Having grandchildren also means that we are growing older! I remember when our first-married daughter Shawni announced that she was pregnant. I was at once thrilled and devastated! Overjoyed, I pictured Shawni fulfilling her dream of cuddling a newborn baby on her shoulder and feeling those sweet, tiny, uneven breaths on her neck. She had always wanted to be a mother, and I was dazzled at the thought that she would finally be able to experience the astonishing (including hard-beyond-description and magical-beyond-understanding) world of motherhood. But then there was the other part. Suddenly, I felt old! Weren't grandmothers supposed to be old people with bifocals and walkers? How could I be old enough to be a grandmother?

I was lucky enough to be in the delivery room when that first grandbaby emerged into the world. After Shawni's wild, whirlwind delivery, not unlike my own nine deliveries, I had a glorious week together with that new little family as I ate up little Max and helped Shawni and David to acclimate to their 24/7 life as new parents.

A couple of months later, Shawni flew home with that precious first grandbaby and, exhilarated, I picked her up from the airport. Max was firmly strapped in his crazy-huge car seat that takes the space of one and a half adults, and I was delighted to sit in the backseat and go "gah gah" over him on the way home. As we pulled into the driveway, I heard Shawni say to wide-eyed baby boy, "Here we are at Grandma's house!" My first thought was: *Is Grandma in there?* It almost took my breath away when I suddenly realized that this was not my mom's house or Richard's mom's house. This was my house—*and I was the Grandma!* The light dawned on me that my life had changed forever!

Twenty years have passed since that day. Just as the gravity of being a mother slowly settled into my mind, now comes the gravity and responsibility of being a grandmother! And along with grandchildren comes the inevitability of growing older. Even though I still feel young, at least in my mind, I'm getting ready to have a knee replaced, and sometimes I have to rock a couple of times to get out of a low chair. Ha!

Even though I don't feel *that* old, I now have grandchildren who know how to bring me abruptly to reality! While visiting with our Boston family a few years ago, four-year-old Peter, grandchild #20, was sitting beside me in the car inspecting my hands. He asked why those blue veins were standing up so high on the backs of my hands. I started to explain that my mom had veins just like that, but before I got through the first sentence, he had already figured out the answer. With a knowing smile, he looked up at me and said in his cute Boston accent, "It's just because you're soupah-old."

"True, Peter. True!"

On another rather "painfully old" birthday, I had just flown into NYC from Zurich, and our son Eli was waiting in a car with his darling four-year-old daughter Zara to surprise me. She was stuffed in the backseat with a congregation of purple balloons (my favorite color) to celebrate my big day. After wild birthday greetings, we started on our way back to their five-story walk-up in Manhattan. As we rode into the NYC traffic, Zara leaned over and began staring at my neck through her little purple glasses. She wrinkled up her nose with curiosity and asked, "Why is your skin all squashed together?" I burst out laughing. I knew exactly what she meant! Oh, the pure, clean, brutal honesty of children!

Although I know that some of you may still be in your forties and fifties, getting older can be stunning. Like the first time we realize we can't see telephone numbers that we've always seen before. Almost overnight, it seems, we need reading glasses. But that is just the beginning. We are terrified when we can't remember names (even though we can usually remember the first letter).

It's actually breathtaking when you suddenly realize that you can't sit cross legged to play with your grandchildren anymore and it takes a while to stand all the way up from the floor.

It's actually breathtaking when you suddenly realize that you can't sit cross legged to play with your grandchildren anymore and it takes a while to stand all the way up from the floor.

I have been in a delightfully stimulating book club for over twenty-five years. We have had fascinating discussions; we have also commiserated about the tribulations and triumphs of our children from the time they were born and have rejoiced over the milestones of our families. As time went on, we empathized about the trials of menopause, worried together about our "issues," and celebrated the successes of our children and grandchildren. About twelve of us show up consistently every month (except the summer months) to talk about a good book and our lives at the moment. This was a prolific group when it came to children. Once we counted up our progeny. Amazingly, the average number of children per mother was six or seven. Through the years, we have served as a huge group of cheerleaders for each other.

Both while and after raising our families, we have all tried to embrace opportunities to give back. Two women have served on extensive medical missions in third-world countries to teach medical staffs how to save newborn babies. One has served with her husband mentoring inmates at the state penitentiary. Many have served our church members and missionaries all over the world as well as large numbers of needy families and refugees in our community. They are writers and thinkers, full of stimulating ideas, and have been contributed great ideas to this book. Each is a little miracle and a marvelous grandmother!

All have great senses of humor. We usually meet for lunch and then take turns leading a discussion on a recent favorite book. Last year we were talking about the perils of growing older. Our hostess just happened to have a small book sitting on her coffee table entitled *The Joys of Getting Older*, which she said she really liked. The endorsement at the top of the cover said, "An inspirational look at the beauty found within the Circle of Life."

This was the endorsement:

"A straightforward, clear-cut how-to book for putting a spark (or two!) back into your life. It truly describes the magical beauty to be found in the twilight years."
—Yule Biyung, author and inspirational speaker

We didn't get the joke until we opened the book. The pages were totally blank! We collectively burst out laughing! It was worth the $5.99 it cost for the joke!

When we quit laughing, one of our book club members seriously suggested that in response to that book, we go around the table and each contribute what we as empty nesters *do* love about growing older. Here is our list:

- My progeny: children and grandchildren. Watching them grow and having fun with them.
- Time.
- The chance to be reflective.
- Being able to plan my own schedule.
- Feeling closer to my husband. Now I am his partner and his defendant.
- Freedom.
- Changing . . . I can think of ways to finally really change and improve.
- Gaining more knowledge. I am building on existing information.

- Discovering the real purpose of life.
- Learning to be a thoughtful matriarch.
- Experiencing simplicity.
- Having time to count my blessings every day.
- Becoming less critical and more empathetic.
- Feeling the power of friends supporting each other.
- Being a cheerleader for my posterity.
- Seeing the fruits of my labors.
- Cutting out things that aren't important.
- Realizing that age is liberating.
- Focusing on things that are really important.
- Seeing dreams fulfilled.
- Finding time for family history.
- Being an influence in the background.
- Having more time for siblings.
- Making life a refining time.
- Having more time for friends, whom I feel are sisters.
- Being peers with my daughters and daughters-in-law.
- Having time to think about each precious soul in my care.

Even though our book club relishes many things about growing older, some are facing difficult physical issues with back or knee injuries. Some have family members with serious health problems like cancer, dementia, and even Alzheimer's (we have already lost one of our dearest book club members to that devastating disease). Still, we all remain optimistic that there are multiple things that we love about this stage of our lives.

I have loved this quote since I was a young mother and find it even more important now as I deal with the ups and downs, joys and crises of grandmothering:

"The greater part of our happiness or misery depends on our disposition, and not our circumstances. We carry the seeds of the one or the other about with us in our minds wherever we go."—Martha Washington

Thoughts?

- In the space below, create a list of the things you love about growing older. Do it with your friends, your husband, or even your children.
- Make a note in your journal or on your phone to remind yourself of how much fun you're having!

Life Is Long

When our children panic about a stage their kids are going through, I remind them that I disagree with the old adage that "life is short!" As I looked back in time to write this chapter, I realize that my position is true—life is long! Twenty years flies by. But what happens in between takes a long time! Interestingly, sometimes we go from one stage to another so slowly that we hardly realize that we have moved on. Your distraught daughter with a colicky baby finally gets what you had to do to survive . . . when *she* was the colicky baby! Whiny children often become responsible adults . . . in time. Super-messy, right-brained kids usually become smart, creative adults . . . in time. Strong-willed, hard-to-deal-with teenagers more often than not look back and realize how crazy and difficult they were and regret the angst they caused you . . . in time.

I wish we were all clever enough to write a book to rival Dr. Seuss's *Oh, the Places You'll Go!* with one called *Oh, the Places I've Been!* I hope you will indulge me as I take a short journey back through my life. My husband and I are getting ready to celebrate fifty years of marriage, and that is l-o-n-g! If this sounds about as interesting as watching someone's home movies, feel free to skip this part.

Our first two years together were spent in Boston while Richard got his MBA at the Harvard Business School and I taught music at a junior high. From there we moved to Washington, DC, where Richard had a demanding job managing statewide senatorial, congressional, and gubernatorial campaigns across the country that required his being away from home four days a week while I held down the fort at home. I was a young mother

> Life is long! Twenty years flies by. But what happens in between takes a long time!

with three kids under four. Life was very long then, and the days were slow! My days were crammed with crying children, dirty diapers, and adorable antics! I thought that life was going to last forever.

By the time we had been married for seven years and had four children, ages five to eleven months, we were asked by leaders of our church (The Church of Jesus Christ of Latter-day Saints) to go to London to supervise missionaries there for three years. I had never crossed an ocean and was a bit daunted about this new "calling," which became quite an astonishing adventure. Over those years, there was never a dull moment as we loved being part of the lives of over five hundred dedicated young men and women. I was twenty-nine and Richard was thirty-one when we left. We had two more babies while we were there. The first one, Jonah, was born via emergency C-section, nine weeks early at 3 pounds, 13 ounces because of placenta previa. It was 1977, before they knew much about how to save preemies. Combined faith and prayers of the whole mission saved the life of our now 6'6" giant of a soul. The next baby, Talmadge, arrived twenty months later with a beautiful, wise, and calm spirit, and he fit into the chaos with hardly a murmur!

When we returned to the United States, we started writing in earnest, and a couple of serendipitous events happened. Our book *Teaching Your Children Joy* spawned an international organization that eventually involved 200,000 parents in Joy Schools, and our book *Teaching Your Children Values* catapulted to #1 on the *New York Times* bestseller list thanks to Oprah Winfrey, who had Richard, me, and six of our children on her show for a whole hour.

To make a long story short, we become full-time writers (in addition to being full-time parents). Because all we needed was some paper and pens (this was before computers), we realized that we wanted to make life with a gaggle of kids a great adventure, so we began to explore the world as much as possible while those kids were still with us. We had lots of frequent flyer miles from previous book tours, so we spent summers in Japan, the Philippines, and Mexico; we built a log cabin from scratch in the wild wilderness of Oregon; and we made vast numbers of memories at Bear Lake, where we had a little mountain cabin in Southeastern Idaho where I grew up.

Richard and I wrote books together during that time, mostly to survive our kids. When we had six kids under ten, I wrote *I Didn't Plan to Be a Witch*, which pretty much captured the essence of my life with that merry mob. As our seventh child joined our family, I began to realize that my time with the kids at home was getting shorter. Loving even the mayhem, I wrote *A Joyful Mother of Children*.

We struggled through the exciting but crazy school years of volatile friendships, bullying, kids running for office and winning as well as running for office and losing. I mourned with a daughter who didn't make dance company in high school and rejoiced with her when she made it after another year of hard work. We had kids who were desperate for friends and those who were saturated with friends. An extremely accident-prone son, who happened to be the same one who was born nine weeks early, was attacked by two Dobermans on a hot summer day and may have lost his life if a good Samaritan had not happened to come by to rescue him. Just before his sixteenth birthday, he was hit by a car on his way to high school and ended up with two mangled legs, which are still not pretty! But those hard times created a beautiful soul.

I thought I would be done with all those hard experiences when the children flew the nest. What I didn't realize was that mothering doesn't end when the children leave. The thrills get more exciting, and the difficult gets different. It gets bigger and better . . . and more expensive!

As kids prepared to leave home over the next fifteen years, there was a long era of opening envelopes with sweaty palms and racing hearts to read what their future would hold after laboring for months over college applications. There was a lot of rejoicing with acceptances and mourning over rejections as each child saw their future after high school begin with the words in those envelopes.

Mothering doesn't end when the children leave. The thrills get more exciting, and the difficult gets different. It gets bigger and better ... and more expensive!

Maybe an even more breathtaking envelope-opening experience happened with another important decision that our children made. They gathered their courage, wrestled with the alternatives, got answers to their prayers, and each in their own way decided to serve as missionaries for our church. Those envelopes held the names of the places that they would be serving for the next era of their lives. They knew they might be sent anywhere from across the state line to across the world. The boys left at age nineteen for two years (usually after their first year of college), and the girls left at age twenty-one for eighteen months. Saren went to Bulgaria, Shawni to Romania, Saydi to Spain, and Charity to England (our same mission). Two of the boys also went back to London (Josh and Jonah), Talmadge served in Brazil, Noah in Chile, and our youngest son, Eli, went to Japan. It was a marvelous experience for them to leave the minutiae of their ordinary lives and learn not only to be totally self-reliant but also to lose themselves and then find themselves through teaching and service as they gained a deep love for Jesus Christ.

To add to the dilemmas that young adults face, those who had returned from missions and graduated from undergraduate universities were struggling to decide about graduate schools and always looking for jobs beyond the make-do jobs they had to have to get their degrees. Some were able to fall into great jobs. Others, try as they might, couldn't find a job, and sometimes even when they did, they hated it and were in search of better ones!

Exciting engagement stories began to occur quite consistently. When Noah was sixteen, we went on a humanitarian trip to South America, which ended with a climb to the top of the mountain above Machu Picchu in Peru. Right then he decided that magnificent spot at the top of the world was going to be the place where he was going to propose marriage to his future wife. He wrote a proposal on a piece of paper, stuffed it in a bottle, and buried it there. We wished him luck when he told us his plan. Sure enough, eight years later, he was standing on that mountaintop again, proposing to his one and only Kristi! There was quite a bit of competition to match that story as engagements ensued.

Then joyful weddings began to dominate our lives—not without considerable angst, in many cases, about the choice of spouse. One couple called it off three times (which caused a lot of heartbreak) before deciding that they were meant for each other. Our kids' marriage ages ranged from twenty-three to thirty, and one is still looking! We had not only beautiful wedding ceremonies but also the inevitable hoopla of the clothes, the invitations, the flowers, the food, the receptions, the disasters, the wedding dinners, the wedding breakfasts, the send-offs, the honeymoons, and then real life and the decisions of where to live and how to get jobs to support themselves.

I must admit that when the last of our nine children left home for college, emotionally I was on a broad spectrum, vacillating between devastation and delight. I was sad to see all those crazy, wild, frustrating, and joyful days of having a gaggle of kids and their friends saturating our home endlessly come to an end. But

I was delighted at the prospect of sending them off and spreading my wings after many years of refining and life-training as a mother.

I must say that I have had the opportunity to catch up with my dreams during those empty-nest grandmothering years. I even took an art class.

I must say that I have had the opportunity to catch up with my dreams during those empty-nest grandmothering years. I even took an art class.

Although we had done a lot of speaking to parents about raising kids based on our mulititude of parenting books while the kids were home, now that the kids were gone, we started to travel in earnest. We circled the globe six times with the international Young Presidents Organization (YPO). They are a group of extraordinary people who became presidents of their own companies (with a required number of employees and yearly revenue) before turning forty. They and their spouses are proactive parents who are eager to do the best job they can to create responsible, self-motivated children who are ready to contribute to the world. That, along with worldwide travel with The Entrepreneur's Organization and international schools, associations, churches, and businesses, has given us such a fascinating and dazzling dive into a world of more than fifty countries and a seemingly endless array of different cultures and religions.

Our first world tour from September 2004 to March 2005 took us to Tokyo, Kyoto, Hong Kong, Kuala Lumpur, Manila, Bangkok, Singapore, Jakarta, Bali, Seoul, Shanghai, Madras, New Delhi, Agra/Jaipur, Dubai, Oman, Bahrain, Cairo, and several Caribbean islands. Now that was my idea of a dream year!

In those fifteen years, we tallied up about two million miles on airplanes, and I loved every minute of it! I *love* airplanes.

Especially when traveling *without* little children! No one can call you and ask you to do things. You can read and write and think and even watch a movie or two uninterrupted.

Our worldwide travels have led us to diverse and marvelous friends. As we have been immersed in their cultures, we have grown to love and respect our new friends' strong faiths that have created strong families. We loved what we learned about the family life of Muslims, Hindus, Sikhs, Jews, Buddhists, and fellow Christians. We have felt in some cases that that they are far ahead of us in demonstrating their devotion and using that faith to create strong families. We have also admired families whose faith is based in their family culture; they have raised beautiful families, some who say they are spiritual but not religious and others who are not spiritual at all but are faithful in raising stellar families. We salute them all for the inspiration they have been to us!

Thinking through that part of our lives, even though it was just a short synopsis, has made me remember again that life is very long! Several lifetimes have occurred in that almost fifty years, not counting our very long lives up until Richard and I met. Life must be long because it takes a long time to produce the wrinkles that life has somehow provided for my face!

I have loved this quote since I was a young mother, and like it even better as a grandmother:

> *"Life is not a journey to the grave with the intention of arriving safely in a pretty and well-preserved piece, but rather to skid in broadside, thoroughly used up, totally worn out, and loudly proclaiming, 'WOW! WHAT A RIDE!'"—Anonymous*

Thoughts?

- If you have not already, write a synopsis of the years of your marriage to share with your grandchildren. They may not know many of the details that you will tell, and they will treasure them in the future.
- Do you record the cute things that your grandkids say immediately? You may think you'll never forget those hilarious little quips, but you probably will unless they are documented!

Taking Care of the Grandfather

For those of you who still have spouses . . .

What excitement and joy we had bringing nine children into the world! Actually, I did most of the "bringing in," but Richard was a great partner in "bringing up." He was a terrific helper with the children when he was home, even though he has never really learned how to turn on the clothes dryer or the dishwasher. Among other things, he was a marvelous bedtime storyteller and was extraordinarily good at teaching children to set and accomplish goals.

I can guarantee that not every day of that journey has been a great big bundle of joy! Richard and I approach every situation from entirely different places and have conflicting ideas about how to do most everything. But we soon realized that we synergized well and that our combined views brought better results. We learned that the challenging times bring joy, maybe even more than the pleasant, easy times, as we honed our relationship. Even though there were days when I wondered if I could go on, the rewards of struggling to create our partnership were excellent, exciting, and abundant along the way.

> **We learned that the challenging times bring joy, maybe even more than the pleasant, easy times, as we honed our relationship.**

Often, those years had a lot of moments of putting the kids' needs before Richard's. While I knew that Richard was my first priority, there were times when the children's needs eclipsed his. While our older children were off producing grandchildren, we still had children at home for many years, so the distractions of life were abundant. When the nest emptied, it was hard to remember that I now had the luxury of putting Richard firmly back into the #1 slot.

We are both still busily engaged in many important issues and projects that take our time and energy. We are still writing, traveling, and speaking and trying to keep up with our expanding family. So the challenge is still finding time away from the phone responsibilities and the internet for each other. I have to keep reminding myself that even though our children and grandchildren still occupy a lot of time, my most important occupation is taking care of their father and grandfather.

I must admit that there are some real challenges in living with a "grandfather" (which has been his chosen title ever since our first grandson called him "Gamfadder"). When I was a kid and my parents were growing older (they were a generation older than most parents), they were often annoyed at each other because they had to repeat everything they said as they became hard of hearing. Irritation filled the air when that happened, and I promised myself that would never happen to me. Richard claims that he has absolutely perfect hearing, but he began having me repeat almost everything that I said. I was frustrated! I became a little less irritated when my children also asked me to repeat what I said. I wondered if my soft voice could possibly be part of the problem. Ha! I'm working on canning the irritation and speaking louder.

What I love about Richard is his great ideas—which is also what drives me crazy! He has too many ideas! It is dangerous to send him off alone on a long trip because he comes back with a bundle of new ideas when we already have way too many! When for some reason we have to take two cars somewhere and I am following him, I always know when he's getting an idea because he slows down. His mind never stops creating new ideas.

Another thing I love about Richard is his passion for adventure! But what makes that challenging is that he can't stay in one place for more than a few days without wanting to go somewhere else. It took me a few years to realize that the things that sometimes irritate me about Richard are also the things that I love most about him!

It seems that "the grandfather'" has abundant idiosyncrasies which are becoming magnified as he ages, while I, of course, am perfect! I won't go into detail, but needless to say, there is some exasperation on both our parts as we are getting older. But they are dramatically outweighed bu the joy of our ever-growing oneness.

I heard a story told by our friend Craig Zwick at a church conference.[1] He spoke about a wife who was bothered by little things that her husband did, and in an effort to help him understand what had been bothering her, she started keeping a list of things that had irritated her on her phone so that at the right time she could share them and he could see what he was doing and change his ways. One day while pondering over her list, the thought occurred to her that documenting his mistakes was never going to change him. He already pretty much knew what she had written anyway. She realized that they did need to work through some things in their partnership, but she knew that she should get rid of her list, as it would only cause contention. She said, "It took me a while to hit 'select ALL' and even longer to hit 'DELETE!'" That story made me smile because I have to admit that I've made these lists many times (at least, in my mind). :)

Still, expressing negative feelings in a marriage is important to do in the right way and at the right time, which I have to say has not always been my strong suit. Richard and I disagree on most of the details of when, where, why, and how to do things, and we both think that our solutions are the right ones! There have been some pretty wild arguments. Luckily, we are also pretty good communicators. When the water gets a little muddy, we have learned to share our feelings in what we call a partnership meeting that we always try to have briefly on Sundays. We are determined to be one in

When we agree to disagree, we think of ourselves as one entity with two parts that together create a circle, parts that compliment and compensate for each other's strengths and weaknesses.

our marriage. That doesn't mean that we don't each have our ideas and opinions, our personalities and our character traits, but it does mean that even when we agree to disagree, we think of ourselves as one entity with two parts that together create a circle, parts that compliment and compensate for each other's strengths and weaknesses. It's a challenge, but that paradigm has saved us from disaster many times!

Lately I've realized how important it is to remember my spouse's love language.[2] Most of you probably know what your spouse's love language is. If not, you'll immediately recognize which of these five things below is important to you and which is important to your spouse:

- Words of affirmation
- Quality time
- Receiving gifts
- Acts of service
- Physical touch

Perhaps an even better list of things to help us remember to truly love "the grandfather" is found in the New Testament as the Apostle Paul talks about the importance of charity. Check yourself with this list of attributes of those who are truly loved as it applies to our spouses.

Charity:

1. suffereth long,
2. is kind,
3. envieth not,
4. vaunteth not itself,
5. is not puffed up,
6. doth not behave itself unseemly,
7. seeketh not her own,
8. is not easily provoked,
9. thinketh no evil.[3]

It's worth thinking about how to keep the flame of love and appreciation alive as we get older. It is not only important for us but for our children and our grandchildren to see that we still love and appreciate each other. They need to know that love can last and that their grandparents aren't afraid to show them that!

Thoughts?

- Have you ever created a list of things that irritate you about your husband? Use the space below to make a list of things you love about your husband. It's a good reminder that the things you loved about him when you got married are still there and that sometimes, the things that irritate you most about him are also the reasons you loved him in the first place!
- Do you know your husband's love language and act on it? Do you practice real charity in your actions toward him?
- How often do you show affection or give compliments to your spouse when you are with your children and grandchildren?

Notes

1. General Conference, Sunday morning, October 2017.

2. From *The Five Love Languages* by Gary Chapman. Chicago: Northfield Publishers, 1995.

3. King James Version, 1 Corinthians 13: 4–7.

CHAPTER 2

Grammie Camps and Fun with Small Groups

T here are so many things to talk about when it comes to Grandmothering. As we go forward in this book, it will be interesting to think together about our own familiy culture and the challenges of adding in-laws and the excitement of the birth of our grandbabies and how much advice to give. We will discuss the inevitability of things that go wrong, the need to take care of ourselves, the issue of entitlement that surrounds these following generations, as well as continuting to create time to remember and reunions after they have left home.

But let's start with the really fun part: ideas to create exciting and memorable times with our grandchildren now!

Little fleeting moments and brief contacts are one thing, but we all know that great moments with children often come while spending large chunks of time with them, having fun and creating memories.

A grandmother who loves capturing moments with her grandchildren shared the following:

> I've kept a "journal" of special moments with each of my grandchildren. One of my favorite moments was when I stayed a few days with Ashley and her children. We went on adventures to the museums, [to the] tumbling gym, hiking, and playing at the house with toys and puzzles and anything they wanted. When it was time to go, I went to my room to pack. When I came upstairs to leave through the front door, Johanna had barricaded the door so I couldn't leave. She had pulled the piano bench in front of the door and grabbed anything else she could find to pile on it so I wouldn't leave.

Speaking of moments, I have to say that being with grandkids when the mom is there is one thing. Taking care of them without the parents is another thing altogether! Preschoolers, especially, take a lot of energy! In fact, I kind of forgot about how much time and energy it takes to take care of two dynamite little preschoolers, even though I promised myself that I never would! A couple of years ago, we were excited to take care of our two youngest (at the time) grandchildren for nine days while their parents went on a vacation they had won. Zara was three, and Dean was nine months. We had so much fun with paper dolls and dress-ups and the zoo and the grocery store and the park, which took a lot of time buckling up in the car. (That always made me long for those days when we just tossed our kids in the big stretch van before the days of seatbelts and off we'd go. But I digress.)

Dean had a nasty cough and couldn't sleep, so we couldn't either. Every other night, Richard and I took turns getting up to comfort him until he could quit coughing. Zara was up at 6 a.m. for the day and was like a super ball, bouncing off the walls, and was more entertaining than a circus performance! Zara and I made cookies one morning. After carefully putting the flour and sugar in our industrial-size mixer, she somehow found the on/off switch while I wasn't looking and turned it on high. I looked like Olaf, the snowman from *Frozen*.

By the end of nine days, Richard and I were exhausted! I have to say that my favorite moment was when the parents burst through the door with open arms to take those adorable kids home!

Let me say upfront that I have been working on the ideas for this chapter for fifteen years. Those who are "beginning grand-mothers" may find some fun ideas here to bond with your grandkids and help them bond with each other as they grow.

Others of you who are older may be too tired or too old or may think you are already with them too much! I say, "Do what works!" You can simplify or you can elaborate. The hope is to flood you with ideas so that you might find something that will work for you and your grandchildren. Some of you will be way ahead of me and have thought of amazing and creative ideas that I would have loved to include in this chapter!

As our married children began to settle into their lives with our grandchildren, all lived in faraway places (with only one exception), and I began to realize that the only time I would have all the grandkids together during the year was the few days before or after our annual four-day family reunion when everybody comes together at our summer home in Bear Lake, Idaho. I could see that time was flying. The grandkids were growing up fast, and I needed to take advantage of those few precious days we had

The grandkids were growing up fast, and I needed to take advantage of those few precious days we had together.

together; I needed to do something fun and memorable with them while also giving them time in small groups to bond with their cousins. The problem was, I couldn't do it for them all at once. There were too many!

Divide and Conquer

Here's how I got started on "Grammie Camps": As more and more grandchildren joined our family, I was struggling for a way to divide them up into smaller groups so that I could interact more personally with them as well as help them to bond with each other. Feeling a bit overwhelmed, I had to come up with a solution to divide and conquer! One day, I visited a cousin (who is also a grandma) living in Star Valley, Wyoming. She took me to a beautiful wooded space on their large farm with a nice gathering spot and a fantastic swing that her husband had built especially for their grandchildren. She had a few grandchildren at that time who joined her there for "Grandma Camp" in the summer to spend some time with just her . . . alone. I was struck with the importance of what she was doing. It was the perfect way to gather groups of her grandchildren for personal interactions. That day, the idea for "Grammie Camps" was born!

The stories that follow have turned out to be more fun than I had ever imagined! Even though I'm only with each small group for less than twenty-four hours each year, we pack in the fun and excitement as well as work and learning! We all look forward to being with each other every summer. I have to admit that I have had the time of my life!

How we acquired the places for our Reunions and Grammie Camps is in Chapter 10. However, if that doesn't work for you, remember that in the long run, gathering your family in any fashion is one of the most important things you will ever do and is worth whatever it takes to make it happen.

In planning Grammie Camps, I've found that it's important to be flexible. I always try to take into consideration all the different moving parts of a large extended family and make sure we do what makes the most sense for everyone each summer.

I divided the kids into groups according to natural breaks in age and established that the kids needed to be five before they could come. Some groups had three grandchildren; most had four or five. At first, we had only about a dozen grandkids. They named their own group, with just a little help from us. Our oldest three grandchildren were called The Old Faithfuls. The next was a group of three who were all born in the same year and were called The Goonies. Then there was a group of three girls called The Babes and a group of five boys called The Bros. As more five-year-olds moved into the system, we created a group of four little girls named The Princesses.

Although every year is a little different, we usually meet on one of the days just before or after our official four-day reunion in July, depending on when families arrive and when they have to leave. On Grammie Camp day, we start our fun together at what we call the Lighthouse, a small octagon-shaped house that we built on a little hill just above our big family home on the lake.

The Lighthouse was built in 1999 to fulfill a dream of Richard's to have an octagonal *glass* house. (Go figure. It has something to do with Thomas Jefferson.) It is a place where Richard and I stay when we go there; it is full of light, with a wonderful view of the lake. We are so lucky to also have this as a gathering place for Grammie Camps.

The kids are ecstatic when it's their time for Grammie Camp, and when we have sleepovers, they love having breakfast together the next morning.

Having started with three small groups, we then went on to four groups and started combining groups to make it doable. A couple of years ago, we added a one-hour party with what I call "the littles" because the toddlers under five were feeling quite neglected and dejected about not having their "party time."

Grammie Camps are a little different every year. In 2016, we had only a few hours together because I was in London helping with the arrival of Charity's first baby right up until the last minute before the reunion. Usually we have sleepovers at the Lighthouse after we finished our activities. Even though it is a small house with only one big room and two bathrooms, the kids camp out in sleeping bags and have the time of their lives bonding with their cousins. The kids are ecstatic when it's their time for Grammie Camp, and when we have sleepovers, they love having breakfast together the next morning. The older kids have become experts in making crepes, which is now our breakfast tradition.

How It Works

In thinking about the things that I could do to engage the kids at Grammie Camp, I realized that it would be a perfect time to share with them the things that I love and then have them participate in those things—hands on. Our time together also usually includes several of the following, depending on the age group:

Happies and Sads: We always start our meetings with each child telling the happiest and saddest things that have happened to them since the last time we met. We learn a lot about each child as they share the hard and the good things that have happened in their lives that year. There is real empathy and rejoicing as they share their lives.

Talent Show: For years, the "talent" was pretty marginal, but now we are getting some real skills! The talent ranges from great piano and violin solos to amazing demonstrations of the use of the kendama and putting together a Rubik's Cube in one minute flat!

Show and Tell: This year, we had two new pets for kids to show off during show and tell, a goldendoodle named Bo Jangles and a guinea pig named Princess. It was a pretty exciting thing for the kids to show off their new pets to their cousins. The grandkids have also shown their artwork, their favorite toys, and their random inventions.

Work: Since I come from families of hardworking farmers on both sides, I wanted my grandchildren to feel the pleasure of working for a reward. (My parents would love this.) There are always plentiful weeds at Bear Lake, so I usually offer a penny for every weed pulled (five cents for the really big ones). They spend about an hour making money by pulling weeds. It is pretty funny to watch the older kids in the group help the younger kids keep track of their numbers. They are paid immediately, and then we all get in the car and go into Montpelier (my hometown, thirty minutes away) to the dollar store to buy something with their hard-earned cash. The decisions are sometimes painstaking. Other times, it is a joy to see them buy something for a sibling with the money they have earned!

Dancing: The younger groups love to dress up and dance. We have dress-ups for both girls and boys and a place to dance to beautiful music that matches the scenery. There is nothing that shows personality more than dancing to great music!

Fun: The older groups all have great memories of going to a fun melodrama at the Pickleville Playhouse about forty minutes away. It is always a hilarious and creative production about and created by the infamous Juanito Bandito. It has become a memorable Grammie Camp tradition.

Art: I love art, and we have had a great time looking at beautiful classical artwork and then painting Bear Lake in the style of that artist in watercolors (for example, the pointillism of Seurat or the impressionism of Monet and Renoir).

Song: We have a silly camp song that all the kids know about Grammie Camp. We usually sing it in the car on the way to the dollar store or the cemetery looking for ancestors or to dinner at a fast-food place. The second verse goes like this (to the tune of "I Love the Mountains").

> *I love Grammie Camp*
> *I love the things we do*
> *I love to learn about*
> *Ancestors brave and true*
> *I love to work and play*
> *With my cousins too!*
> *Boom de ata, Boom de ata*
> *Boom de ata, Boom de ata*
> *Grammie Camp, Grammie Camp*
> *Grammie Camp, Grammie Camp*
> *YEAH! [shouted]*

Memorization: Memorization is almost a lost art! So a couple of months before Grammie Camp, I like to challenge the kids to do some memorizing for a prize. Some years, they memorize scriptures; other years, they memorize quotes. For the younger kids, the quote or scripture is short and the reward is Gummy Bears. The older kids, who are memorizing longer, deeper things, get something more substantial like a new game or a fun new toy. I have always loved bribery. :)

The prizes are a small incentive, but competition to get it right amongst the cousins has also been fun to watch!

Our all-time favorite quote in our family is from Teddy Roosevelt. Several of our older grandchildren now have this memorized word perfect:

In the battle of life, it is not the critic who counts; not the man who points out how the strong man stumbles, or where the doer of deeds could have done them better. The credit belongs to the man who is actually in the arena, whose face is marred by dust and sweat and blood; who strives valiantly; who errs, who comes short again and again, because there is no effort without error and shortcoming; but who does actually strive to do the deeds; who knows great enthusiasms, the great devotions; who spends himself in a worthy cause; who at the best knows in the end the triumph of high achievement, and who at the worst, if he fails, at least fails while daring greatly, so that his place shall never be with those cold and timid souls who neither know victory nor defeat.

My favorite scripture is found in the Book of Mormon in Helaman 5:12. The little ones learn only the first phrase, but most of kids over about ten can rip this off without a mistake.

And now my sons, remember, remember that it is upon the rock of our Redeemer who is Christ the Son of God that ye must build your foundation; that when the devil shall send forth his mighty winds, yea, his shafts in the whirlwind, yea, when all his hail and his mighty storm shall beat upon you, it shall have no power over you to drag you down to the gulf of misery and endless wo, because of the rock upon which ye are are built, which is a sure foundation, a foundation whereon if men build they cannot fall.

Another favorite quote is from Shakespeare and has comes in handy for the kids when they face adversity in their lives. We love talking about how this quote might apply to their lives. Some kids have reported daring to try out for the basketball team or running for office at school after rehearsing this little gem in their minds:

Sweet are the uses of adversity,
Which, like the toad, ugly and venomous,
Wears yet a precious jewel in his head.
And this our life, exempt from public haunt,
Finds tongues in trees, books in the running brooks,
Sermons in stones, and good in every thing.

—William Shakespeare, *As You Like It*

Music: One year, I gathered a list of my favorite classical music on Spotify (with the help of daughter Saydi) and sent it via email to all the grandkids from ages ten to seventeen. During a contest at Grammie Camp, I offered cash rewards for recognizing each composition and another one if they could name the composer. On the days before Grammie Camp, it was so great to see the kids gathering in corners here and there, listening and memorizing the music along with the composers' names. I only played about a thirty-second segment of each one for the test, and the kids wrote the name of the song and the composer. It was so fun and money well invested!

I thought ten compositions would be good, but our excellent musician Saydi suggested twenty. We settled at eighteen. Fewer might have been better, but Saydi's ten-year-old daughter Hazel was the winner with fifteen of eighteen compositions, complete with their composers. Several were not far behind.

Many people have asked for the list, so here it is:

1. *Carnival of the Animals: Aquarium* by Camille Saint-Saëns
2. *Peter and the Wolf* by Sergei Prokofiev
3. *Brandenburg Concerto No. 3* by Johann Sebastian Bach
4. "Clair de Lune" by Claude Debussy
5. *Symphony No. 9* ("Ode to Joy") by Ludwig van Beethoven
6. "Spring" from the *Four Seasons* by Antonio Vivaldi
7. *Star Wars Theme* by John Williams (this was, by far, the favorite)
8. "Ride of the Valkyries" by Richard Wagner
9. *Appalachian Spring* by Aaron Copland
10. *The Well-Tempered Clavier* by Johann Sebastian Bach
11. *Moonlight Sonata* by Ludwig von Beethoven
12. *Fantasia on a Theme by Thomas Tallis* by Ralph Vaughan Williams
13. *Adagio for Strings* by Samuel Barber
14. "Flight of the Bumblebee" by Nikolai Rimsky-Korsakov
15. *Scheherazade* by Nikolai Rimsky-Korsakov
16. *The Moldau* by Bedřich Smetana
17. *A Little Night Music* by Wolfgang Amadeus Mozart
18. "Morning Mood" by Edvard Grieg

Ancestor Stories: As will be discussed in great detail in Chapter 7, the value of teaching our children about their ancestors is enormous. Knowing stories about the lives of those who came before them gives them resilience and grit. I have tried to put this concept to work when I have a captive audience once

> **One year, for an art activity, we created a big family tree on large canvas with acrylic paints.**

a year at Grammie Camp. Each year, we have talked about a different ancestor's life. Sometimes we act out stories, which makes it more memorable. One year, for an art activity, we created a big family tree on large canvas (about four feet by two-and-a-half feet) with acrylic paints. The tree has three parts: the trunk, nine big limbs with smaller limbs branching off of the main limb, and sixteen roots that go down and branch off into the earth. Each group helped me to do a different part of the tree.

After the painting dried, we taped a picture of Richard and I on the trunk, a picture of each of our children and their spouses on the large limbs, and a picture of each grandchild in that family on the smaller branches. Below the earth line, roots stretched down with pictures of my parents on one side and Richard's on the other. The branches continue until we have sixteen roots with pictures of an ancestor on each root. (Keep reading for instruction to see a picture of the tree.)

A Mega Year

Last year, I was determined to let my grandchildren know more of the memorable stories of the wonderful ancestors who came before them. (For more about teh impact of telling these stories, see Chapter 7. But how could I teach them to know those wonderful people *personally*? I didn't want to just tell them a story about an ancestor, which they would probably forget, as I had done in the past.

I got an idea and decided to go a few steps beyond my former efforts for Grammie Camp that year. About a month before we met, I assigned the name of an ancestor to each of the kids and let *them* do the research on their lives on familysearch.org or wherever they could find information. Then on the day of Grammie Camp, they were to "come back from the dead" and actually *be* that person. They were to be ready to tell the story of "their lives" to the "audience" (their group).

At the time I was planning this Grammie Camp, our son Noah and his family were in transition from California to Utah and were staying with us until they found a home. When I explained the idea to our nine-year-old granddaughter Lyla, her eyes lit up and she immediately came up with the perfect name for Grammie Camps that year . . . The Ancestor Museum!

Then she and her eleven-year-old brother McKay helped me plan *the prizes* for doing a good job, which, of course, are very important!

We had only had three days for all the Grammie Camps, so I consolidated the kids into just three groups, organized according to age. We are amazingly fortunate that the Lighthouse, where we hold Grammie Camps, was only a twenty-minute ride from where my father's family, who settled the little town of Bloomington, were buried, eighty minutes from where my mother's family, who settled Star Valley, Wyoming, were buried, and eighty minutes the other direction from where Richard's family were buried in Logan, Utah. Each day after the kids' presentations, we got into Noah and Kristi's twelve-seat sprinter and headed for "their" gravestones at the cemeteries.

This year, mothers were invited for the ancestor stories, since they needed to know some of these stories too. It was great to have the moms along for the ride and to take pictures! It was also crucial to have their help with a group of nine of their kids while we ate hamburgers and raspberry shakes for dinner at the famous LaBeau's Drive-In after our visit to the cemetery. Since our time was so limited and the numbers so big (and since this grandma is getting older . . .) we didn't do sleepovers that year.

> *If you want to see some beautiful photos taken during these three days of Grammie Camps and the kids' presentations, as well as a picture of the family tree the kids helped me create, go to **71toes.com/grammie-camp**.*

If you're interested, here are the schedules that I sent to each group of mothers for our Grammie Camps this year. The instructions, the plans, and the gifts for the kids are all there. I'm just putting in these schedules for all three days so you get an idea of how this went.

Grammie Camps 2017

The Year of the Ancestor Museum

Group B: Ancestor Museum—Tuesday, July 11
Members: 10–12-year-olds
Special Presentations and a Trip to Star Valley
ATTENTION: Mothers are invited.

I will be sending each child the name of an ancestor that they will need to look up on familysearch.org so they learn some interesting things about his/her life. Then on that day, the kids will need to "come back from the dead" and "become" that ancestor as they tell some interesting things about "their" life to the "audience."

9:00
Just the kids will meet at the Lighthouse and we will . . .

1. Review the Grammie Camp song
2. Talk about their Happies and Sads for this year.

3. Receive a special prize for reciting Helaman 5:12

9:45

The mothers are invited to join us for The Ancestor Museum. Each member of this Grammie Camp group will become a speaker at a "museum" and tell us about the person they have become for the day as well as some interesting stories about themselves. They should start with when they were born and when and where they died. They should focus on things that were hard for them in their lives! Mothers can add things they may know and ask questions of the speaker. Each story will be about a person who is buried in the Freedom, Wyoming, Cemetery.

Everyone will "come back to life" one at a time and tell us all about what their lives were like. Costumes are welcome but not necessary!

11:45

We will go on a journey to Star Valley (about eighty minutes away) to see where "they" lived and what they did when they were kids. In the car, we will learn more about Star Valley and the courage and character of our relatives, who were some of the first settlers in the valley.

1:15

We'll eat lunch at a fun Mexican restaurant in Afton.

2:00

We will visit my cousin Nada who lives in Thayne (twenty minutes away from Afton) in her house where Grandma Hazel lived with Nada's family for several years, when Nada was young, while Grandma Hazel was teaching school. She will share stories about Grandma Hazel and her life growing up in Star Valley. Nada (who is eighty-three) will play for us on the piano, hand out words to old-time songs so we can sing along, as well as do a little yodeling, which she learned from our Swiss ancestors. Grandma Hazel taught Nada to play the piano by ear, and Nada became an outstanding musician! She also knows a lot about Grandma Ida and their family.

3:30

We will go to Freedom (about ten minutes away) and find the cemetery (which is located in a beautiful setting that looks a lot like Switzerland, where they came from). Each grandchild will locate "their" lovely pioneer gravestones. On the way back, they'll be able to see the house that Grandma Ida helped Grandpa Ray to build and where she and her two little babies died of influenza. There is a great ice cream place in Star Valley where we'll stop for a treat on the way home.

Gift: Each year, since I don't really give much to the kids except for their birthdays and Christmas, I try to think of a little gift they would like that would remind them of that year's Grammie Camp. Thanks to McKay's suggestion, each member of this group was given a puzzle box. Opening the box took some thinking. When they did, they found a secret drawer with the scripture they had learned in one drawer and a package of fruit snacks in the other.

6:00 or 7:00

We'll return for dinner with everyone.

GROUP C: Ancestor Museum—Wednesday, July 12
Members: 5–10-year-olds
Special Presentations and a Trip to Bloomington
ATTENTION: Mothers are invited.

1:30

We will meet at the Lighthouse and start with a welcome to our two new members of Grammie Camp. Next, there will be a pet show-and-tell and then a short talent show.

2:00

The older kids will teach the young ones the Grammie Camp song. Then we'll hear about the best thing that has happened to them this year as well as the saddest thing. We'll also talk about Helaman 5:12 and have them recite the first phrase: "And now my sons, remember, remember that it is upon the rock of our Redeemer who is Christ the Son of God that ye must build your foundation." Those who can do it word perfect will get to share a raspberry shake at dinner in Garden City. If the youngest ones can't quite do it yet, they will get prizes anyway.

3:00

We invite the mothers to join us. Each child will have been assigned a name of one of our ancestors who are buried in the Bloomington Cemetery. Please help them to find information and a story about that person on familysearch.org, ancestry.com, or from other sources you may have. They should pretend that they are coming back from the dead to tell us about their life on earth as though they are telling people who are coming through the museum, starting with where they were born and when they died. As they prepare their story, help them focus on things from their life that were really hard for them! Moms will be allowed to ask questions and help a bit if necessary. I have pictures and certificates and journals of those ancestors that they could share with the group. After the stories, we'll go for a scavenger hunt in the Bloomington Cemetery to find "their" graves. Moms are invited but not required to come to the cemetery.

5:30

We'll go to LaBeau's for dinner and be home by 7:30.

> *Gift:* Again, cute Lyla had a great idea for the gifts for this group this year. She was incredulous that I had never heard of Beanie Boos (look it up on Amazon if you don't know either). They are just cute, inexpensive, very small stuffed animals of every variety. Lyla helped me pick out just the right animal to give each child. When they were handed out at the end of their presentations, I told them that they needed to remember their ancestor by naming their Beanie Boos after the person they "became" that day. It was a riot to see each child fall in love with their Beanie Boo!

Party for the Littles: Thursday, July 13, 9:30–10:30 a.m.
Members: 0–4-year-olds

Ancestor stories, games, crafts, and water balloons.

MOTHERS OR DADS ARE INVITED—in fact, babies' moms will be needed!

Group A: Ancestor Museum—Thursday, July 13
Members: 13–17-year-olds
Special Presentations and a Trip to Logan

ATTENTION: Mothers and Grandfather are invited.

1:30

We will first have a short session for Happies and Sads for the year and what they are looking forward to for the coming year. Prizes will be awarded for repeating Helaman 5:12 word perfect.

1:45

Parents are invited to join and hear presentations by kids about the ancestor that they have been assigned to research on familysearch.org. Each grandchild should try to "become them" while they tell "their" stories. They should each be ready to give a short talk about "their" lives starting with when and where they were born and died and a sketch of their life as though they were giving a talk at a museum. They should focus on things in their life that were hard for them.

2:30

We will move the museum tour to the Sprinter, and we will drive to Logan, stopping at the Summit to read May Swenson's poem (she will be one of the people that we will have learned about) and then the Logan Cemetery where all those people they have "become" are buried. Grandfather will then conduct a tour of *his* life growing up in Logan, with a drive by his elementary school, junior high, and high school, and with a short stop at USU, where Grammie and Grandfather met and fell in love. We'll have dinner at the famous Bluebird Café, where we celebrated Grandma Ruthie and Grampa Dean's fiftieth wedding anniversary (even though he had been gone for many years). We will return to the lake by early evening.

A letter was sent about a month before we met with the parents with each child's ancestor assignment. I do have to say that, because one of our families was living with us for a couple of weeks before the reunion, I was able to help some of those kids with their stories while their parents were looking for a new house. Also, I didn't see anybody roll their eyes (while I was looking) about this assignment. And I did hand a three-page paper written by our son Eli when he was in high school about the life of one of the ancestors to one of the teenagers who had flown in just before we started and didn't get the message about her assignment. She did a great job by the time it was her turn!

We had three days that I don't think any of us will ever forget! The kids were spectacular telling about "their" lives and loved finding "their" graves in the cemeteries. My darling eighty-three-year-old cousin, whom my mother had lived with for several years when she was a single schoolteacher in Star Valley, handed out a list of words to "old time songs" and rallied the kids to sing their hearts out while she played like a champ with only chords for music, as my mom had taught her to do! She yodeled, and they were grinning from ear to ear as she entertained them!

Help from a Single Son

One of our sons is not married. He is in his forties and has thirty kids whose lives he changes every year as their third-grade teacher at a charter school in Arizona. He adores kids, and kids adore him! One of the highlights of our Grammie Camps the past few years has been the planned entrances of Josh. In addition to being a teacher, he goes the extra mile to learn and teach outside the classroom. Several times a year, he holds "Astronomy Nights." He has a wonderful telescope, and he invites his students and their parents to come back to the school on nights when he knows they will see marvelous things in the sky! He introduces what they are going to see on the computer before they actually see it in the sky. It is a "heavenly" experience, as everyone is filled with wonder at what they see through the telescope.

The highlight for the Grammie Camp kids is when Josh comes up to the Lighthouse on a blazing starry night, gets them oriented to the sky on his computer, and then shows his nieces and nephews the wonders of the night sky through a small telescope that we have up there. It is something they will never forget.

In addition, Josh always teaches his kids at school how to make rockets. One year, he did that for two different Grammie Camp groups and then showed them how to launch them on our big lawn the next day. I think the girls were more excited than the boys as they decorated their fancy rockets and sent them up into the sky with powerful engines!

When weather permits and when Josh can come early or stay late, he also shepherds a Grammie Camp group for a sleepover on Richard's sailboat. Nothing is more exciting than those nights on the boat when he shows them the wonders of the night sky and lets them stay up late to watch a movie on his computer. Josh was named "Teacher of the Year" by the American Leadership Academy charter schools in Arizona in 2017. I love having his wonderful help with Grammie Camps!

> **Nothing is more exciting than those nights on the boat when he shows them the wonders of the night sky and lets them stay up late to watch a movie on his computer.**

Notes from Kids

Before we leave the Grammie Camp topic, I just want to share a few of the cute thank-you notes that the kids have sent in years past after they get home.

Here's something ten-year-old Eliza wrote about her memories of Grammie Camp (spelling and punctuation not corrected):

I love Gramie Camp. I enjoy it so so much. I enjoy the activities like picking weeds and going to the store and getting my rewards for it. I also like the prizes like candies and things for each other. I like sleeping over because I can be with my cousins becase they are nice to me. I also like learning about my ancestors because I can be like them. I enjoy learning about being brave and strong. I really like the ones about boats and journeys to a new land. Like the ones ware you leave all your things and go on a boat. My favorite story is learning about Grandma Hazel and how she was tough and so good at music. I'm so glad gramie made up Gramie Camp.

By Eliza

PS. I love the song.

From fourteen-year-old Elle:

Dear Grammie,

I loved laughing with you at Grammie Camp. I loved going to Bandito with you and getting those great shakes! I'll always remember it.

Love, Elle

From seven-year-old Claire:

Dear Grammie,

Thanks so much for Grammie Camp. I thought it was so fun. I loved looking at the stars and learning about ans-esters with the big tree. I wouldn't be here without you guys!

Love, Claire

From thirteen-year-old Grace:

Dear Grammie,

Thank you soooo much for bringing us to Bandito every year. We always have so much fun at Grammie Camp and I'll always remember it. And thank you for always cleaning up after us (which we should do ourselves).

Love, Grace

And from eight-year-old Lucy:

Dear Gramie,

Thank you for Gramie Camp so much! Thank you for the rockets, and the dancing, and most of all . . . Gramie's Classical Music Challenge!

Love, Lucy

And just to prove that boys write thank-you notes too, this is from Silas (nine):

Dear Grammie,

You make everything fun, even if we feel sad. Like just this year, at Grammie Camp you had Josh come over and show us how to make rockets.

Love, Silas

Thoughts?

- Am I crazy? (These events will have to be adjusted as I get older. Darn! It takes a lot of energy, but this bonding time with our darling grandchildren is priceless! I really am having the time of my life!)
- Wherever you are in your grandmothering life, what have you or could you do to facilitate your relationship with your grandchildren while they bond with their cousins? (I wish we could sit and talk about this so you could give me your ideas too!)

Twelve-Year-Old Motor Home Trips

George and Lenore Romney (Mitt Romney's parents), whom Richard used to work for and who were lifelong friends, told us once about one of their family traditions, which was taking a group of their grandchildren on a trip in a motor home on or near the year they turned twelve. They lived in Michigan and took the kids from Michigan to Utah to Washington, DC, in a motor home. They loved having two or three kids at a time all to themselves for the long journey. You can teach kids a lot and learn a lot about them when you have a captive audience.

We adopted this idea. Some of our grandkid groups named themselves based on these trips. When our first three grandchildren were within a year or two of twelve, we borrowed my sister's huge motor home and took Max, Elle, and Ashton to the Yellowstone Park area, and thereafter they became know as "the Old Faithfuls." We loved the hike to Jenny Lake and were amazed at Old Faithful and Artist Point. But probably our most memorable moment was when we were all settled down for bed, reading a book in that big motor home, and a park ranger scared us as he knocked loudly on the window where we were reading. He then came to the front door to tell us that it was totally illegal to park where we were and we needed to leave immediately. At midnight! We drove on back out of the park (because apparently it takes months to get a permit to park a big motor home in Yellowstone Park).

They loved having two or three kids at a time all to themselves for the long journey. You can teach kids a lot and learn a lot about them when you have a captive audience.

Another memorable moment came the next day. The kids were so sad that they were going to miss the midnight showing of one of the releases of a new Harry Potter movie. As we passed through Afton, Wyoming, we were all overjoyed to see that the movie was playing in that obscure little place—at midnight. Ashton, who was the most excited of all, sadly fell asleep before it was over. After the late night the night before, he was "dead as a doornail"! We almost had to carry him out to the car afterward!

Again, the kids came up with cute thank-you notes:

Thanks for the wonderful time on the adventure to Yellowstone Park in the Motor Home. It was fun to see Old Faithful and to see Harry Potter.
    Love, Elle

It was so fun to eat in the Motor Home. It was probably a big deal to take us there. I want to do that with my grandkids!
    Love you, Max

Our next group of three had their trip a few years later. This time, we rented a little motor home and went from Bear Lake to Lagoon, a great amusement park near Salt Lake City. We camped overnight on the way. Though Richard and I were a bit dubious about how much fun it would be, standing in long lines for rides on a sweltering summer day, it turned out to be hilarious fun! I have to admit that we didn't go on all the rides, but we went on some that were definitely not on our wish list and had a great time! It was joyful to watch the kids go wild over the fun they were having. That group became known as "the Goonies."

Our bonding days with those kids on our Motor Home Trips will never be forgotten. They not only bonded with us—they bonded with each other! Little moments from those halcyon days often crop up in our conversations with each other as the years have gone by. There are private jokes just between us that keep us laughing as we remember.

Other Small Groups

One other thing we did to help small groups of cousins to bond was to assign them to help with the work at reunions. A chart was made by whomever was in charge of the reunion that listed the groups and their responsibilities, with squares to check off when their jobs were done. Those who got the most "checks" won a sleepover on the tennis court at the end of the reunion. Each group had a name and was assigned things like loading the dishwasher, emptying the dishwasher, cleaning and polishing the counters, sweeping the floor, vacuuming, and putting away all the toys at night. With that many people together for the days of the actual reunion, it was helpful for the adults not to have to do all the cleanup and helpful to the kids to realize that there is "no free lunch."

Your Ideas

I realize that this is kind of a lot! Remember that I have been thinking about and coming up with ideas for Grammie Camps and gathering kids together in small groups for many years! It takes time and thought and energy. But I always remember what Christopher Robin said to Winnie the Pooh:

> *"You're BRAVER than you believe, and STRONGER than you seem, and SMARTER than you think!"*[1]

For those of you who are beginning grandmothers, I hope these ideas are hopeful, not overwhelming. For those who have been grandmothering for more years than I have, I wish I could hear your own great ideas for getting your kids together to learn and have fun!

I realize that I am talking to grandmothers who probably don't have the multitudes of grandchildren that we do! Here are a few ideas for getting smaller numbers of kids in groups together for fun and learning.

- A friend who is an expert quilter gets her grandchildren together in a small group to do things that I couldn't do in my wildest dreams! Here is what she says:

I only have a few grandchildren and still have unmarried children, but I do love to help them with quilting. I signed all my granddaughters up for quilting classes. Then they came down and helped me with our annual Quilt Walk. They actually finished their own quilts to display on the last day. All of them have a passion for sewing and creating. I have different age groups come and spend a week with me. Each day is scheduled for learning something new, and then in their spare time, they relax and have fun with each other.

- Other grandmas have regular sleepovers with their grandchildren in which they create memories and bond with their cousins (and their grandma). One grandma loves taking her grandkids to concerts, even rock concerts, while others invite small groups over for cooking classes. Richard and I have so much fun taking one family at a time to movies. Afterward, we enjoy some food together so we can talk about the good and bad things about the movie. We love to hear their opinions!

Thoughts?

- Your own ideas for interacting with your grandchildren are the best! What ideas have you tried that are working for getting your grandchildren to bond in groups?
- Consider the things that are most important to you when it comes to teaching and having fun with your grandchildren. What will they remember?

Notes

1. Milne, A. A., K. Geurs, and C. Crocker (writers) and K. Guers (director). *Pooh's Grand Adventure: The Search for Christopher Robin* (movie). Walt Disney Television and Buena Vista Television, 1997.

CHAPTER 3

One-on-One Adventures

"**D**elight!" That is a word that encapsulates the fun of personally connecting with just one grandchild at a time—just you and that one special child! In the process, we get to know them and love them and put some magic in their lives. As Alex Haley says:

> *Nobody can do for little children what grandparents can do. Grandparents sort of sprinkle stardust over the lives of little children.*

Maybe the most important thing about a one-on-one relationship with each grandchild is to let them know how much we love, support, and adore them! At a funeral for a beloved grandmother, all three grandchildren who were asked to speak each in turn shared that they were always quite sure that they were their grandmother's favorite grandchild. I was struck by how important it is that we let our grandchildren know that they are dearly loved by their grandmother—even (and maybe especially) those who may, at different stages in life, be difficult to love!

We need to actually let them know that we are delighted by their successes and concerned about their trials. A short note or a text to a teenager who is excited about a big dance at school or worried about taking the ACT test goes straight to their hearts. Telling them that we are praying for them or thinking of them with concern and love when they are going through a difficult trial creates a special bond as we let them know that we are with them, if not in person, in our thoughts. Those are the things that they will remember.

Probably the best advice is "If you love them, tell them!" Specifically! How often do you just flat out say, "I love you so much! I love your creativity, your goodness, your courage, and the way you treat your friends"? Your compliments are most helpful when they are specific and sincere. Whether it's just a sentence or a comment now and then or a written note to tell them something you noticed about them that is admirable, it is what your grandchildren need most from you.

Sometimes their responses to your compliments will surprise you. When I recently told a ten-year-old granddaughter how smart I thought she and her siblings were, she said, "Oh, it's just that we know how to pay attention and our parents teach us a lot."

I'm not saying they need a trophy for every little good deed, but those grandchildren at that funeral knew specifically what their grandmother loved about them. Often, we can be more objective than their parents, who sometimes can't see the beautiful view of their children from the trenches!

As you can imagine, for me it can be a little tricky to arrange private times with thirty-one grandchildren who are living all across the globe. We are blissfully happy that our wild travel schedule allows us to see them often and that their own travel addictions get them to each other and get us together as families several times a year. Even when we are with our grandchildren, though, I have realized that it's easy to get caught up in conversations with their parents or catching up with adult family members we haven't seen for a while and leave out the kids.

As our grandchild "quivers" were filling up, I began to question how well I really knew each of our grandchildren and wondered how I could get them "out of the clump" and into my life as unique individuals. Right about then, Richard and I were invited to present a workshop at a conference in Columbia, South America, where teachers and administrators of charter and private schools from the upper regions of South America and all of Central America gathered ideas to hone their skills. Richard and I were invited to conduct a workshop on *The Entitlement Trap*, but we were told that we would be welcome to attend any class that we found interesting. I attended a class presented by a stellar private school teacher, who talked about the challenge of not thinking of your classroom as a group of kids who need to be taught but as a group of fascinating individual people who need to feel that you know and admire as individuals with ideas and interests that you want to know.

The Importance of Asking Questions

The teacher advised us to recognize and analyze each child's main methods for learning. Are they creative? Practical? Or analytical? She pointed out that we need to connect with right-brain and left-brain learners in different ways! She didn't realize that she

Ask not only what their favorite things are but what scares them and what worries them. Ask them about what they'd like to become and what they'd like you to know.

was talking to a grandmother who had more grandchildren than the teacher had children in her classroom, each with their own way of learning and embracing life. I loved what she said and was determined to do better to connect with each grandchild according to the way they saw the world!

Her most urgent plea was to ask questions. All kinds of questions. Ask not only what their favorite things are but what scares them and what worries them. Ask them about what they'd like to become and what they'd like you to know.

She gave me the key to knowing more about our unique grandchildren. Since we are "questionnaire people" anyway, a questionnaire for each child seemed like a perfect solution to getting to know them better. We see them several times during the year, but our bulk of time together is every summer during July. Just before Grammie Camp one year, I sent out a questionnaire with some questions that I thought even the youngest ones could answer. The questions are below, with along with mostly one- or two-word answers from our nine-year old granddaughter. Her answers are actually quite insightful and sometimes pretty amusing. (Spelling and punctuation are not corrected.)

- What do you love? *To read*
- What do you fear? *Rattlesnakes* [We had seen several that summer at the lake.]
- What makes you happy? *My family*
- How happy are you on a scale from 1 to 10? *7*
- What do you worry about the most? *Being*

uncomfertabul [This was a revealing word coming from this granddaughter. She was "uncomfortable" with a lot of things in her life at that moment.]

- What are three things you are thankful for? *Family, the gosple and the world.*
- What is an example of your kindness to others this year? *I gave my baseball ticet* [ticket] *to my brother because he rely wanted to go!*

Just before our reunion more recently, Richard and I sent out questionnaires to all our grandchildren who were eight and older. What we got back was fascinating. Here is the questionnaire:

Name:

1. Contact information and social media (put in information on everything you use)

Text (phone number):
Twitter:
Snapchat:
Instagram:
Other:
Which of these reaches you fastest?

2. Two things that you love to do (or that make you happy):

3. Favorites

color:
food:
sport:

movie:

musical instrument:

singer:

actor:

game:

school subject:

New Testament hero:

Old Testament hero:

Book of Mormon hero:

4. Eyrealm Mission Statement

[This has to do with our family mission statement, which will be explained in Chapter 4 and has now filtered down to the next generation.]

What are you going to do to BROADEN?

What are you going to do to CONTRIBUTE?

What are you going to do to LOVE MORE?

5. You

Describe yourself in 3 words:

Your best friends right now:

What are two of your gifts (things you are really good at)?

Something you wish you were good at but are not:

I like being myself because:

What is one recent example of kindness?

What are you afraid of?

How happy are you right now on a scale of 1 to 10?

What do you worry about?

6. Your future

Three careers or jobs you might choose:

Your longest-range goal:

One thing you are looking forward to this year:
Something you want to improve upon next year:
Two things you will look for in your future husband or wife:
Where would you like to live if you could live anywhere?
What are three things you know you will do in your life?
What are three things you are sure you will never do?

7. Spirituality

What do you ask for most in your prayers?
What do you thank Heavenly Father most for?

8. Admiration and Examples

What is one thing you look up to and admire in your dad?
What do you admire most about your mom?
In one of your cousins?
In one of your uncles or aunts?

9. What is one more important thing about you that did not come out in any of the questions above?

One very precocious ten-year-old grandson sent back some fascinating, honest, revealing, and sometimes hilarious answers to the questions. Here is a sample, starting with Section 5, from his questionnaire:

Describe yourself in 3 words: *Smart, funny, creative*
What are two of your gifts (things you are really good at)? *Hiding and coming up with many ideas.*
What do you wish you were good at? *Hypnotizing*

I like myself because: *I am awesome and grateful to be above ground.*

What is one recent example of kindness? *I saw a guy alone in the corner at recess and went over to talk to him.*

What is something you want to improve upon next year? *Hypnotizing*

And on the last question—"What is one more important thing about that you that did not come out in any of the questions above?"—he had a sweet admission, which was something his parents had been worried about: "I'm not very active." (Meaning that he would rather sit and read than be outside playing).

Even though not every kid replied to every question, the answers we got were insightful, fun to read, and good for us to know as grandparents.

Richard, who is an excellent questioner, was having fun asking our eleven-year-old Eliza questions one day when he had taken her out to lunch. He asked her what was something that she would never do. He was fishing for something like "I'll never take drugs" or "I'll never get in a car if the driver has been drinking," but no. The answer was a complete surprise.

"I will never ride a bike naked in public!" she declared emphatically.

Totally taken off guard and trying not to laugh, he said, "Eliza, why would you say that?"

Her answer came quickly and with conviction. She said "When we were in San Francisco last year, we saw a big parade of bicycles, and there was a guy there riding his bike naked. And I decided right then and there that I would never do that!"

"I will never ride a bike naked in public!" she declared emphatically.

While we were talking about asking children questions in a meeting with friends, one of the grandpas said that he had fun asking questions on a long car ride with a grandchild. Then when he couldn't think of any more questions to ask, he asked her to ask *him* questions. That spiced up the conversation a lot!

Our discussion group then talked about how important it is to have our grandchildren ask *us* questions, which prompted a grandma in the group to tell us this story:

> *I have a granddaughter who called me one day with a question I wasn't expecting. She said, "Grandma, can you do the splits?" I burst out laughing and then asked, "Why did you ask me that question?" The child said, "Because my mom told me that your mother can still do the splits, and she is ninety-seven, so I was wondering about you."*

The group laughed out loud, and someone asked, "Can she still get up?"

Grammie Dates

Questionnaires are one thing, but face-to-face communication is the best. When I visit families one at a time, I like to take each grandchild on a Grammie Date. It's great to talk to them one-on-one in their own environment. Those little dates are usually not long. Even an hour (or half an hour with a three-year-old) can reveal lots of information. The teacher referred to earlier suggested we remember to use positive affirmations and to say things like "I love your ideas about . . ." or "You are so good at . . . "

I love this quote:

"Grandmas don't just say 'That's nice'—they reel back and roll their eyes and throw up their hands and smile. You get your money's worth out of grandmas." —Anonymous

When we visit our son in Hawaii, I like to take each of his five grandchildren out one at a time for a little alone time. Sometimes we go to a place that fits with their interests. Their ten-year-old Elsie is an artist, through and through! When she is not reading, she is creating something amazing! On a Grammie Date with her, we walked into a little artist's village only about ten minutes from their house in Maui. We wandered through the plentiful art galleries that fill the streets. It was pure delight to see her inhale what she saw. From a store with hundreds of magical-sounding wind chimes blowing in the wind to paintings produced by heat, she was in her element! It was a day we'll both remember.

Sometimes I just take the kids out to lunch and ask questions. Here are snippets from a conversation I had at lunch with eleven-year-old Camden. (It's a great idea to take notes while they talk. It makes them feel that what they are saying is valid and important! They are pretty pleased when they see that I'm really interested in their responses and actually taking notes, not just trying to make small talk.)

I keep my notes on my phone, so I got it out and started asking questions.

Me: Camden, what do like best about living in Hawaii?

Camden: I love surfboarding and boogie boarding because the water is so warm! It's a perfect temperature here all year! And it's easy to make friends.

Me: What is the hardest thing about living in Hawaii?

Camden: It's far from relatives, and it's so expensive!

Me: What do you miss most since you moved here?

Camden: I miss Teresa. [She's his other grandmother; she thinks he's the coolest thing since sliced bread, and I can't disagree.]

Me: What don't you like about living here?

Camden: Homework! It is one of the stupidest things ever made!

Me: What do you like best about your mom?

Camden: She doesn't give you very bad punishments. She teaches you music. She has lots of friends and talks a long time with them.

Me: What is the worst thing about your mom?

Camden: Same as that last sentence!

Me: What is the best thing about your dad?

Camden: He encourages us to do any kind of sport, and he helps us when we are having a really hard time.

You probably wouldn't be interested in four-year-old Poem's favorite color or her favorite food, so I've cut to the chase and included just a couple of insightful things that came from her mind while we were on a walk together. Her answers were perfect.

Me: What do you like about your mom?

Po: She's nice and beautiful and makes me food.

Me: What do you like about your Dad?

Po: I like the scripture study and he makes great food.

Me: What is one thing that would describe your sisters and brothers?

Po: Ana (fifteen)—polite; Camden (thirteen)—really annoying; Elsie (ten)—good at art; Ezra (three)—playful.

Sometimes as you question your grandchildren, they offer unexpected words of wisdom. On a recent date with Po (who is now seven) we were sitting on a bench talking and sipping fruit drinks we had just bought when I noticed there was an ant floating in my drink. She peered in and then looked up at me with a toothless grin and said, "You know, ants are good for the soul."

Questions that require an answer of how they feel are especially important. I gained some really insightful information from a Grammie Date in Arizona with twelve-year-old Claire, who had gone through a really hard year. Below is a condensed version of what I learned.

Me: What was your hardest experience this year?

Claire: Being the only one who got cut from my competitive soccer team.

Me: You must have been heartbroken. How do you feel about it now?

Claire: After I cried for a while, I decided to try out for a different team, and I got in!

Me: Good for you! That is so inspiring! So what is your biggest worry right now?

Claire: I'm behind in some classes, but I've figured out a way to catch up.

Me: Good job! I can't wait to hear the results! What are you afraid of?

Claire: Doing a back tuck? [She had developed a fear of doing a very skilled and dangerous move in her gymnastics class. Smart girl . . . I would be terrified too!]

Me: Did you quit gymnastics?

Claire: No, my mom knew a coach and he helped me conquer my fear. But I think I'm ready to go to another sport.

Me: What was your best memory of living in China?

Claire: When I was introduced to my school class in China.

Me: What was your worst memory in China?

Claire: The first week I was there, I was bullied and they wouldn't let me play soccer.

A wonderful deep discussion followed about the things she had learned that year, which would never have happened without a one-on-one encounter. It helps me see into their souls, helps me see their problems, and lets them know I love them.

> *"It is only in the heart that one can see rightly.*
> *What is essential is invisible to the eye."*
> —*Antoine de Saint-Exupéry,* The Little Prince

Sometimes the best interchanges with grandchildren happen via the internet. We were on our way to Spain to see one of our families who take off every other year or so for a grand adventure. This family had been traveling all over Europe with five kids, including a one-year-old, for about three months in an old vegetable oil–powered Mercedes G Wagon that our son Jonah had bought after they arrived. Sometimes they stayed at nice

Sometimes the best interchanges with grandchildren happen via the internet. hotels because his wife Aja is a guru at getting points for hotels. Sometimes they stayed with friends and family. Sometimes they were at campgrounds. Aniston, an incredibly durable fourteen-year-old, took it all in stride, made friends wherever she went, and tried to be helpful as possible, although I'm sure she had her moments.

They had just rented a house in order to put the kids in Spanish schools so they could learn the language. I was so worried about Ana (Aniston), who is brilliant but had been homeschooled most of the past few years. She would be starting her first day of high school in a new school, where she would be taking all subjects, including Spanish literature and chemistry, in Spanish, of which she had a very limited vocabulary! I asked her a lot of questions in an email because I was pretty worried about what she would be facing. Here was her response:

> Hi grammie!!!!
>
> I cannot wait to see you!!! I just got back from my first day of school!!!! my first class was really overwhelming but after that it was great!! it's nice because in math and chemistry the terms are pretty similar. I made a few friends, some of which were in all my classes and helped me figure out homework and stuff.
>
> Our house is great. it's SO SO SO nice to have my own closet and a bed!!!
>
> I love you so much!
>
> Ana

This was my response:

Oh man, Ana, I'm so glad to hear from you! Thanks for the info. Of course I knew you would handle this with grace and pizzazz as you always do, but it's just great to see it in writing! How are the other kids doing? So happy about your bed and closet. There nothing that makes you more grateful for little things like that than being without them for so long.

I love you so much and can't wait to have you in my arms in just a few days!

Forever,

Grammie

Creating Special Occasions

One of my favorite one-on-one experiences with a grandchild was with Hazel (my mother's namesake). She lives in Boston and is as bright and unique as they come! She is a born manager and loves being in charge of things because she pretty much knows what to do in any given situation, which sometimes creates a little rift between her and her mom. When she was eleven, she was already pretty "techie." She created her own blog, which you can find at faultsofmymom.blogspot.com. After you giggle about that title, don't worry: one of her first posts is titled "Wait, Re-Wind: My Mom is Awesome." Her comments are fun and funny and insightful!

Hazel also has an email account. That year, I was asking her regularly about what she was reading. Here is an email interchange between Hazel and me during this fun little period as reading buddies. (Spelling and punctuation are not corrected.)

Dear Grammie,

Right now i am reading little women on the kindle it is really long! it is so surprising how proper girls had to be back then!!! My mom says when I finish little women I can watch the movie and go on a field trip to Luisa may Alcott's house!.

love, Hazel

Dear Hazel,

You Lucky Duck! I'm so glad that you are reading Little Women! *It's one of my favorites! Louisa May Alcott is incredible! You are so lucky to live so close to where she lived and wrote. You are going to love her house! Your mom has the best ideas! If you want to read a short synopsis of her life, you can click here: http://www.biography.com/people/louisa-may-alcott-9179520#synopsis.*

Thanks for keeping me in the loop on your reading. I LOVE it!

Love you,

Grammie

As our communications proceeded, I decided to join her; I not only read the book, but I also arranged to fly to Boston and be with her and her mom on the trip to Concord to see Louisa May Alcott's house. We looked forward to our time together with excitement for months. Her mom, Saydi, and I had time to finish the book, and on March 10 that year, I arrived for our "Little Women Day" in Boston. Our trip to Orchard House (forty-five minutes from their home) was pure delight! Hazel, her "faulty" mom, and I had a day that none of us will ever forget. After a lovely breakfast in a two-hundred-year-old inn near Orchard House, we toured the house where Louisa wrote the book as the characters came alive

> I decided to join her; I not only read the book, but I also arranged to fly to Boston and be with her and her mom on the trip to Concord to see Louisa May Alcott's house.

to us! Louisa May Alcott had grown up with her now-famous father Bronson Alcott and her delightful family in Concord, Massachusetts, where Henry David Thoreau and Ralph Waldo Emerson also lived. We soaked in that fascinating era of transcendentalism and explosive revolution along with the joy of learning more about the creation of *Little Women*. We were book-bonded forever!

Another delightful way to spend one-on-one time with your grandchildren is to read *with* them.

> *"You are never too old, too wacky, too wild to pick up a book and read to a child!"—Dr. Seuss*

Julie and Eli live in New York City with two small children, right next door to a public library. Julie always has the most delightful books ready for me to read to our grandchildren (ages four and two) when I come. I love exploring the magical world of creativity and fun through the eyes of so many wonderful writers and artists with two of my favorite little people (one at a time). Here is a list of Julie's favorites, with a short explanation of each book:

- *Journey* by Aaron Becker. Wonderful journey of imagination to make with your grandchildren, with beautiful artwork! There are also other books by Becker called *Quest* and *Return* that go along with *Journey*.
- *The Adventures of Beekle: The Unimaginary Friend* by Dan Santat. The imagination in this one is adorable.
- *This Is Sadie* by Sarah O'Leary. Basically, this book lays out the magical world of being a child.
- *My Father's Dragon* by Ruth Stiles Gannett. This is actually a short chapter book, but my parents read it to Zara last summer for a for a week, reading a chapter each night.

- *Animal Manners* by Barbara Hazen. (This book is out of print, and I had to find a used one on Amazon. Perhaps you can find it at a used book store. I read this book growing up, and it is seriously the most quotable book I use for my kids. It's all about manners, and it has cute rhymes I can repeat to remind them about their manners. This might be enticing for a grandparent.)
- *Should I Share My Ice Cream?* by Mo Willems. This is a great one to get your grandkids to laugh.

Other delightful books to read with young grandchildren are:

- *How to Babysit a Grandma* by Jean Reagan
- *The Book with No Pictures* by B. J. Novak
- *The Day the Crayons Quit* by Drew Daywalt

If you live close enough or stay with your grandchildren long enough, here are some chapter books for elementary-age kids that our son Josh, who is an outstanding teacher and lover of books, recommends:

- *The Miraculous Journey of Edward Tulane* by Kate DiCamillo
- *Because of Winn-Dixie* by Kate DiCamillo
- *Tale of Despereaux* by Kate DiCamillo, Newbery Award Winner for 2003
- *The One and Only Ivan* by Katherine Applegate, Newbery Award Winner for 2012
- *Holes* by Louis Sachar, National Book Award Winner for 1998 and Newbery Award Winner for 1999 (also great for middle school kids)
- *Chronicles of Narnia* by C. S. Lewis (which are timeless and our family's all-time favorite series for children)

One of the most memorable and delightful one-on-one experiences was with a sixteen-year-old granddaughter. During a twenty-minute ride in a small truck, she told me all about her first boyfriend and the long time it had taken them to even dare to hold hands. Then, with peals of laughter, she told me about her first kiss. She even gave me a peek at her private Instagram account so I could see her squealing with delight on her way home after that once-in-a-lifetime experience.

Thoughts?

- What are the things that you'd like to learn from your grandchildren by asking questions?
- How often do you encourage them to ask you questions?
- Have you recorded your fondest memories of one-on-one experiences with your grandchildren? They would love to read about it through your eyes someday.
- List the books you have loved reading with your grandchildren.
- Record and treasure those one-on-one experiences.

Great Ideas from Other Grandmothers

Some of us have made mistakes with some of our children and regret not getting it quite right. Grandparenting is a chance to do some things that maybe we didn't do so well or didn't have the time or energy to do with our own children. As Sunie Levin said:

If you made your mistakes, nature's given you another chance when you're a grandparent.

We all wish we had done something different when we look back at our lives with children, but our grandchildren give us an opportunity be better and do better!

The rest of this chapter will be ideas from smart grandmothers who have designed some insightful and fun ways to bond with our grandchildren one on one. Sometimes those little things we do with a grandchild one on one are more important than we think. Someone has said:

Enjoy the little things in life because one day you will look back and realize that they were big things.

Some of these are direct quotes, and some are recounts of stories that friends have told me:

"Teenagers are so busy that it's a little harder for grandmas to work with them one on one. Not many of them pay attention to email anymore. But those who have phones do pay attention to texts! I love texting my teenagers just a line or two once a week or so to let them know that I'm still here and I love them!"

"Sometimes I text my grandson when I know he's at high school and say, 'Hey, this is Nana, but you can tell everyone it's from your girlfriend.' Sometimes I like to tease those high school kids by saying, 'Can I come and have lunch with you at the cafeteria?' just to give them a scare!"

One grandmother, whose grandchildren mostly live nearby, said that when her grandchildren walk into her house, she doesn't allow them to just walk by with a quick "Hi" on their way to play with their cousins or the toys. They know that they must stop and look her straight in the eye and say, "Hi Nana," loud and clear! Somehow looking each other straight in the eye helps each person to really see into the soul (at least for the grandma), and it is her way of connecting one-on-one with each grandchild as they arrive. Along those same lines, teaching children to look people straight in the eye is a great job for a grandma. They will probably respond to your training better than they would their parents. It's such an important thing to know how to do, especially for children who are quiet and shy.

A grandmother who loves nature and the outdoors tells her grandchildren over eight that they can have a two-day, one-night adventure with her and their grandfather once a year. They can choose whatever they want to do as long as it is within driving distance. Not unexpectedly, the kids usually choose somewhere that involves nature and hikes and often camping out. Those precious times spent together with only one grandchild are never to be forgotten!

"My grandchildren, who live next door, get lots of special attention one at a time by being with me in my kitchen and yard. They help me water flowers, fix meals, and serve Grandpa. Our three-year-old, Trell, comes in the back door most mornings, still in his jammies, and wants to make popcorn in the microwave. I have taught him how, and he loves it. Grandpa makes a huge deal about how wonderful it is. Trell just beams as he hands the popcorn to his grandpa, sucks on his binky, and heads back through the field to his home."

"I've kept a photo scrapbook of each grandchild. It is their favorite book to look at when they come to visit. Last year, I added a two-page life story to the obituary of their four great-grandparents plus Bill's funeral program [her husband passed away of cancer at age sixty-two] with his life sketch and my 'I Am the One' poem that tells about how I felt about him."

"Now that I have retired, I have discovered the sheer joy of letting a toddler (who is just beginning to formulate words) lead you around by the hand and notice what he notices. One toddler found it fascinating to take walks around the neighborhood on the curb (like a balance beam). Another liked to point out the airplanes (we live underneath a flight path). One found it endlessly entertaining to push tiny cars and trucks down the plastic slippery slide in the back yard. It's a challenge to find one-on-one time with grandkids who are busy in school, etc., but the ones I played with when they were two keep asking for sleepovers."

"We have a divorced son living with us, and [he has] three children who spend weekends with us. The three of us who are adults coordinate with each other to give them some individual time with one of us as much as possible when they are here—either running an errand or doing something they choose. It can be a challenge, but no matter what, we have reading time with them individually."

A very proactive grandma who has realized the importance of telling the stories of her life to her grandchildren

> Now that I have retired, I have discovered the sheer joy of letting a toddler (who is just beginning to formulate words) lead you around by the hand and notice what he notices.

says that she has written fifty bite-size stories that can be read to her grandchildren at bedtime. The children love the stories, which create a special bond with her grandchildren.

"I feel so strongly about finding opportunities to interact one on one. I don't think there's any other way to get to know each other. Since I don't live in the same town as each of my children and grandchildren, I make it a point to visit them or have them visit me one family at a time. It's a special time when Grandma comes, and we do lots of fun, special things. It's different if I come as a babysitter for their parents for a week and have to make them do their routines, homework, put them to bed. I like to form fun memories that they associate with Grandma. If I come to Utah, where several of our families live, I'll still just do something special with one family at a time."

> I like to have an affectionate nickname for each of my grandchildren that reminds me of them. It is a fun way to have a "secret connection" just between us.

"All except one of our grandchildren has grown to love genealogy. They have done lots of research to find ancestors, which they are genuinely excited about! Genealogy has been the best one-on-one experience for me as we enjoy looking for ancestors together. We get so excited when we find something or someone we've been trying to find!"

"I like to have an affectionate nickname for each of my grandchildren that reminds me of them. It is a fun way to have a 'secret connection' just between us."

An amazingly dedicated grandmother was driving a little six-year-old granddaughter to her private school and her activities, which involved a three-hour ride round trip with her granddaughter. The grandchild's mother was literally plugged into the wall, attached to a feeding tube in her bedroom. It was her lifeline as she survived the first few months of a horrendously difficult pregnancy.

When that dedicated grandmother could see that the mother was soon going to be able to join "the land of the living," and when she was well enough to resume the driving duties, her grandmother said to her delightful granddaughter, "I'm going to miss our rides and our talks a *little* when your mom is able to drive again, aren't you?" The grandma was a little disappointed when she answered, "No!" Until the next moment when she said, "I'm going to miss this a *lot!*" What a special, bonding, terrifically hard, but once-in-a-lifetime experience for this grandmother and granddaughter!

An excellent violinist herself, a grandma who has been thrilled by classical music all her life loves taking one grandchild at a time to the symphony. They look forward to the event for several weeks and love having time to exchange emails and texts and do some research about what they are about to experience together in listening to some of the great music of the world!

Sleepovers are this grandmother's specialty. She loves having her ten-year-old granddaughter on a weekend to enjoy cooking and playing and reading together. At the moment, she only has one granddaughter who is the perfect age for a sleepover. After an evening of fun, they hop in "grandmother's feather bed" together and share stories and sometimes deep thoughts about life. This grandmother knows more about the worries and joys and loves of that granddaughter than anyone I know!

Another grandmother with lots of grandchildren has a "Grandchild of the Week" (kind of like the "Star of the Week" projects we used to do with our kids). At the beginning of the week, she puts the grandchild's picture somewhere where she will see it often as a reminder to do something special with that child when they live nearby or send a note or a handwritten letter or small package to those who live farther away. She also texts the older grandchildren to let them know that they are very important to her and that she is thinking of them.

> A birthday is a great time to let your grandchild know exactly what you love about them! I like to send them a birthday message that is not just a "Hallmark card."

"A birthday is a great time to let your grandchild know exactly what you love about them! I like to send them a birthday message that is not just a 'Hallmark card.' In fact, I send an email or even a text that includes specific things that I love about them. I know they love the little gifts I send, but they tell me as they have gotten older that the messages of love and encouragement I have sent them are much more important than any of the gifts that are soon forgotten!"

"I live very far away from my grandchildren, which is why I love technology! I can send them a short voice text message or a link to something I think they would be interested in. Sometimes I take just a minute to send a voicemail or a text to older children and teenagers to say something I love or admire about them, and I know they'll get it almost immediately. I love sending voice messages to my preschoolers and FaceTiming with them so they'll know my voice and my face the next time I see them. Electronics are my number-one tool for keeping in touch with my grandchildren one on one!"

And here's something from a grandmother that I don't know, but it's worth including:

My granddaughter came to spend a few weeks with me, and I decided to teach her to sew. After I had gone through a lengthy explanation of how to thread the machine, she stepped back, put her hands on her hips, and said in disbelief, "You mean you can do all that, but you can't figure out how to play Angry Birds on my phone?" :)

I hope you have found something in all these suggestions from marvelous grandmothers that will help you do better and be better as a grandmother. I know my mind has been opened to new ideas and new ways to bond with my grandchildren! Expressing our support to our grandchildren one on one during their hard times, our joy in good times, and our unequivocal faith in them at all times are some of the most important things we will ever do. As grandmothers, we can be their champions, their assistant coaches, and their cheerleaders whether we live next door or are halfway around the world. We can make them feel loved and courageous and strong and treasured, unconditionally.

I love this quote by Maya Angelou: "People will forget what you said, people will forget what you did, but people will never forget how you made them feel." Substitute the word "grandchildren" in place of "people" in the quote, and it becomes more powerful! Grandchildren will forget what you said, grandchildren will forget what you did, but grandchildren will never forget how you made them feel.

Thoughts?

- What ideas for one-on-one experiences have occurred to you as you have read the ideas of other grandmothers?
- Would you have to change your opinion about one or more of your grandchildren to truthfully be their champion?
- Contemplate how you make your grandchildren feel, including those who may be worrying you. *"We should all have one person who knows how to bless us despite the evidence; Grandmother was that person to me."* —Phyllis Theroux

CHAPTER 4

The Importance of a Strong Family Culture

Thoughts about Family Culture

I n the mayhem of motherhood, it's hard to appreciate the magnitude of the family culture you are creating within your home and family. Now that you are a grandmother, you can look back and appreciate some of the things that you didn't even realize you did to create your family culture. *Wikipedia describes a family culture as "an aggregate of attitudes, ideas and ideals, and environment, which a person inherits from his/her parents and ancestors."* There are so many attitudes, ideas, and ideals that we bring from the families we grew up with. That combined with the family culture our spouse brings to the table creates a unique family culture of our own.

Still, that culture is not set in stone. It continues to evolve. In our own case, as years passed, our family became more aware of nutrition and tried to make eating well part of our family culture. Every morning, Richard made a smoothie with fruits and vegetables, juice, yogurt, nuts, and anything else he could find that looked healthy. He started adding *lots* of carrots, kale, and spinach, and those smoothies were sometimes *too* creative. They began to look more like mud than a smoothie. One morning, the kids were actually choking on his concoction. It tasted horrible! Spicy! They had to spit it out. We were mystified until we realized that what he thought was a frozen banana was actually a frozen spicy sausage!

Our family culture grew and evolved over the years, much like the smoothies—mainly healthy, sometimes muddy, and occasionally a little too spicy!

Think with me for a few minutes about your family culture when you lived at home with your parents. Was it a culture of faith, of fun, of rules, of responsibility, of systems, of sibling rivalry, of character building, of chaos, of anger, of angst, of too little time, of lots of tenderness, of dynamic goals, or a combination of all that plus so much more?

How much of that family culture became a part of *your* family culture as you raised your own children? Some of you reading this have probably come from dysfunctional homes. You may have had to start from scratch to create a functional and enriching family culture. After seminars with mothers and grandmothers, several inevitably come up afterward to say that they are grateful for the ideas we have suggested for a happy family because they came from homes where alcohol and drugs and abuse were the family culture. Kudos to those brave souls who are determined to be the change in the trajectory of their families.

Creating a strong, functional family culture is no small task! As you read, think of the good things you did to create a strong family culture that created stability and strength while your children were home that are now being passed on to the families of your children (even though you may not have realized what you were doing at the time). Let's look at a few examples.

Family Meetings

Let's explore a couple of things that my sister Lenna (who is twelve-and-a-half months younger than I am) did to create a family culture that has had staying power. Family meetings were a big part of their family culture. Early on in their marriage, when her husband Bruce was under a lot of pressure at work, he called a meeting of their kids to explain that he was going into a big project at work and was going to have work long hours. He told them that they may not even see him for a while but that their mom would be there to take care of them and that it was their job to work hard, get good grades, take care of their jobs in the house, and be responsible for their actions. But no matter how busy he became, he always found time for regular meetings.

Those family meetings became even more important when there was a crisis or one of the children needed help. Bruce emphasized that their family was a team and that when one member was in trouble, they would work together until they came up with a plan to help, which they did over and over again as their family grew and difficult situations arose. Everyone rallied and came up with ways to help the one in need.

Meetings became part of their family culture. Little did he know that those gatherings and the advice Bruce gave in that poignant meeting described above would be one of the most valuable things that he could possibly have left with his family, because he passed away unexpectedly at age fifty-seven, just after their last child had married.

Those adult children are among the most responsible adults that I know. Even though they won't be "seeing him" for a very long time, they have followed his advice and have created beautiful families and become incredible people! Lenna is a marvelous matriarch and continues to call meetings when needed. One of her sons-in-law, who came from a very difficult family, couldn't believe it the first time he was included in a family meeting, which included the adult kids and their spouses. At that time, they were trying to come up with solutions to help one of Lenna's children with a serious problem. This son-in-law had never heard of a family meeting, and he couldn't believe the good that was accomplished in one hour as they all joined as a team to help the one in need.

When I asked Lenna how she has been able to maintain a strong family culture and keep her kids unified and loving each other, even after Bruce was gone, she had this to say:

> Even though we have dealt with difficult issues like divorce, depression, and serious illness, I have really worked on not judging their actions or opinions. And I try to just keep loving them unconditionally, no matter what! We meet every Friday night for dinner with those who can come and usually just enjoy catching up, but when someone in the family is in need, we are still a team, and together we figure out specific ways to help. Our continuing meetings are the key to our success.

Thoughts?

- How have you used family meetings to strengthen your family culture?
- Would it be advisable for you, as the grandmother (perhaps with your spouse), to suggest a family meeting to solicit help from your children for a family member who needs it?
- Record memories of your family meetings below.

Family Traditions

Social scientists have proven that fun is an important part of so-lidifying relationships. Along those lines, traditions and rituals are a powerful component of a family culture. We call them the glue that holds families together. Traditions create lasting emotional bonds and a certain energy that is shared not only during the event but in the memory of it too!

Whether you realize it or not, your family is loaded with traditions that you started that have now become part of your family culture. Every family has traditions. When we talk about traditions to audiences, eyes of parents and grandparents alike light up. They love sharing what they have done to bring back memories of having fun together. What follows are brief explanations of the traditions our kids grew up with that have filtered down to their families.

One of our most memorable traditions has always been at Christmastime. The first is something we call The Nazareth Supper. We started this when our children were small and loved to role play. On Christmas Eve, we dressed everyone in costumes that started with simple head scarfs and became more elaborate over the years. We pretended that we were in Nazareth, gathering for the last dinner at the house of Mary's parents before she and Joseph departed for Bethlehem. All the little girls relished the chance to be Mary, and one of the boys usually volunteered to be Joseph. Richard and I were usually Mary's parents, and the other guests were relatives or friends of the family, and sometimes "Biblical characters" were invited to join the dinner.

Whether you realize it or not, your family is loaded with traditions that you started that have now become part of your family culture.

The fun began when we were seated for dinner. The candles were lit and lights turned off while we enjoyed a simple meal similar to what they might have enjoyed all those years ago: fish, hummus, grapes and cheese, falafel and unleavened bread—and sometimes I found a honeycomb. I'm sure it wasn't totally authentic, but it created a wonderful and peaceful atmosphere on Christmas Eve.

The guests were free to ask questions of Mary and Joseph and Mary's parents. Their imaginations ran wild, and we got some pretty amazing inquiries. At the end of the dinner, we sent Mary off on the donkey (played by Richard), and we journeyed to Bethlehem, where the nativity was enacted—complete with angels and wise men with makeshift crowns and a little manger where our newest baby was swaddled and laid down on a sheepskin, wondering what in the world was going on!

We didn't realize when we started that little tradition that it would play out not only for years in our own family but would have its own life in the families of our adult children! Our oldest daughter, Saren, made simple but beautiful costumes for every family to use. Some Nazareth Suppers became exotic and more authentic, while others were simplified. Since it's impossible for most of our children to come home for Christmas anymore, we usually visit their homes and love watching their take on the Nazareth Supper and the depiction of the nativity in each home. We love pictures and videos of favorite moments from their homes on Instagram and FaceTime. I suspect that some of our grandchildren will have their own version of that tradition, maybe even after we are gone.

Other favorite rituals were birthday traditions. (We had so many kids, we had to do something special for them at least once a year, right?) Richard's tradition was a favorite. His birthday is October 28, the height of the autumn leaf season! When we started his tradition, it was just a matter of going out to the nearest park with lots of trees and playing in the fallen leaves. We buried the birthday "boy." After a few seconds of lying there silently, he would jump out, much to the delight of the little kids! We gathered piles and jumped in them and stuffed leaves down each other's backs. As time went on, the celebration got bigger and bigger. Friends were invited. Kids jumped out of trees into leaves and raked piles as high as an elephant's eye.

The year Saren and Shawni were missionaries in Bulgaria and Romania and Josh was at college, Richard received three envelopes in the mail, and to his surprise, a leaf dropped out of the girls' envelopes with notes saying that they would be jumping in the leaves with the orphans they were working with or with missionary companions to honor his special day. In essence, they reminded him, *Even though I'm far away, remember that I'm still part of our family!* The third envelope from Josh also contained a leaf, but no note (this is a guy). He knew that his dad would know what it meant! :) Now grandchildren are jumping in leaves all over the world on October 28 and sending pictures via Instagram to honor Grandfather's birthday.

Thoughts?

- What are the traditions that have strengthened bonds of your family culture (informal traditions like a simple family dinner every week count).
- Consider whether or not traditions like unconditional love and being non-judgmental are part of the culture of your extended family. If not, how can you be the change?
- Would it be possible for a Grandma to suggest a fun new family tradition? :)

A Culture of Service

We have encouraged families all over the world to create a "mission statement" with their families. I'm sad to say that idea didn't occur to us until our older children were teenagers. With the urgings of our dear friends Sandra and Stephen Covey, who are the "Mission Statement Gurus," we took our kids away for a weekend for the explicit purpose of creating a family mission or vision statement that encapsulated what our family was about and what we hoped to accomplish together.

After a long, elaborate process that included lots of ideas from the kids and several efforts to simplify, we came up with a three-word mission statement for our family. It was simply "Broaden and Contribute." When we posted those three words on our refrigerator door on a piece of paper with a magnet, we had no idea what that would do for our family culture.

To us, *broaden* meant getting the best education possible in order to broaden our view of the world. It meant broadening our understanding of different lifestyles, having compassion for those in need, and celebrating the mighty faith that is shown in different cultures and different beliefs than our own. To us, *contribute* meant that it was our job to give back because we have been blessed with so much.

For a family meeting, we had the kids do some research on world poverty. They reported that nearly half of the world's population—more than three billion people—live on less than

> After a long, elaborate process that included lots of ideas from the kids and several efforts to simplify, we came up with a three-word mission statement for our family. It was simply "Broaden and Contribute."

$2.50 a day. More than 1.3 billion live in extreme poverty—less than $1.25 a day. According to UNICEF, 22,000 children die each day due to poverty. Over 805 million people worldwide do not have enough food to eat.

The kids knew we lived in a comparatively luxurious house in a nice neighborhood with plenty to eat. They knew they had privileges only a tiny percentage of people in the world did, but Richard and I felt compelled to give them a glimpse of the real life of those who live in poverty.

The next year, we prepared the kids for a different kind of Christmas. We wanted it be one that was more about giving than receiving. But as it turned out, we received a lot more that we gave! We went to a village in the Altiplano (high plain) of Bolivia, where we helped to dig trenches in rock-hard soil with picks and shovels at 14,000 feet so that villagers could have running water in their village for the first time.

The kids had so much fun after their work day when they played with the darling little village kids. We were invited into their 10x6-foot dirt-floor homes with no windows, and the Bolivian children loved seeing Polaroid pictures of themselves. On New Year's Day, before we left, we turned on the first water faucet ever in the middle of that little village. When the water gushed out of that faucet, the villagers were astonished! But the look on the faces of our children were priceless! It was an extraordinary eye-opening and bonding experience we will never forget.

That was the beginning of a long series of humanitarian expeditions. During school holidays and occasionally for a week in the summer, the kids made bricks and built school desks in Africa and helped plant gardens and went into poverty-stricken homes in the mountains of central Mexico with CHOICE Humanitarian (**choicehumanitarian.org**).

I know what you might be thinking: *That has got to be exorbitantly expensive! Our family, and now our extended families, could never afford that.* But you would be surprised. We got discounted group airfares, ate food prepared by the villagers, and slept on the schoolroom floors and sometimes in tents. Some of our trips turned out to cost less than a family trip for a week to Disneyland.

We had no idea how far our little attempt at a family mission statement would go. As years passed, their devotion to humanitarian service didn't stop when the children left home and started their own families. The culture of service has thrived in the next generation. Humanitarian service has now gotten into the blood of our grandchildren!

Our Arizona family traveled just over the border (ninety minutes) to Mexico one Christmas Eve and helped, along with about fifty other people, build three houses for needy families over the Christmas holidays. They took their five kids and had the time of their lives learning how to build cinderblock houses and playing with the village kids. To see how they did it, go to *71toes.com/house*. You can also visit the Families Helping Families website, if you're interested, at *fhfmexico.org*.

They stayed in motels, and because they lived so close, that adventure was a lot cheaper than Disneyland!

Recently, members of our families have gone to India to help with a wonderful project there called Rising Star Outreach (*risingstaroutreach.org*). It is an extraordinary nonprofit organization that, among other things, has built a beautiful school for children whose families have been stricken with leprosy and would otherwise not be able to attend school. Our oldest grandson, sixteen-year-old Max, completed his Eagle Scout project there. He raised money for books that could be bought in the country, and among other things, he hand-carried a book for each child that they wanted most to read in English, *Pippy Longstocking*. To see Max surrounded with beautiful, happy children in India, go to *71toes.com/giving*.

Our next oldest grandson, Ashton, did his Eagle Project in the orphanage in Bulgaria where his mother served while she was on a

> We didn't have to go across the world to contribute to the lives of others. There were friends and neighbors in a different kind of need right under our noses!

mission. She had been working to raise funds for this and many other orphanages in Bulgaria since the day she returned home. Their organization is called One Heart Bulgaria. Ashton had been in charge of their family's annual Children for Children Concert for many years to raise money for the orphanage. (Details on raising the money are found in Chapter 9.) Finally, he was able to see the orphanage and, among other things, present them with a computer that he had raised money to buy as part of his project. To see the good work this grandson did, go to *looslifamily.blogspot.com/mission-accomplished*.

During those early humanitarian expeditions, we discovered that several of the families we traveled with were supported by grandparents who wanted their children and grandchildren to have these experiences, even when they weren't able to go themselves. In Chapter 9, you will see that see that our family members can apply for a matching grant from a fund that Richard and I have set up for the purpose of helping our grandchildren help others. They can also apply if they see other great causes that require financial aid.

Of course, there are many other ways to contribute and serve others that don't require any money at all. Our greatest awakenings from these experiences was that we didn't have to go across the world to contribute to the lives of others. There were friends and neighbors in a different kind of need right under our noses! Even though our children and now grandchildren are busy with their lives in school and work and involved with their own friends, there's always time to lend a helping hand. In family meetings, we used to challenge our kids to sit by someone in the cafeteria that week who looked as though they needed a friend and start a conversation. Such great stories emerged from those experiences that they are now encouraging their children to do the same. It has been a courageous and outstanding learning experience. Those stories from kids who have found somebody in need in their own realm are eye-opening and maybe more important than the ones we learned in those countries far away, because they have ongoing opportunities to make a difference in someone's life.

Come to think of it, this culture of looking for someone who needs help in your own world started with my mother. When I was an awkward seventh grader, several times a year, we would have dances at school. I hated those days! I was the epitome of a wallflower, with funny hair and salmon-colored cat-eye glasses. I was never asked to dance and hated that hour of misery. One day, when I knew "the dance" was going to be that day, I begged my mother to let me stay home! I told her that I had a stomachache (which I did), but she managed to get to the bottom of what was going on right away. She challenged me to find someone at the dance who was also sitting on the sidelines, looking more miserable than me, and start asking questions. I could see that my mom wasn't going to let me stay home, so with a heavy heart, I reluctantly dragged myself to the school.

Within minutes of when the dance started, I found my girl. I was ultra-shy anyway, and the thought of talking to someone I didn't know, especially her, was worse than my misery! I was terrified. She was an albino with pure white hair and buck teeth; no one ever talked to her. It took me quite a long time to summon the courage to go sit by her and even longer to ask the first question. But to make a long story short, she became a good friend, and we supported each other. She died because of health reasons as a young adult. I'm so glad my mom helped me find her!

Ways to cultivate a family culture of service are everywhere. And it is a special delight to serve with your grandchildren! Last Christmas, while visiting our grandchildren in Arizona, we had the opportunity to go to one of the largest homeless shelters in America. It was heartwarming to see our grandchildren bravely serving food to and engaging with the men and women who came in for lunch. They were amazed at the stories they heard and that most of them were just good people who were dealing with horrendously hard lives.

I have an incredible friend who is a grandmother in her eighties. She has been my idol for many years. The second-most enjoyable thing in her life has been serving others. The first is serving others with her grandchildren. She is consistently helping at the homeless shelters and refugee centers with a grandchild in tow, and she loves working with her grandchildren to make cookies, find warm clothing, and make infant-care kits that she drops off at humanitarian service centers. Her life has been one full of glorious, usually anonymous service!

---

*You can find many wonderful ways to serve along with your grandchildren in your own town, anywhere across America, at **justserve.org**. You'll be amazed at what you find. Have fun!*

Thoughts?

- Did you have a family mission statement or mantra? Maybe you have one that is part of your family's tradition that has never been formally written. In retrospect, if you could write one now, what would it say?
- As a grandmother, what can you do to strengthen your family culture based on the values you have always held dear?
- Here's a challenge I'm offering, not just to you, but also to myself: think of ways to give service with your grandchildren!

Adjusting Your Family Culture as Your Family Expands

When our children began to leave home (not because of the smoothies) and began to create their own lives and families, we realized that our own culture now needed to be a big "umbrella culture" broad enough to accommodate the new traditions that our children were developing in their own families.

Our umbrella culture needed to include loving and caring for our children who are still single as well as our married children and their children, amidst all their ups and downs. It had to be an umbrella under which understanding could abide, no matter what the circumstances, even if there was disagreement or rebellion. That umbrella culture of love and acceptance stabilizes our family against the wind that swirls around us, and it remains a constant source of protection, even though our children are out there completely enveloped in their own lives.

The remainder of this chapter includes ideas for creating an umbrella culture that will strengthen your family. As our families change, so must we, darn it! After many years of "being in charge," we are now in an era that is about "going with the flow."

> **Our own culture now needed to be a big "umbrella culture" broad enough to accommodate the new traditions that our children were developing in their own families.**

Instead of telling our kids what we think they should do, the water is much smoother if we give advice sparingly and usually only when we're asked for it. And perhaps the most important part, as they move off into their own realms, is keeping in touch with their feelings and needs.

Flexibility

I've been working really hard on something (sometimes with gritted teeth) since our children have gone and come back and as we have visited them. It's something that I think is really important to keep everybody feeling good under that umbrella: it's called *flexibility*. It is something that can keep our "umbrella" from flying away in the wind!

As children leave, work, marry, and have their own lives and children, life gets complicated. There are so many things that are planned and then changed. So many schedules that need to be considered. So many opinions that are firm. So many mothers with different rules. All require flexibility!

With the minutiae of our big family, I find myself realizing over and over again that I'm not really in charge anymore. Or even when I am, like when I'm planning a family dinner at our house, I recognize the fact that ideas and schedules will ebb and flow and plans will change as we go along. My busy grandchildren and their pesky parents keep changing their minds about what will work. The days of doing things my way, on my timetable, are over!

This story from a friend is a perfect example:

> This summer, while we were having our extended family reunion, a couple of the families changed my plan of having a family meeting because they wanted to go camping. I was upset, but I didn't say anything because we were spending quite a bit of time together in other ways. They had their reasons and needs, and I just had to respect that even though it wasn't how I had pictured it in my mind, at least they were cooperating *some* of the time.

So go our lives as grandmothers!

I have found one word that keeps popping up over and over again as plans change and I'm disappointed when someone can't come or when some whole event has to be changed because of a major conflict. The word is **Whatever!** I have that word engraved on a rock on my desk to remind me that nothing (except that word!) is ever set in stone.

Another word that Richard and I love is *serendipity*. Richard has written *books* about it! It is a word coined by Horace Walpole in the 1800s. The definition is "a state of mind wherein a person, through awareness and sagacity, frequently discovers something better than that which he is seeking."

As grandmothers, we need to let serendipity take over when dealing with our families. Rather than feeling upset about a change of plans, we need to embrace serendipity. The concept is that if you're really looking for it, a change of plans will eventually help you find something better than the original plan.

To illustrate, a friend writes:

I guess we need to learn how to give as much enthusiasm to Plan B as we would have given to Plan A. Being flexible is such a great human trait. Think of it. What makes each person's life path great? Our ability to change, grow, adapt, and enlarge or change paths altogether. So, for something as small as a Sunday dinner in which the roast burned, we can have tuna sandwiches and eat them on the back lawn as a picnic. Plan B at its best.

Thoughts?

- How flexible are you?
- Do you join me in thinking that it is a huge relief to just think "whatever" and let it go?

- Challenge: Look for opportunities to experience serendipity in your life. Learn to love situations that haven't turned out as planned but worked out better in the end. It keeps life exciting. :)

Advice and the Use of Duct Tape

In a hilarious article called "Grandmothers Should Be Seen and Not Heard," Anne Roiphe says, "Not speaking your mind is the number-one commandment for would-be beloved grandparents. Silence on certain issues is not just the golden rule—it's essential." She goes on to say, "Ah, my poor tongue is sore from being bitten."

If we look back at our own parents and our grandparents, we realize that parenting has gone through an enormous evolution during the past two generations. In the world of our grandparents and great-grandparents, children were often to be "seen and not heard." One friend confided, "When I went to visit my grandparents as a child, I was basically ignored. I went off to play with my cousins, and I don't remember ever having a conversation with my grandparents. They told me what to do, when to stop interrupting, and where to sit, but there was never any person-to-person communication. They were just 'my grandparents.'"

For most of us, that is pretty much a thing of the past. Relationships have changed for the better. Over the years, we have tried to actively include our children in our conversations. As they grew older, we welcomed and respected their

One of the hardest things about watching our children as they create their own cultures with their spouses and with their children is knowing whether or not to give advice!

opinions. Things have also changed as we watch our children's parenting with both admiration . . . and, sometimes, with a strong urge to give advice. I think you'll agree that advice is tricky!

One of the hardest things about watching our children as they create their own cultures with their spouses and with their children is knowing whether or not to give advice! We often think we know exactly what would "fix" things that aren't working, but should we tell them? It's a dilemma! It can undermine or break a relationship. Negative comments can create feelings of offense and incompetence and lead to less communication in the future. I have often thought that it would be good to take along some duct tape that I could put over my mouth when I feel something that could be offensive coming out. Even more important, I need to carry it for Richard's mouth! :)

A young friend shared a few things with me that her parents were saying about her only child that were meant to be helpful but came across as sharp criticism. Her parents shared very clearly what they thought about her parenting. They expressed criticism directly to her and said things like, "You just can't say no!" "Your child terrorizes you!" or "That child is too sensitive!"

This is not helpful! As grandmothers, we have to admit that those thoughts may have also crossed our minds with our own children's parenting, but usually, we are able to contain ourselves!

Even if we are pretty sure we have the answer to their problems, giving advice on "how to do it" (especially unsolicited) is the last thing our kids usually need. Still, not giving advice is hard. As

> Even if we are pretty sure we have the answer to their problems, giving advice on "how to do it" (especially unsolicited) is the last thing our kids usually need.

grandparents, it is so temping to say things like "Just say no!" or "Can't you see what's happening here?" or "You've got to let him know who's the boss!" or "She needs to know that the consequences for disobedience are swift and unalterable!" When those thoughts come to our minds . . . it's time to get out the duct tape and slap it over our mouths!

I've found that the best thing I can do when a parent is exasperated with a child who is misbehaving is to give them confidence in finding a solution. It's great to talk situations through with your kids when help is solicited, but unless you feel that the child is in danger of serious consequences, it usually works to say something like, "I know this child might be driving you crazy right now and you may think he is going to end up in the penitentiary, but this is just a stage. He will eventually be able to control his behavior. Strong-willed children are the ones who make great contributions in the end, and messy kids are usually the most right-brained and artistic ones!" Positive affirmations are by far the best way to breed confidence and stimulate healthy relationships.

We had a few feisty kids that must have driven my parents—our children's grandparents—crazy! I don't remember my parents ever giving me any advice about how to handle our children. My dad would never say a word. And my mother didn't bother us with her opinion. She went right to the source! One of our daughters was a whiner. She was nine years old and still whining and crying about something incessantly. It drove us all crazy, but try as we might, we couldn't get her to stop. When she was about ten years old, my mother took her aside one day and very seriously told her that she was willing to give her $10 (which was worth a lot more in those days) if she could go for one whole week without whining. Those brown eyes lit up, as she was very aware of her need for money! Believe it or not, she quit whining! There were occasional slip-ups after that week, but she figured out how to distract herself when she was tempted to start whining. It was sort of a miracle!

Occasionally, we may see our children using parenting techniques that may actually be damaging to our grandchildren. There may be a place for a gentle reminder. I love this story by one of our church leaders, Joseph Brough, about his wonderful grandmother:

> One of [God's] most beloved tools in guiding his children is righteous grandparents. My father's mother was such a woman. On an occasion that took place when I was too young to remember, my father was disciplining me. Observing this correction, my grandmother said, "Monte, I believe you are correcting him too harshly." My father replied, "Mother, I will correct my children as I want." And my wise grandmother softly stated, "And so will I." I'm pretty sure my father heard the wise guidance of his mother that day.[1]

There are more than just discipline issues with our grandchildren that beg for advice with our children. Our grown children face big decisions about jobs, cars, and houses. Richard and I have entirely different methods when it comes to giving them advice. If our children sincerely ask for help, I do give some suggestions. We reason together and try to come up with some solutions. I try to always end our conversation with "Just go with what feels right. I know you will come up with a good solution to this problem."

I try to always end our conversation with "Just go with what feels right. I know you will come up with a good solution to this problem."

Richard's personality doesn't work that way. He is dying to give advice. In fact, he can't help himself! He has to do it! That roll of duct tape in my pocket comes in handy on such occasions so I can slap a piece over his mouth when he starts to "wax eloquent" with advice. (Just kidding. Sort of. :))

He is certain that he can think of solutions that they may not be able to see. He came to grips with his own shortcomings in sharing advice early in our experience with married children, so he decided to call a meeting of the children at a family reunion. There he offered a deal for giving advice. In fact, we ended up calling it a "pact." First, he told them that it would be impossible for him not to give them advice when he felt it was needed. Their part of the pact was that *they would not be offended* by his advice when he told them what he really thought they should do. But his part of the pact was that *he would not be offended* if they didn't follow his advice.

Actually, both sides of the pact have worked out well. Usually Richard's advice is well taken, and it often helps with the solution they are looking for. But I have to admit that it is a special delight to our kids when they have not taken his advice and been right! Our oldest daughter and her husband first settled in Silicon Valley and were concerned about buying a small house for what seemed to us to be an astonishingly exorbitant amount of money. Despite both of our adamant urgings that it wouldn't be a good idea, they bought the house, fixed it up, and sold it five years later for double the price they paid. We loved our piece of humble pie!

Thoughts?

- How good are you at biting your tongue when you know that your advice is only going to create bad feelings?
- Do you dare give advice with sensitivity when you feel that a child is being mistreated?
- Is it easy to replace negative thoughts with positive affirmations? If not, is it possible to train ourselves to do so?

Questionnaire

As you may have noticed, Richard and I are big on questionnaires! Last summer at the end of our reunion, we had a dinner for just the nineteen adult men and women in our family. During the evening, Richard handed out a questionnaire entitled "The Three-Generation Partnership: Where Parents Are Managers and Grandparents Are Resources and/or Consultants)." We had been guessing at how much help with their kids and how much advice our children would like to have. We knew that some were more receptive to advice than others, and we tried to be sensitive to that, but we thought it was time we quit guessing and just ask. The last thing we wanted was to be labeled "meddlers"! Each of the parents as well as our single son were given a questionnaire to fill out.

Each spouse answered separately, and no one saw anyone else's answers. They just said what they thought. There were opportunities for comments at the end of each section. The responses were fascinating! Some were predictable, but there were some surprises. Here is what we included in the questionnaire:

Questionnaire

How can we, as empty-nest parents and stewardship/consultant grandparents, be of help, support, and assistance to you and your family?

Advice: I would welcome input or counsel (pick one) . . .

____at your initiative on whatever you observe or feel is needed.

____only as I request it.

____only on an action or in a situation where you perceive danger or serious consequences.

Teaching my kids: I would welcome your help (pick one) . . .

___in any teaching situation you see or create.

___only when I request it.

___on things we have discussed and agreed on—a teamwork approach.

My kids' needs: I think the best way to keep you up to speed on our kids is (pick one) . . .

___You initiate questions and inquiries about how my kids are doing in various areas.

___I will initiate communication about my kids, their progress, their needs, and my concerns about them.

___We should have, in person or by phone, a regular "five-facet review"[2] of each of our kids and take a teamwork approach to helping them and maximizing their potential.

The answers, for the most part, told us that our kids welcomed our input and help with their kids. Most welcomed it at any time. A few wanted input only when requested. We were cautioned about talking about sensitive topics without their approval, and one mostly just wanted more help with babysitting. It was fascinating . . . and useful!

Thoughts?

- Would a questionnaire like this be helpful, impossible, or absurd for your children?
- If you think it would be intrusive, what else could you do to encourage your children to let you know how they feel about your involvement with their children?

Conclusion

Grandmothers are often the kingpin of a family culture. You are anything but irrelevant. I am always inspired by funerals, especially funerals of grandmothers. Grandchildren often speak of their grandmother's wise influence, their great advice, their love, and their faith as having been a beacon of light in their lives. Their children speak of them as champions and saviors. As you have read this chapter, I hope you have considered your own family culture and have realized how important you have been and will continue to be in creating your family culture.

This year, I visited with one of my cousins who knew my grandmother Nellie much better than I did and was close to her until Grandmother Nellie died. She told of having struggled as a teenager with self-esteem and was hanging out with some girls that were not good for her. In a quiet conversation, Grandma told her that she was very worried about the friends she was keeping and strongly advised her to find new friends. My cousin said that if her mother had told her that, she would never have listened, but coming from her beloved grandmother, it made sense. She found new friends, and it changed her life forever.

Grandmothers are often the kingpin of a family culture. You are anything but irrelevant.

Thank you for being the light, the umbrella, the force, the influencer, the advisor, and the champion of your family!

Thoughts?

- What are the important things that you have done in your own family to create a strong family culture?
- At your funeral, what will your grandchildren say you did to create your family culture?

Notes

1. April LDS 2017 General Conference, Saturday morning session.

2. *How is Jimmy doing physically, mentally, socially, emotionally, and spiritually?*

Chapter 5

Adding In-Laws and Babies

A friend told me that when her kids started to marry, she and her family chose not to call their new family members in-laws. Instead, they called them "in-loves"! I think that's such a fun idea, especially if you really love all your in-laws! Since this chapter was already written when she suggested that, I'm going to leave it as is, but if you like, you can make the substitution in your minds as you read. Ha!

In our family, as weddings rolled out, we found many ways to appreciate our children-in-law! Our first in-law got the baptism by fire into our family. Poor David was trapped in a car for seven hours with Richard driving from Jackson Hole, Wyoming, to Salt Lake City, Utah, just after he had asked for our daughter Shawni's hand in marriage, and Richard was interviewing all the way! It would have been fun to be a fly on the roof of that car! It takes a

> **As our in-laws began joining our family, we were so grateful not only for their unique personalities but also for the interesting and new perspectives they brought to the family.**

long time to get from Jackson to Salt Lake (plus, Richard intentionally missed a turn, and they took a little detour). After that, one of the reasons that we knew we loved David so much was that he survived that ride with flying colors!

As our in-laws began joining our family, we were so grateful not only for their unique personalities but also for the interesting and new perspectives they brought to the family. They have added so much to our family and have brought their own unique extended families into our realm! As more in-laws began to arrive, the lens of their personalities came into focus and we realized what perfect partners they were for our children as well as stellar future parents. They made them so much better! I'll briefly introduce our couples so you can recognize them a bit as their stories pop up throughout the book.

Shawni and **David** met at BYU. They have made their home in the Phoenix area with five kids and a dog named Bo Jangles. Two have already left home: a son is on an LDS mission in Taiwan, and a daughter is studying at BYU–Hawaii. Recently, the family spent a semester in China (since David works there half time anyway), which did a great job of broadening the kids' horizons!

Saren met **Jared** in Boston, where they were both in college. He is a farm boy from Idaho, much to the delight of my farm-girl-from-Idaho heart! They started their family in San Jose, CA, and had five kids in just under five years, including identical twin boys. We're glad they survived! Those five are now thriving at ages 13–18, and they live in Odgen, Utah.

Jonah also found **Aja** in Boston while they were both going to school. They are true adventurers and have lived in Las Vegas, New Zealand, and Washington state before their current location in Maui. Last year, they spent six months traveling all over Europe with their five kids in an SUV, and they did it all on a shoestring budget!

Saydi met **Jeff** in Washington, DC, where they were both working. They had loved their schooling in Boston and ended up going back there for twenty years! This year, they are on an adventure with their four kids, taking care of a one-hundred-acre farm near Half Moon Bay, CA, where they specialize in goat milking, plant cropping, beekeeping, and homeschooling.

Talmadge met **Anita** while they were both working in New York City. After a one-year "humanitarian honeymoon" in Mozambique and India, they returned to NYC, where their daughter was born. They now live near Anita's hometown in Switzerland where Tal is in sales management for a European company in several countries all over the world.

Noah met **Kristi** at BYU–Hawaii, and they got engaged at the top of the world at Machu Picchu. Their first three children were born in New York City, where Noah placed an online language-learning program in the NYC schools. Three more children were born after a move to California. They have just moved to Utah and are starting an exciting new international company.

Eli met **Julie** on a study abroad program in Jerusalem. They married and moved to Washington, DC, where they both worked until the arrival of their first baby girl. A dream move to NYC has both of them adoring living near Central Park. They are scrambling to keep up with a second child with a third one on the way in a fifth-floor walk-up on the upper west side of Manhattan.

Charity found **Ian** in San Francisco, where she was working and he was finishing his PhD. After a roller-coaster romance, they realized that they couldn't live without each other, married, and traveled to six continents and ten countries in eighty days just before Ian began his demanding job in London, where they now live with their adorable one-year-old and another on the way.

Babies Dropping Down from Heaven

For me, one of the sweetest joys of being a grandmother is being at or near the births of our grandchildren. When I have been lucky enough to watch the actual births on a few occasions, there was a clear feeling that heaven was near. Except for the nine times I have given birth to our own babies, nothing has given me more joy than watching these new little grand-spirits emerge into the world. It's as close to heaven as we'll ever get on earth!

After the flurry and initial relief of the end of labor and the joy and glory of the first moments of entry into the world, the baby born in a hospital is usually whisked away to a warm bassinet and left alone until the nurses arrive while the mother is being cared for. I love that moment when I can grab the tiny, flailing hands of that newborn to let them feel that they aren't alone as I privately welcome this precious child into their new world. It only lasts a minute, but it's a minute that I never forget as I feel the grasp of that confused little hand and let them know that someone who loves them is there.

> I love that moment when I can grab the tiny, flailing hands of that newborn to let them feel that they aren't alone as I privately welcome this precious child into their new world.

On one such occasion, there was a strange development. As I was holding hands, I counted those ten sweet tiny fingers and then checked out the toes. On newborn Lucy's right foot, I kept counting to six. *One, two, three, four, five . . . six,* I kept repeating in my mind. Finally, I asked Lucy's daddy, David, to come and count those toes. He counted and got the same number. We were stunned. For the first few months, the doctors assured Shawni that children are often born with extra digits, which are easily removed. But markers for her normal progress didn't add up, and by Lucy's first birthday, they knew she had a very rare condition called Bardet-Biedl Syndrome.

Lucy is the light of our lives, but sadly, she will probably lose her own light in her eyes within a few years. Blindness between nine and fourteen is normal for kids with that syndrome. Her parents, along with others who have children affected with BBS, have now started a foundation called Families Fighting Blindness to find and gather information from parents all over the US whose children have the syndrome to aid in research. More details about our lovable Lucy are found in Chapter 6.

We've had grandchildren born all over the world: from New Zealand to London, from Los Angeles to New York City, from San José to Boston, from Gilbert to Fairfax, from Las Vegas to the Olympic Peninsula, from Washington, DC, to Maui. I thrill at the memory of being there at or shortly after each birth. Each delivery is different and earth shaking, and every mom's preference is different. I won't bore you with *all* the details, but I will tell you about three of the more spectacular deliveries.

Some of our mothers call for epidurals for the pain when things get really rough—which I looked forward to several times, but my babies flew out too fast. Only two epidurals actually worked in time for the delivery (one actually worked *after* the delivery), and I have to admit that one out of nine deliveries was peaceful and calm, which was pretty nice!

On the other hand, many of our daughters and daughters-in-law are adamant about having absolutely natural childbirths.

Several have had midwives and doulas and have taken classes, read books, and are "over the moon" about giving birth at birthing centers, where the lights are low, the music is ethereal, and a loving doula talks them through the process of giving birth. Saydi is one of those "naturals," even though the birth doesn't always go as planned.

In a warm birthing tub in Cambridge, Massachusetts, she was laboring with her second child when the midwife told her that she would have to get out of the tub to deliver the baby because she hadn't had an HIV test! As the pains became very strong, she suddenly said, "I think I'd better get out of the tub and move to bed." She stood up, and as I turned to leave the room, I heard a big splash and was horrified, as I thought Saydi had fallen in the tub, only to realize that *the baby* had actually "fallen out" *into* the tub! The doula scooped him up while we were all stunned with the sudden change of plans. When we felt secure that both mother and baby were doing great, we couldn't stop being amazed at little Charlie's dazzling dive into the world!

With Saydi's last baby, she had better luck at the birthing center. I watched with awe and wonder during her little Peter's water birth. As he emerged from the birth canal and up through the water of the tub, I could see his little face coming up to the surface in perfect peace to greet his calm and joyous mother. It was as ethereal as watching a total eclipse of the sun, except better! Heaven was there.

We watched another spectacular birth at 3 a.m. from our Park City home on Eli's iPhone as the courageous Julie delivered their first baby vaginally and . . . breech! The baby was delivered by a well-trained team of doctors in Washington, DC, who knew exactly what to do. We simply could not contain our anxiety and excitement as we watched, holding our breath and praying, as Zara's little feet emerged first! Although Eli was very discreet about the details of what we saw, Julie is an exceptional nurse and was somehow brave enough to allow several OB/GYN interns to watch the experts do that astonishing delivery.

It's important to document those births, not only for the parents but also for the grandparents. When Eli's children are born, he asks me to write a letter to them about our first days together. He saves my recollections online to be read on future birthdays.

A friend from Switzerland told me that her daughter asked her to write a letter to her firstborn granddaughter to be delivered to her on her eighteenth birthday. In the envelope, that grandmother deposited one hundred francs and left a message that said if she was still alive on that day, they would go shopping!

Thoughts?

- What are your best memories of the births of your grandchildren?
- Have you written your thoughts so your grandchild can treasure your perspective later in life? If not, consider it!

Taking Care of the Mama

Every mother-daughter and daughter-in-law situation is unique at the birth of a new baby. There is no "one size fits all" way for a grandma to help with babies. Every expectant mother's wishes should be carefully discussed before the birth of a baby. Some women want their mothers or mothers-in-law in the delivery room, and others want their mothers to wait in the waiting room or wait until later to help. Some first-time mothers don't know what they want until it happens.

It's also important to be sure that your son/sons-in-law are comfortable with the arrangements you've made with their wives. One son-in-law admitted that he was pretty apprehensive about my coming for a whole week when their first baby was born, but afterward, as I was departing, he was so dear in expressing his sincere thanks for our exciting and unforgettable days together.

But for me, the next best thing to being there at the birth is being able to take care of the mom (and dad) while she takes care of the baby during the first week or so after birth. Usually I stay for the first week after the baby is born when it's our daughters having the baby, and then wait until the mom of our daughters-in-law leaves after that first week to get my turn during the second week with the newborn. Sometimes I'm lucky enough to be the first responder with daughters-in-law when their mothers are not available. On one occasion, the other grandma was helping a family who had another grandbaby on the very same day. And another's mother was living in Switzerland and couldn't get there, so I got to step in. In any event, I am thrilled every time I get to spend a few days with a newborn and their family.

We have so much fun together, even as we deal with the multiple issues of having a new baby. All have breastfed their babies, and since breastfeeding is harder than labor and delivery for me and our daughters (who seem to have those same genes), I can offer some advice, along with the help of lactation consultants. The daughters-in-law amaze me with their plentiful supply of milk!

Probably the best thing I have to offer during those first tenuous days as they worry about issues that always come up with a newborn are these words: "That's normal."

Probably the best thing I have to offer during those first tenuous days as they worry about issues that always come up with a newborn are these words: "That's normal." Most of the issues are predictable, but some are so different that we call the midwife, doula, or doctor for answers. All of it is fun for me!

To be honest, I think what I love most is watching the babies sleep during those first days. Their eyes are closed, but soon they start with rapid-eye movement, which I am convinced means that they are dreaming. What do they have to dream about except where they've just been, I ask you? They inevitably smile and then smile again. I am certain that it isn't gas. They are talking to the angels. Once I was sitting late at night with our second grandchild Elle, when she did that rapid-eye movement/smile thing over and over again with her twitchy little smile, as though she was talking to someone. The parents were gone, and it was dark and quiet, when suddenly she laughed! I'm not kidding. Just as I wondered if I had imagined it, within a minute she laughed again. She was having a great conversation with somebody on the other side of that veil of forgetfulness that William Wordsworth describes so beautifully in his "Ode: Intimations of Immortality." I love this thought, although in quoting it, people usually leave off the last and most important line. It goes like this:

> *Our birth is but a sleep and a forgetting:*
> *The Soul that rises with us, our life's Star,*

Hath had elsewhere its setting,
And cometh from afar:
Not in entire forgetfulness,
And not in utter nakedness,
But trailing clouds of glory do we come
From God, who is our home:
Heaven lies about us in our infancy!

Call me crazy, but even now, I can't read that without tearing up!

Helping with first babies is delightful because the mom (and dad) and baby get all the attention. I love cooking with a new baby in-house. It's my chance to try new recipes and enjoy some good food together. When other children are added to the mix, and some happen to be picky eaters, I go with the mother's suggestions for food, but I am *still,* even after all these years, not too sympathetic to fussy eaters. I give them the opportunity to make their own peanut butter sandwich if they don't like what I've prepared. No offense taken (hopefully on either side).

I often look back with fond memories at the days when my mother and mother-in-law used to come and help with a new baby. Back then, though, we usually lived in places that were foreign to them, and they would never dare drive to the grocery store. I made sure that lots of food was packed in the fridge and freezer to keep us all happy until I was well enough to go out myself. Whatever works for you is great. Just for the record, though, nothing gives me more pleasure than being in the household and helping with a newborn!

I'm including comments below from a few of those mothers with whom I shared those intimate first few days of the life their newborns . . . because Julie thought I should. :)

From our youngest daughter, Charity, who was living in London at the birth of her first child:

Becoming a mom with my mom was one of the very sweetest experiences of my life. It was extremely comforting and empowering to have her with me as I waited for labor to begin, progressed through labor, snuggled my newborn for the first time, and then tried to figure out what the heck I was doing during those first surreal and sleep-deprived days of motherhood. Besides being such a huge supporter mentally and physically, she cleaned the house, made meals, and convinced me to sleep while the baby was sleeping. I will cherish the days we spent together around my son's birth forever, and I'm so looking forward to that precious time with Mom/Grammie when future babies come along.

From our daughter-in-law Kristi:

Taking the leap of leaving home and figuring out who I am has been one the most beautiful, eye-opening, tender, stretching, and sacred experiences in my life. Becoming a mother has added more dimensions to that than I thought was possible. Having the help and support of my own mother and wonderful mother-in-law has meant more than the world to me. We don't have a manual for life, but we have something even better—our mothers! The time spent with them during those first few days after welcoming a new baby are forever etched in my heart and in my husband's and other children's hearts as well.

We had a child that came to us with a special heart that has needed intervention with some hospital stays. All four of her grandparents selflessly came to our rescue on several occasions during this process. One set stayed home and helped with the baby's four siblings while the other stayed by our side at the hospital and offered much-needed support.

Here is a message from our Swiss daughter-in-law, Anita, who gave birth to a daughter in NYC. This is what she remembered most about our week together:

1. You made wonderfully healthy food.
2. You let us "be."

Love that Anita! :) And finally, here is a kind note from daughter-in-law Julie that made me laugh:

Whenever I tell my friends that my mother-in-law has come to help with both my babies, they are very surprised. They proceed to tell me stories that I can't even believe about dealing with new babies and mothers-in-law. Granted, I live in New York City in a very small space, and so when someone comes to visit, it is a very intimate situation.

I believe it has been successful for two reasons: The first is that she refrains from any interference or judgment. I can imagine how silly my husband and I must have acted with our first baby, being so worried about little things. We probably even corrected the way she was helping with the baby. Thinking back, I am pretty embarrassed—since Linda has had nine babies of her own and could not be more of an expert! But we all know that the first-baby journey is one we all have to go through, and her non-judgmental presence helped so much with my recovery.

The second reason is that Linda did whatever was needed. If we were out of milk, she was the first one out the door in the morning, down four flights of stairs, to get it. She grocery shops, cooks, cleans, picks up my favorite treat, sends us on our first date night. It is wonderful to have someone who can do the day-to-day thinking for me while I just focus on the baby. I am incredibly grateful for my mother and mother-in-law during this amazing, wonderful, yet incredibly difficult week with a new baby.

Thoughts?

- How do you feel about being at the births of your grand-babies? How does the mother feel? It's fun to ponder and remember those joyous memories!
- How do your sons-in-law feel about the help you pro-vide after a birth? (It never occurred to me that they wouldn't be thrilled to have me!) :)
- If it isn't always possible to be there physically, what do you do to connect with the baby and the parents after the birth? What do you do to help your children during this massive transition?

Gathering Daughters and Daughters-in-Law

Let's start at the beginning with MFME, our acronym for the women in our family: the Mothers and Future Mothers of Eyrealm. You may be wondering about the backstory on the word *Eyrealm*. When Richard and I were married, I gave him a wide gold wedding band so that I could have the words "The Higher Realm" inscribed on the inside. We had agreed that we wanted to reach higher and be better as a couple than we had been as individuals. As our family grew larger, "higher realm" morphed into Eyrealm, which we thought would be a good name that would include all the people in "our realm." When we started having group activities with our girls, which eventually included our daughters-in-law as they came in one by one, we called our little group Mothers and Future Mothers of Eyrealm or MFME.

As our older daughters left for college and missions and study abroad experiences and jobs, I started to worry about whether I had taught them enough about the importance of motherhood. Did they know (especially since I wrote a book called *I Didn't Plan to Be a Witch* when all the kids were home :)) that being a mother is the most meaningful, magical, magnificent job in the world, even though it is also the hardest job and often involves complete mayhem?

Since many people now think that other things like high-paying jobs and adventure travel are a lot more fascinating

> As our older daughters left for college and missions and study abroad experiences and jobs, I started to worry about whether I had taught them enough about the importance of motherhood.

and fulfilling than motherhood, I wondered if my daughters knew that the wild and raucous ride I had experienced with them as their mother was the most adventure I'd ever had. Had I taught them how important it is to remember that there is a time and a place for both motherhood and meaningful contributions outside the home? Did they know that no matter what else was going on in their lives, their families were most important? I got worried. We needed not only to talk but also to have some fun together away from our everyday lives.

> **We needed not only to talk but also to have some fun together away from our everyday lives.**

By the time we actually started having official retreats once a year in 1996, Saren and Saydi were still single and working, and Shawni was married with a little one-year-old and pregnant with her second child. And our baby, Charity, who was our caboose that came after four boys, was a preteen.

As we started our little group, we were looking forward to some future fun together. Since most of the girls were on the East Coast, we usually used one of their apartments as a home base for our meetings once a year, and we found places (restaurants, parks, and museums) to discuss each other's lives, motherhood, and share the world we were living in at present. We met first in Washington, DC, in 1996, and then Fairfax, Virginia, in 1997.

In 1998, I started calculating and realized that before long, more of our children would be getting married and having children and that we would soon be inviting in-laws to join us. I realized that if we were ever going to be able to get away again without a lot of children in tow or a lot of babysitting involved, we were going to have to catch that moment in time and go on a dream trip to Europe. It was a moment in time we had to grasp! We used frequent flier miles, found cheap hotels, rented a car that was perfect for five, and had an absolutely crazy and delightful week driving around Europe on a dime! Shawni's husband David was able to take care of their only child and our only grandchild, one-year-old Max, while we were gone.

We had a hilarious experience with driving, especially in Rome. To give you a picture, here's a little dialogue between the girls and I that Saren recorded while I was driving and they were navigating. Do you sometimes wonder how we survived without GPS in our cars and on our phones? Well, this is the answer:

Girls: Stop here, Mom. STOP RIGHT HERE OR WE'LL GET LOST!

Me: I can't stop *here*!

Girls: Yes, you can; just STOP! Turn left on this street. Oh! It's one way. Just go anyway!

Me: I used to feel bad about going down these one-way streets the wrong way, but it doesn't bother me anymore!

Me: Okay, now this should be the main street that leads out of Rome. Oops . . . stairs! Should we just drive up the stairs? This looks like a pretty big road on the map! [Said while driving down the tiniest alley we've ever seen.]

Shawni: Mom, you're such a good driver. You haven't hit one thing!

Then there were the everyday happenings:

Shawni: Do they have real toilets? I love real toilets!

Saren: Look at that village! Look at that castle! You guys! Wake up and look at this!

Charity: Let's get some of that 'gel' stuff [gelato].

And in the days before Airbnb:

Me: The guidebook was right. This place *is* humble, and it *does* smell like your great-grandmother's house!

Saren: This bed is like sleeping on a trampoline.

We five adventurers had so much fun on a very small budget! It was a trip we'll never forget, *and* it was the beginning of a long line of excellent MFME confabs! In 1999, we met in Boston, and in 2001, Saydi was getting her master's degree at Columbia, so we met in New York City, where we had some fascinating and rousing discussions about the importance of motherhood. By then, we had our first daughter-in-law, Aja, who was studying anthropology at Harvard, so she and Saydi told us about some of the fascinating classes they were taking. Going to a show with that crowd was too expensive, so we splurged on a lovely dinner out to discuss our future as the Mothers and Future Mothers of Eyrealm.

That year, I asked everyone to fill out a questionnaire while we were together. Looking back now, I wonder how I dared ask some of the questions you see below. But the answers were very insightful, and they have all have loved looking at them again and again as the years have gone by. They either laugh at their naïveté or are pleased that they got it right. Here is the list of questions:

Questionnaire

1. For those who are not yet mothers: What are you looking forward to most about being a mother?
2. What do you think will be the hardest part?
3. For those who are mothers: What surprised you most about being a mother?
4. What is the hardest part?

5. How many children would you like to have (knowing that you can't always have what you want)?

6. What was your most memorable experience this year?

7. What do you think you'll be doing five years from now?

8. What should be your criteria when you ask yourself whether or not you should have a child?

9. What do you dream of doing?

10. What is the most important thing to look for when searching for a marriage partner?

11. What is the most important thing to remember when you are a mother?

12. If you could have lunch with three people in all the world (alive or dead), who would they be?

13. If you could go anywhere on earth, where would it be?

14. What do you love most about what you're doing right now?

15. What do you worry about?

16. If you had a magic wand, what would you change about yourself?

Here are just a few of the responses, which may make you smile and remember your own early motherhood. This from a first-time new mother:

What surprised you the most about being a mother? Breastfeeding, how little newborns sleep, how indescribably fun it can be much of the time, how much more I love my husband now that we share a special love for someone.

What was the hardest part? Never having time for yourself; everything is so much more complicated.

As mentioned before, every few years at MFME, I hand their responses back to them and let them digest what they thought when they were younger and then fill out a new one. It was fascinating for me to read the original ones as I was writing this book. After seventeen years, lots of children, and "water under the bridge," some of the things they wish they could change about themselves have changed and others are still working on the same things (as we all are). Many of their dreams have come true, and others have changed what they thought they wanted.

After we ran out of frequent flyer miles, I began to figure out how we could continue these meetings. There were two main hurdles to getting together: time and money. Since most of our Eyrealm women are spread out all across the country without extra travel funds, it would have been impossible for them to be able to get together, because most retreats would involve flights and food. As our numbers grew, we also needed accommodations bigger than the tiny apartments of our daughters. The dilemma was how were we going to get all these women, who were working with children and budgets, together when they couldn't afford it.

Many years ago, when we finally had a little money to invest, I decided to delve into the stock market. I bet it all on one stock: Apple! Much to my delight, that money soon started multiplying. As the years went by, my humble and generous parents passed away and left their little farm to me. (Other small parcels of land went to my siblings.) When Mom and Dad had gotten married, Dad bought a little farm in Montpelier, Idaho, and, to add additional income, went to work doing backbreaking work for the county highway department while I was growing up. He built a barn and sowed and harvested wheat and alfalfa hay on the land surrounding it. I clearly remember driving trucks and tractors to pick up bales of hay in the field from the time I was eight.

He and my mom held that piece of land dear, and we had so many memories of kittens being born in the haystack, feeding chickens, gathering eggs, and riding our great old horse, Foxy. The farm was located in the southeast corner of Idaho, where the economy was depressed and the prices for land were low, so I rented the land for many years, mostly to hang on to the memories. But when I saw the coming need for money to be able to get our daughters and future daughters together for important gatherings, I reluctantly sold the farm and invested the funds, which again grew substantially.

Our gatherings are not extravagant, but they are extraordinarily delightful! I am confident that my parents are thrilled as they look down from heaven and see that they have provided a wonderful way to get these women of Eyrealm together to talk and bond and enjoy learning from each other as we discuss life and deep thoughts, as well as their most important role: motherhood.

I have friends who do something very similar with their daughters on a smaller budget, because it's not about where you go—it's about being together.

Another friend said, "Regardless of the resources, if it's a priority, you can figure out a way to make it happen. These times together are priceless! You couldn't pay me a million dollars to miss out on the family things that we've done together."

And another friend, who works daily with desperate refugee families and the homeless, reminded me that "we all live in Disneyland!" It's true that wildly dysfunctional families and families whose lives may be in danger are living in a different world. "But," my friend reminded me, "there are problems in 'Disneyland' too, a lot of which could be helped by taking time to talk about and work out problems in functional families. Everyone needs a time and place to vent and commiserate, especially with those they love."

If, because of your health or financial circumstances, you cannot go somewhere exciting or even meet with your daughters in person, there are ways to "gather" at a distance via the internet. The important thing is communicating and spending time together, wherever you are or whatever you are doing.

Usually our MFME gatherings are only three-and-a-half-day events (counting travel) because there are so many complications with growing families. One year we could only squeeze out twenty-four hours to be together without the kids after the last day of our reunion. We left about a dozen little kids with Richard and a couple of the dads who were still there and went to Lava Hot Springs, a well-known little nook in Southeastern Idaho about an hour and a half away where we could swim and soak in the natural spring hot tubs and talk about books and ideas and movies we'd loved. When we got home, Richard was tending and the kids were all happily playing on the beach, eating a breakfast of hard-boiled eggs. (Richard likes to simplify.)

It was so fun to add in-law daughters as time went on. Our in-laws have taught us so much and are adored by our family. Before we meet, we decide on a book that we want to read and share together. Some of our favorites have been *The Alchemist* by Paulo Coelho, *Surrending to Motherhood* by Iris Krasnow, and our recent favorite, *Gift from the Sea* by Anne Morrow Lindbergh. Since the explosion of great information on the internet, we have loved sending each other articles, podcasts, and TED Talks to read or watch before we get together so we can discuss them when we meet. We love the interaction so much and our time together is so short that sometimes we even decide which article or post or podcast we're going to discuss at which meal. The discussions are lively, and we don't always agree on everything, but that's part of the fun! During the time we are together, we also try to go on a hike to glory in nature, and we attend a wonderful cultural event.

As time has passed, our women have become very difficult to gather, given that we have kids all over creation!

The discussions are lively, and we don't always agree on everything, but that's part of the fun!

At the moment, we have families in Zurich, London, New York, Boston, Arizona, California, Hawaii, and Utah. Lives got busy, and we decided that we could only pull off our gatherings every other year. Probably the crown of all our MFME gatherings happened in the fall of 2015, when Tal and Anita moved to Switzerland, Anita's childhood home.

I must admit that it took a lot of planning—and some money—but it was *so* worth the trouble. The girls were responsible for finding the very best deal they could on airfare using money from the MFME fund (mentioned earlier) to reimburse them. I paid the very reasonable hotel bills, considering our numbers, and Charity kept track of all the food charges while we were together. All those costs were put on one credit card, the owner of which was delighted to get the points. All the girls were happy to reimburse her for their own food.

We all met at the Zurich airport, and after renting two cars, we arrived in about an hour at the sweet little town of Schmiedrued, where my great-grandparents Samuel and Verena Goldenberger lived and worked and went to school (see their story in Chapter 7). That little school has now been turned into a village museum, and Anita arranged for us to meet with the curator and translated for us during the tour. He was obviously proud to show us what life would have been like while our ancestors were there. Julie had six-month-old Dean in tow, and it was such a thrill to sit with him on the well-worn wooden steps of the school that our grandparents and great-grandparents had once tread! It was so fun to show our girls where their roots came from and to show the in-laws a glimpse of the blood that runs in their children's veins!

Another of the highlights was arriving at Anita's hometown, a ski resort called Flims. We visited with her wonderful parents, who were still living in her childhood home. We had met them only briefly at the wedding six years earlier, so it was a memorable reunion for all of us.

I do have to say that it was stunning to travel together through Bavaria, and we were delighted to go on The Sound of Music Bike Tour in Salzburg. I guess the locals were getting pretty annoyed with all the tourists belting out "The Hills are Alive" in their city streets, so we weren't allowed to sing until we were outside the city limits. And then we let loose! That night, we heard an inspiring concert in the same room where Mozart and his father had performed 250 years ago!

It was the trip of a lifetime for us!

If, by now, you are feeling sad or discouraged because, for whatever reason, you could never do something like this, the following takeaway can give you hope: the most important thing about that trip was not the places we went or the things we did. Here are our oldest daughter Saren's thoughts on that trip:

> Perhaps the most important part of the trip was that we talked—a lot. We had great conversations as we drove from place to place, alternating who went in which of the two cars. We talked over meals and gathered in one of the hotel rooms each night to talk late into the night—even when we were so tired and knew we should really go to bed. We each shared the best and hardest things going on in our lives right now. We talked about what books we've read, good movies we've seen, what podcasts we've listened to, and all that we've been learning. We talked about our children and helped each other come up with ideas for handling various things going on with our kids. We laughed a lot. Oh, how good it feels to laugh with these women I love so much!

If you want to see our trip to Switzerland in living color, go to Shawni's blog at 71toes.com/mfme. If you've already got more than you want to know, I totally understand! :)

There are so many ways to have fun with daughters and daughters-in-law that are packed with fun and a lot simpler. One grandma I know takes her daughters and daughters-in-law to Swiss Days, which is a fun family event in Midway, Utah, every September. They stay overnight, eat out, and have a grand time catching up. Others take their girls to the beach for a weekend or even just go out to dinner once a month. If your daughters and daughters-in-law are widespread, consider what you can do to bring them together, even if it is over the phone or online. Whatever you do, it will be worth the effort!

Thoughts?

- Are you already doing something like this, or does your unique situation make it impossible? (I know that our situation is extremely rare, especially because we have four daughters and four daughters-in-law.)
- Do you dare get together with just your daughters without hurting the feelings of the daughters-in-law? (Fortunately, each of our daughters-in-law have a least one sister and a great mother that they can spend time with on their own. So occasionally, I get together with just our daughters and the in-laws plan their own gatherings for their side of the family.)
- Perhaps you have only one daughter-in-law or none at all. Maybe your daughters and daughters-in-law don't mesh well. Or there could have been a difficult divorce that threw a wrench in the works. What could you do to work around that?
- Whatever your situation, are there things that you could do to create a bond with these women in your life as well as help them to bond with each other?

In-Laws Having Their Say

Let me move on to a fun thing that has bonded all our in-laws who all came from different gene pools, backgrounds, and viewpoints. Not only were *they* different, but we Eyres were a little different too! After a few reunions with our whole big group, Jonah's wife, Aja, came up with a great idea: a group just for the in-laws of Eyrealm. This organization meets in the hot tub one evening at every reunion. I think they spend most of their time talking about how to deal with the crazy idiosyncrasies of the Eyre Family, with whom they are inextricably connected! :)

Aja was immediately elected the president, so she explains the process here:

> I was the first daughter-in-law to join Eyrealm. Shortly after I married into the great Eyre clan, my brothers-in-law and I decided to start our own "club" to counterbalance the other family clubs like Mothers and Future Mothers of Eyrealm and Fathers and Future Fathers of Eyrealm. So we called our club PILE, which stands for Present In-Laws of Eyrealm. We would excuse ourselves for PILE "meetings" one evening of the reunion and then just go relax and get food and talk. It was great fun.
>
> As more members "joined" PILE, we did take our meetings a little more seriously and were able to use it as a time to vent, to advise, and to commend each other. But we stayed true to our original purpose of giving us all time to relax and de-stress.
>
> As a result of our club and the discussions and memories I have had with my in-laws, I really love the other PILE members like they are siblings. We share very similar issues since we are all married into the same family and to similar personalities. The PILE get-togethers are a highlight of family reunions for me.

There was a period of time when Richard and I were speaking often on cruise ships. We told the directors that we didn't want to be paid—we just wanted to take some kids with us for free. We took our sons on one cruise, our daughters on another one, and our daughters-in-law on another one. On the latter, we learned so much about our sons that we didn't know! Our daughters-in-law were great sports and had a great time bonding in their own cozy little room. Although not all of them could arrange to go on these trips, we loved having those who could. We are still working on a trip with the in-law sons; their schedules are harder. Someday, we'll make that happen!

Embracing Co-Grandparents

Maybe all you readers won't feel the same, but we adore all the parents of the children that our children have married! Before the babies came, they were just good friends, but as those babies began to drop in, we have realized that their best title is *co-grandparents*. After all, we will be joining with them for weddings, baby blessings, baptisms, and reunions for the rest of our lives, and the thing that we will always have in common is our grandchildren.

None of our co-grandparents live near us. They live in Idaho, Arizona, California, Switzerland, and Texas, and two couples have lived in London and Brazil for extended periods of time. We always send all of them our annual Thanksgiving cards, and when we are anywhere near them, we try to meet them for a meal. They have all had fascinating lives, and we love them for the amazing children they have raised. We have different backgrounds and personalities, but we adore them all!

Richard likes to write our co-grandparents a personal note once in a while just because we miss them. It's a fun relationship that's a little more than a friendship because we share that precious commodity called our grandchildren! We have made certain that our daughters- and sons-in-law know that we admire, respect, and are inspired by their parents!

Most of our grandchildren don't live near their other grandparents. But a couple of them do, and I must admit that we are a little envious when we see our grandchildren bonding with those grandparents all year long. It has made me realize that they may be a bit envious of us when we have those kids for an extended time in the summer. Everyone is accepting of the other's circumstances (at least, as far as we know).

For us, the best part of having those great co-grandparents is that they share their extraordinary gifts and knowledge of things that are unique to them with our co-grandchildren! Those are things that go beyond what we could ever teach them. And we love them for sharing their time, their love, and their genes!

Thoughts?

- What is your relationship with the parents of your children-in-law? (We haven't experienced a divorce [. . . yet . . . crossing fingers], but of course, that would make co-grandparent relationships much more complicated.)
- How do you feel about the time you are able to spend with your co-grandparents and the time that your grandchildren are with them?
- How do you keep in touch with them?
- There are many situations with co-grandparents like estrangement, different lifestyles, and even death. What are the ways you have reconciled those issues?

CHAPTER 6

When Things Go Wrong

When I mentioned this chapter to a friend, she smiled and quipped, "Wrong? What could go wrong? These are my grandkids!" It seems that most grandmas have reasons to rejoice; their lives are filled with fun things, exciting things, and joyful things. But there are also things to worry about: things that haven't gone as expected, the inevitable crisis, or even the full-blown disaster!

When people ask me how our children are doing, I always answer, "Everyone's great except the ones who are in crisis this week!" They usually don't ask for details, just nod their heads to acknowledge that they have the same regularity of problems in their own families. With as many children and grandchildren as we have, it seems that somebody is always in distress. Trouble,

> **Difficult issues are always present in our growing and expanding families. Hard times come to all of us.**

heartache, and even tragedy come with the territory of having a family. As grandmothers, we share the weight and sorrow of worries which are now often beyond our control.

In this chapter, I won't be pointing out who in our family has anxiety, who loves their spouse but doesn't like them very much on some days (which could cover most of us), who has teenagers who are rebellious, who has the concerns about starting a new business, who is in what we call "limbo" about what their next move in life will be, how many have had miscarriages and several failed rounds of IVF procedures, who has a hard time with decisions, or who has worrisome physical issues. But those kinds of difficult issues are always present in our growing and expanding families. Hard times come to all of us.

Trials

We've had our share of trials, but probably the longest-lasting one has been our granddaughter Lucy's struggle with a genetic syndrome that causes blindness and huge issues with her weight, among other serious problems. Below are the deep feelings that Shawni recorded when she heard the sure diagnosis when Lucy was a baby.

> Nothing can really prepare you to get a phone call from the geneticist telling you that your child has a really rare syndrome that will change her life, and that of your family's, forever . . . even if you and your husband already knew it in your hearts.

And as much as we kind of knew it was coming, I do wish the geneticist would have at least told me to sit down, or find a quiet place . . . I mean, she *must* have been able to hear the chaos going on around me on a Friday afternoon when my house was filled with the whole neighborhood.

I'll never quite forget standing there, folding laundry, trying to squelch the tears that were burning to come out amidst my kids and their friends asking intermittently for a snack, help with their roller blades, wanting a drink, etc. I know kids have an automatic button that tells them they need to start talking to an adult the second she gets on the phone and not give up (at least mine do), and usually I can multitask. But not that Friday. Not while I felt like my whole world was suddenly swimming around me.

Those are the moments in all our lives that we never forget; they change us forever. As we have researched this syndrome and realized how fragile our genetic makeup is, it has made us wonder how any of us are born "normal" (if there is such a thing). Lucy is expected to have a normal lifespan. She is a plucky, bright artist and has become the light of our lives, but there are scary and unknown difficulties that we will all be facing with her in the future. (For details of Lucy's story, see Chapter 8.)

Regarding the life of another friend, imagine how life shattering it would be if you were told that your grandchild had no chance to survive after birth. I have a friend from my youth who has experienced this incredibly difficult circumstance with her baby grandson. She tells the story like this:

Little Thomas was born with osteogenesis imperfecta or brittle bone disease with a life expectancy of fifteen minutes to twenty-four hours. His parents were sent to neonatal hospice before his birth to prepare for his death and burial. He was born with essentially every long bone in his body broken—some breaks occurring before birth.

He has surprised everyone with miracle after miracle and is now two years old! However, he still has a break roughly every 3–6 weeks. In fact, both arms were broken by a doctor who was trying to do an exam while TomTom was resisting. He breaks that easily. When he breaks, Shane and Rachel (his parents) diagnose, treat, splint, and immobilize the break on their own. It's kind of useless to keep running him to the hospital each time.

As things progressed, he has had several surgeries: tracheotomy, feeding shunt, etc. He wasn't released to go home until Shane and Rachel were adept at managing the machines for those issues. Kent and I have been trained on them also, but I pray that all will go smoothly when I'm in charge. I dread having to do an emergency trach replacement. He also developed hydrocephaly and needed to have a shunt placed. Kent and I try to stay close at hand in case of an emergency.

Miraculously, Thomas, who has been so dearly loved and meticulously cared for, has started going to his nursery class on Sundays in his tiny little wheelchair, created especially for him at Shriner's Hospital, which he can manipulate himself. He is bright and usually happy and has been an enormous blessing to his family, but his condition is a bit like sitting on a time bomb waiting for the next bone to break.

Sometimes trials come in multiples. Let me share two stories from heroic grandmothers whose lives have had trials that they could never have imagined on their wedding days! For some, when it rains, it pours!

My first friend's story reminds me of Job in the Bible with her litany of incredible trials that have lasted over many years. You may not believe it, but in the past five years, she lost four siblings to cancer and a beloved teenage granddaughter to failed kidneys. Surviving that tragic loss, along with helping her daughter and that family through the grief, was a dark and all-consuming process. The next son in that family, also suffering with kidney failure, had a seizure that left his sixteen-year-old body with the mind of a five-year-old, and their younger twin boys are awaiting kidney transplants.

In addition, her husband's health has never been good. With very low liver and kidney function, it has been impossible for him to work for a very long time. Then, to add to her load of trials, she was diagnosed with breast cancer and was fighting for her life with chemotherapy and radiation treatments that made her wish she would die.

By now, you must be thinking that I'm making this up, but actually, this is just the beginning. Her husband then fell down the stairs and subsequently had a stroke, limiting the use of his leg, among other things. Then, while using his walker, he fell and broke his hip. She spent thirty-two days, the entire Christmas season, her body still weak from chemo, sleeping by his hospital bed.

What a blessing that she had wonderful children who supported her and her husband through these trials. Cancer-free (so far), she still only leaves the house for a few hours every week, as she cares for her disabled husband. Certainly, those wedding vows that say "for richer or poorer," "in sickness and in health," and "for better and for worse" have a profoundly deeper meaning than they did on the day they were married!

Twelve years ago, my sister Lenna's husband, Bruce (fifty-seven), was diagnosed with stage four stomach cancer at 9 a.m., and he died at 1 p.m. that afternoon, surrounded by his stunned family of seven children and their spouses. Without going through all the details surrounding the untimely death of this remarkable man, who had done so much good, had rescued so many from despair, and had been so generous, I just have to say that Lenna's life has not been a bed of roses since he left. But she has risen to the task and has been the heroic rock of the family ever since. She helped their children create new businesses, since Bruce had been the supporting pillar of the family business he had owned. She has also helped two children navigate their way through divorces.

Somehow, she and her ever-supportive family lived through the enormous trials that come with a four-year-old granddaughter being diagnosed with leukemia. Adorable Cami endured years of crucial but debilitating chemo treatments and was finally declared cancer-free . . . for nine months . . . before a relapse and then more excruciating years in hospitals, with a complete bone marrow transplant and more horrendous chemo and radiation treatments.

While a dear little friend of Cami's, also suffering with leukemia, passed away, she survived. Now, as a twelve-year-old, the adorable and vivacious Cami gave an astonishing speech at the Give Kids the World Black & White Gala at Disney World in Orlando. She had been the recipient of her dearest "wish" by the wonderful Make-a-Wish Foundation when she was going through the depths of her treatment and now had to the opportunity to thank them and tell her story on the big stage to the many donors and parents at the gala. This was a wonderful story of "beauty for ashes" as the once ashen-gray, bald child who came so close to death was now sparkling with energy. Her enthusiasm must have given hope to so many other families whose children are or will be going down the precarious path she trod!

The most interesting things about all these grandmothers is that you couldn't find more optimistic, upbeat grandmas in the world. Even though there have been days of devastation and despair, they have managed to be able to survive their storms with courage and determination and even with a sense of humor when "little things" go wrong! Louisa May Alcott put a beautiful optimistic spin on dealing with the storms of life. She said:

I'm not afraid of storms. I'm learning how to sail my ship!

As grandmothers, we have inevitably sailed through a lot of storms. And we have learned so much from navigating each one. We know how to sail, even when the wind comes from different directions. Now it is so much easier to help our children and grandchildren steer their way safely through their storms.

Although many of the trials in these three cases involve physical issues, there are so many other kinds of trials, including the epidemic of mental illnesses that is currently raging among families and the heartache of children and grandchildren who make bad choices or choices that will be stumbling blocks to their progress. Often there are immediate or extended family members who have struggled with severe anxiety, alcoholism, drug use, and unending grief over a loss.

Sympathy and Empathy

We all have family members who are going through a very difficult time. We find ourselves wringing our hands and wondering how we can help. Do we need to show sympathy or empathy?

Dr. Brené Brown describes the difference. She says, "Empathy fuels connection. Sympathy drives disconnection." If you are interested in knowing more, visit *youtu.be/1Evwgu369Jw* to find a clever and enlightening cartoon on empathy. She describes sympathy as a way to express feelings of sorrow for the loss of others without really getting involved. She describes empathy as seeing that someone is in a very dark hole and *climbing down in the hole with them*; there, you tell them that you know how it feels to be in a dark place where it seems that there is no way out and that you are there to be with them to empathize and give your support.

In *I Thought It Was Just Me (But It Isn't)* (2008), Brown references nursing scholar Theresa Wiseman's four attributes of empathy:

- To be able to see the world as others see it—this requires putting your own "stuff" aside to see the situation through your loved one's eyes.
- To be nonjudgmental—judgement of another person's situation discounts the experience and is an attempt to protect ourselves from the pain of the situation.
- To understand another person's feelings—we have to be in touch with our own feelings in order to understand someone else's. Again, this requires putting your own "stuff" aside to focus on your loved one.
- To communicate your understanding of that person's feelings—rather than saying, "At least you . . . " or "It could be worse . . . " try, "I've been there, and that really hurts," or (to quote an example from Brown) "It sounds like you are in a hard place now. Tell me more about it."

I share Dr. Brown's belief that when those we love are in distress, they are not usually looking for a solution. They are looking for someone to feel deeply sorry for their situation or their loss, someone to express sincere support as well as sadness that they are having to go through this trial. It's especially helpful when we have experienced something similar. I know that when

I am upset or worried about something, I don't want Richard to do what comes naturally for him, which is to immediately start giving a solution to the problem. I find myself saying, "I know what I have to do. Just tell me that you know it's tough and that you feel sorry for me!"

> When those we love are in distress, they are not usually looking for a solution. They are looking for someone to feel deeply sorry for their situation.

One of the best ways to help others in such situations is to see the big picture; we must try to look beyond what seems to be the problem and try to discover the *real* problem. For instance, often the reason a child or grandchild makes a worrisome decision is not what we think. We judge people based on our perceptions rather than theirs. Once we look at what is beyond what we actually see, it helps us to view the big picture rather than the one that we can conceive according to our own perceptions.

Sometimes it takes years to figure that out. One grandmother whose son was clinically depressed and just wanted to sit in a dark room, curl up in a ball, and die thought it might be helpful to read him an excellent, upbeat article from a magazine that made her feel better, thinking it might make him feel better. Now, after he has had years of therapy that brought her son back to life, she has realized how ridiculous that must have seemed to him in his hopeless state! There are things going on in the lives of those we love that we don't know and could never guess. Withholding judgement and sometimes finding help from someone who has experienced a similar trial or finding a well-trained therapist can help get a person you love out of a "dark hole."

Sometimes family members respond in ways that are not only puzzling but downright offensive. It can be mind-boggling, but we need to work with real dedication to figure out what is creating his or her picture of reality. A friend tells this story:

> Several years ago, one of our sons' relationships with each of his siblings as well as us became quite strained almost immediately after his marriage. Invitations to family events became more and more frequently declined until the siblings weren't seeing him at all. The family only saw him and his family very briefly at birthdays and Christmastime, just long enough to exchange a gift and a brief strained conversation. Mostly we all were sad about it and frustrated—not being able to ascertain exactly the reason why or communicate about it with him.
>
> A couple of his siblings also became quite angry. They were reacting in anger over the loss of their relationship with him. Sometimes they would share their feelings with us, and after validating their exasperation (we felt it too), I would tell them, "We don't understand why he is behaving this way, but there is little more we can do about it except to keep loving him until he can share his feeling with us. The important thing is that you work through your anger so that if he needs us, you aren't still angry with him and can welcome him with love and understanding."
>
> Sure enough, several years later, his marriage failed. His wife had been extremely controlling and intimidating to the point of mental illness. He had felt worthless and hopeless. Now jobless and homeless with three confused little children, he has turned to us and his siblings, who have all received him with open arms.

Sometimes adversity in our own lives is the greatest tool for feeling real empathy for others. In the end, often "things going wrong" turns out better than "things going right!" People who have been blinded or maimed through accidents or disease are the best teachers for those who are beginning of a life without sight or legs. Think of the magnificent light that Helen Keller has been to those with disabilities and Nelson Mandela and Corrie ten Boom to those who have been physically or even mentally imprisoned.

When we have truly been in the same dark hole with someone who has had multiple miscarriages, or lost a child or grandchild, we can empathize with compassion and persuade them that that there will be a bright future, even a "perfect brightness of hope,"[1] because we have been where they are and have eventually survived with a love for life restored.

Thoughts?

- Do you help family members and friends in trouble with sympathy or empathy?
- What lessons have you learned from trials in your life that have taught you how to truly empathize with others?

Worry

An interesting thought occurred to me when I was worried about something. I was listening to the thousandth advertisement on TV for a newly discovered drug to help recover from an ailment. At the end of the advertisement, there is the inevitable list of things that could be possible side effects of taking those drugs, including the fact that if you take this drug, you might die.

It made me think that there are also similar side effects that are created by the worries that keep popping up in our lives. I went online to find just a few of the side effects listed for medications on the internet and had to giggle as I realized that many of them were perfect descriptions of the side effects of worry! I think you'll agree (and it might make you smile):

- Fast, pounding, or racing heartbeat
- Puffiness of the eyelids
- Headaches
- Trouble sleeping
- Mental depression
- Paranoia
- Nightmares
- General feeling of discomfort
- Heartburn
- Weakness
- Nervousness
- Weight gain
- Weight loss
- Anxiety
- Confusion
- Difficulty with speaking
- Indigestion
- Depersonalization

- Quick to overreact emotionally
- Irritability

I am no therapist, but the following tips for worry about things that have "gone wrong" have helped me to be calmer both when I am in a frenzy as well as when worries first begin to crop up in my mind. Here is a list that might help you with the same thing:

1. Create a worry period. If you're worried about something, set a time limit to worry. Set an alarm on your phone or a timer on your stove, and when it rings, distract yourself with another thought and go on with your day.

2. Ask yourself if the problem is solvable. If it is, come up with a doable plan to work it out. If not, dismiss it.

3. Accept uncertainty. Remind yourself that you have no control over an uncertain situation. I like to "cast my burden" and have faith that the Lord can see the big picture when I can't and that, in the end, things will work out for the best.

4. Challenge anxious thoughts. Practice optimism by reminding yourself that most things aren't permanent, pervasive, or personal.

5. Be aware of how others affect you. If there are certain people who create the worry, spend your time with others who are more optimistic.

6. Practice mindfulness. Take a yoga class or learn how to meditate in a way that will relax your mind and help you be more aware of reality.

Sometimes getting past worry for a major event just means giving the story time to unfold. Very early in a pregnancy of our wonderful daughter-in-law Kristi, we learned that our little granddaughter Mila was going to have to have surgery within minutes of when she was born in at Children's Hospital in Los Angeles. It was a huge worry! We were told that her left ventricle was not large enough to function well, and they could see a faulty valve and a hole in her heart on the ultrasound. An expert team of doctors and nurses whisked her away in an incubator immediately after she was born to prepare her for surgery.

It was a worry that had persisted throughout the pregnancy, and everyone in the family prayed for that little girl every night right up until the moment she was born. Amazingly, the doctors were able to insert a stint into the hole and adjust the valve somewhat during that surgery with catheters without open-heart surgery, which to us was nothing less than a miracle! Our baby Mila was on meds and sleeping a lot for two years. She scooted on her bottom instead of crawling and walked very late.

The happy ending of that story is that at age two and a half, Mila was again a candidate for an extremely technical surgery to correct ongoing issues. After much deliberation, the parents gave their consent, and one of the finest pediatric heart surgeons in the world did open-heart surgery on our darling Mila. Richard and I went to LA for the surgery and sat with Noah and Kristi in the waiting room, worried sick about several possible scary issues that could come up during surgery. Suddenly the surgeon threw open the door of the waiting room after only one hour and fifteen minutes. He broke the tension in that room very quickly as he announced, "I carved out a lot of tissue in the left ventricle. I closed the hole. I fixed the valve. She should be good to go for the rest of her life."

We were stunned! Noah and Kristi were overjoyed and immediately jumped to their feet and hugged the doctor, who clearly was not a hugger, and he was gone. We were over the moon with joy and gratitude.

But If Not . . .

In that case, worry was a catalyst for prayer, and our prayers were answered. As deliriously happy as we were on that day, we realize that those kinds of prayers or wishes are not always answered as we would have hoped. Surgeons make mistakes, accidents happen, people die—despite fervent prayers. What about good people who pray or wish fervently for miracles that don't happen? What about those who don't survive a tragedy? What about those who are wronged by someone in a way that changes life dramatically?

I understand that some of you may not believe in God, and you may have found different answers to those questions than I have. But hopefully you can be patient and understanding as I explain the source of my peace. It is my belief that the answer to those previous questions lies in three words from the Old Testament story uttered by three faithful men—Shadrach, Meshach, and Abednego (what a list of names!)—when King Nebuchadnezzar was about to cast them into a fiery furnace because they would not worship his golden idols. The three went peacefully, saying that if it was God's will, they would be delivered from the fire, *but if not,* they would remain faithful and never worship the king's idols.

Those three words are so critical for me when I haven't received the miracle or even answers that I have pleaded for in prayer. If that miracle comes, I am so grateful, *but if it does not,* I am committed to remain faithful to a belief that God knows what my future holds and acknowledges my faith with love, no matter what the outcome.

I believe that I can earnestly pray and sometimes my prayers are answered according to my hopes and desires. Other times there is a different path in store for me. And sometimes the greatest blessings come when that prayed-for miracle does *not* happen.

> Sometimes my prayers are answered according to my hopes and desires. Other times there is a different path in store for me. And sometimes the greatest blessings come when that prayed-for miracle does *not* happen.

In the end, I spend a lot of time worrying about things that I have no control over, and it wears me out physically and mentally! Trusting that everything will work out for my good is called faith. But it's so hard to put into action, especially when conditions are dire. Trials, and the worries that go with them, seem to come up almost daily in the lives of our children and grandchildren: I can think of a handful of things right now, just off the top of my head, that I'm worried about regarding our family. Some are real reasons to be concerned, and others are what Richard calls "silly worries." He is an incurable optimist and always knows that, in the long run, whether things turn out as we want them to or not, it's going to be okay. It's a great gift to be able to "cast [my] burden[s]"[2] in times of need and "wait on the Lord"![3]

One other thing: During times of worry and concern and loss and grief, I really believe that angels surround us to witness what is happening and comfort us. Maybe they even direct our thoughts more than we know! Those angels may be ancestors like the ones I will introduce you to in Chapter 7. I have felt their comfort and assurance that things are going to work out for my good.

Thoughts?

- What do you do when you realize that you are worrying about things that you have no control over?
- Have you experienced difficult and even life-threatening issues? How did you cope and heal?
- Could you sincerely say "But if not . . ." and accept the outcome?

Guilt

One of my best friends had a gentle son. The son had siblings who were highly motivated and aggressive self-starters. My friend didn't realize it at the time, but this son had some learning disabilities. He struggled through elementary school and labeled himself "a loser." When he got to high school, he gravitated to friends that were also "lost," and they began doing things that were dangerous for their mental and physical health. He began smoking and taking drugs and got involved in a crowd that was destructive to his life. His mother struggled to help him get through high school as he found that some subjects were easy while others seemed impossible. He was a good worker and responsible in many areas, but his early experimentation with alcohol had led him to an addiction. In the process, he had damaged his brain function.

As an adult, he married and divorced and became estranged from his two sons, and he was riddled with guilt. He was a dependable worker and did a great job while he was there, but he lived alone, went home every night alone, drank himself to sleep, and woke up not feeling well but still showed up for work on time every day. His family continued to rally around him, supporting him with love and confidence. His mom went to countless addiction programs with him but with no success.

Finally, one day, he had had enough. Even though he had been through several drug and alcohol addiction programs, finally, on his initiative, he went to his mom and asked her to help him find a place that could help him give up his addiction and get back to real life! He is well on his way to a new life. His mother never gave up on him, and she and his siblings rallied around him and have come up with creative ways to keep him occupied and on track.

In a deep talk with his mother recently, he told her about things that she never knew had happened, both in his mind and in his behavior with friends. She was amazed at some things that he told her and felt guilty that she hadn't seen some of his issues in time to help him. That mother was a champion in doing things to help him along the way but had no idea the depth of what he was going through. She continues to do a terrific job of encouraging and sustaining him through his recovery, but she is also coping with guilt for not seeing the warning signs and being too preoccupied with her other kids to realize that he was in deep trouble.

Taking on guilt about a child that has gone astray reminds me of something that happened to Richard and me when we were attending a Sunday School class in a country church in Dingle, Idaho, near where I grew up and where we now spend our summers. It was during a class about parenting difficult children. We were as quiet as mice in the corner as we listened to the class discussion. A "city slicker" who was visiting that day seemed to have all the answers to the questions that the teacher posed. "Well, this is how we did it with our son who was the student body president..." or "We had a daughter who was the valedictorian of her class and knew just how to help a friend . . ." or "Our son was the quarterback on the football team when that very thing happened!" By the end of the class, the guy was getting pretty annoying with the stories of all his perfect kids.

On about the fifth comment from this proud father, a little farmer on the back row with a bolo tie and cowboy boots stood, faced that bragger squarely in the eye, and said with a smile, "Excuse me, brother, but God must not a' thought too much of you as a parent, sendin' ya all them easy kids!" The class burst out laughing! Richard and I couldn't resist a "Right on!" first pump.

The message was clear! Some kids just come to earth easy to guide and armed with self-esteem, but I believe that God also sends some of his most difficult children to the parents most able to help, knowing that if anyone can help them, those parents can! That thought is a terrific way to release a lot of guilt about what we "coulda, woulda, shoulda" done! We do the best we can with the information we have at the time. If you have a difficult or rebellious grandchild, perhaps that same little man could say to you, "God must have thought quite a lot of you as a grandparent, sendin' ya that tough kid!"

We need to remember that our children come as they are. I believe that we all came from a pre-mortal life, where we have already developed much of our personality and character. As grandmothers, we can continue to love and support and believe in our kids, but we have to remember that children come as they are.

Some kids (and grandkids) are obedient and compliant and are doing great, while others have to do everything the hard way in the school of hard knocks! We believe that God entrusted us with these children because we were the best ones to be their parent and give them the best chance to succeed. I thank him for the stewardship.

If you are feeling guilt about a child or grandchild, get all the help you can, spiritually and professionally, from all those you trust, but remember that most often their choices are their choices and not your fault.

Thoughts?

- What process does your mind go through when you feel guilty about something that you think you may have neglected to teach a child before they left home?
- What are your solutions for releasing yourself from guilt?

Divorce

No chapter called "When Things Go Wrong" can conclude without referring to divorce! Although we haven't experienced a divorce in our children's lives so far (knock on wood), we certainly have close family members who have! Research shows that the best thing for children when their parents are breaking up is the love and support of their grandparents; a strong relationship with a grandparent can significantly ease the grandchild's suffering.[4]

It is well documented that grandparents can have a powerful influence for good in helping struggling families. Researchers studied and ranked ways grandparents spent their time with their grandchildren.[5] I'm including the top six. It is interesting to compare these things with the time you spent with your grandchildren this year.

1. Joking with or teasing the child
2. TV-watching
3. Sharing information from the past
4. Advice-giving or problem-solving
5. Teaching skills
6. Taking day trips together

It's interesting that a lot of that time is spent having fun and, in the process, passing on values that are important. Grandparents can give advice and help children deal with things they are going through that troubled parents would not be able to provide. And along the way, it is crucially important for the grandparent to refrain from saying anything derogatory about either parent to the child, no matter how childishly or irresponsibly the parents may be acting!

> Along the way, it is crucially important for the grandparent to refrain from saying anything derogatory about either parent.

While parents are stretched to the limit with their own needs and the children may be acting out with rudeness or sullenness, grandparents, and I have to say especially grandmothers, can play a significant role in giving the child a sense of security, self-worth, and a feeling of wellness through praise, empathy, and confidence in a good outcome, no matter what!

Grandparents can also be an anchor for blended marriages as they provide much-needed stability in the difficult transition of putting two different families together. More and more often in today's world, young families move back into the house with the grandparents where grandmothers can lend enormous support. Grandparents can be the secret potion that gives grandchildren stability and even a little magic!

Possible Solutions

So what do we do when things go wrong? No two stories are the same . . . and no two marriages . . . and no two families . . . and no two grandchildren. It is impossible to give advice that fits every situation, but the following four suggestions would probably apply to most of us.

Stay C.A.L.M.!

The friend whose son who had removed himself from the family writes this:

> When I got the distress call from my son that he was out of state, out of work, leaving his marriage, and needed a place to come with his three children, my head and emotions were spinning. I stopped at the temple [a place of peace for those in the LDS faith] with much humility and pleading in my heart about how to proceed in such entirely unfamiliar territory. While I was there in prayer,

thoughts formulated in my mind in such a way to form the acronym C.A.L.M.

C for clarify: separate facts from emotion and realize "it is what it is."

A for act: move forward without hesitation once the facts are clear and you know what you need to do.

L for love: find the love—in the midst of all of this, there is still love.

M for mitigate: diminish the negative.

That was almost three years ago. Recently, in the midst of a day still full of the challenges of that divorce and its impact on the three children who are in our home along with their dad, our son, I remembered those thoughts that were so clear that day—an answer suited so specifically to me to help me be able to move forward—and I realized the acronym was still the answer I need today.

Never Give Up!

We had just finished a parenting speech, and people were lined up to talk to us. There were two lines, and I was greeting one while Richard greeted the other.

He tells the story like this:

One lady, back a bit in my line, was sobbing. I wondered what I might have said to hurt or offend her. When she got to me, she was still crying, and I asked what was wrong.

"I've lost my son," she sobbed.

"What do you mean?" I asked.

"Well, he's just gone. He's eighteen, so the police say he can do what he wants. He says he hates his family. We know he has drugs, and he's just disappeared. We have not heard from him for two months."

I struggled to know what to say or how to comfort her, but I tried to empathize. A bit clumsily, I put my hand on her shoulder and said, "So you've pretty much given up on him, then?"

Suddenly, there was a change in the woman. She stopped crying. She straightened up and squared her shoulders. And she met my eyes for the first time. "Given up?" she said, almost defiantly. "He is my son! I will never, ever give up!"

Where I had seen almost pathetic sorrow, I now saw strength. This was a noble, committed mother, and while she was stricken with grief and worry, the thought of giving up on her son would never occur to her. She taught me a great lesson about determination that day. I told her then something that I had never fully understood before: "Because you will never give up, you *will* have reconciliation with your son. I don't know if it will be in a month or a year or in ten years or after this life, but you will be together again in love."

To those who believe in eternity and in family bonds that never die and who never give up, there is no failure—there is only delay. If your heart is aching about things that have gone wrong with a child or grandchild, remember these two great quotes from Winston Churchill: "Success is the ability to go from failure to failure without losing your enthusiasm." And "Never, never, never give up!"

Time Will Help!

To mothers and grandmothers who have done everything right but are losing their children to the world, remember that life is *long*! And eternity is very, very long! Someday we will be able to see the big picture of our lives as God sees it. We will realize why we, along with our children and grandchildren, have had to go through hard times and appreciate the valuable lessons that we learned through our tribulations. We wouldn't ask for our heart-aches, but we wouldn't give up what we learn through them for anything. And in time, the loss of a spouse or grandchild, divorce, or health concerns will all be worked out.

Enjoy Where You Are!

Parenting is the hardest and most important job on earth. Grandparenting is a close second. Lots of things can go wrong with your own life as well as with the lives those you love. Growing older is not for the faint hearted! But life at this stage is also beautiful! Our dearly beloved friends Larry and Virginia Stevens are in their mid-eighties and have taught us one of life's most valuable lessons as we have grown older. They have every reason to complain! Larry has Parkinson's disease, which never fails to progress further and further with extremely difficult physical disabilities. Virginia has intense and incessant back pain that doctors can't help her with. They feel that she is too old for surgery, and pain meds create side effects that are worse than the pain. The only thing that helps with the pain is walking. So she walks several miles a day, usually just around her house, making cookies for people in need or reading the scriptures "on the run."

They both always have smiles on their faces and are ready to face another difficult week ahead when we see them on Sundays. One day, when Richard and I expressed sorrow for their trials, Larry smiled from his walker, only barely able to raise his head enough to whisper this advice: "You know, you only have *one chance* in all eternity to grow old. We have to enjoy it!" Right on, Larry!

To conclude this chapter, consider the things that have "gone wrong" in your life as you ponder these thought-provoking quotes:

"There is no education like adversity." —*Disraeli*

"Start by doing what is necessary; then do what is possible; and suddenly you are doing the impossible." —*St. Francis of Assisi*

"The greater the obstacle, the more glory in overcoming it." —*Molière*

"Use what you've been through as fuel; believe in yourself and be unstoppable!" —*Yvonne Pierre*

"Adversity is the diamond dust Heaven polishes its jewels with." —*Thomas Carlyle*

Thoughts?

- What are your best ideas for helping your families, who may be struggling with divorce or blending a family? What about embracing a family who has moved in with you? A whole book could be written about those three things, right?
- Do you just pray for help, or do you plead and beg for help? Do you really listen for answers?
- Are you sometimes tempted to give up on things that are difficult to deal with in your life?
- Are you enjoying your life enough as you get older?

Notes

1. The Book of Mormon. 2 Nephi 32:20.

2. Psalms 55:22 KJV.

3. Psalms 27:14 KJV.

4. Webb, Jodi M. "Helping Grandkids Survive Divorce." The American Grandparent Association. https://www.grandparents.com/family-and-relationships/divorce/helpinggrandchildrenthroughparentdivorce.

5. "Larger Role in Families Looms for Grandparents." *Deseret News*, July 21, 1995. https://www.deseretnews.com/article/430011/LARGER-ROLE-IN-FAMILIES-LOOMS-FOR-GRANDPARENTS.html.

CHAPTER 7

The Secret Ingredient That Gives Your Grandchildren Grit

Bruce Feiler has become one of my favorite authors in the past few years. He "gets it" on the importance of a *family narrative*. His *New York Times* article called "The Stories That Bind Us" made the hair on my arms stand up![1] It expressed exactly what I had been advocating for many years. Like a microscope with a knob you can turn to bring things more clearly into view, it brought the importance of our children knowing their family history into focus. Mr. Feiler's research as well that of that of many others concluded that children who know about their family narrative or the stories of their family and feel that

The single most important thing you can do for your family may be the simplest of all: develop a family narrative.

they belong to something bigger than themselves are more resilient when faced with difficult experiences, are better able to deal with stress, and have higher self-esteem and confidence when experiencing trauma in their lives.

After searching for and thoroughly scrutinizing the "secret sauce" that holds families together, and after examining team-building techniques for companies in Silicon Valley and even in the military, he writes, "A surprising theme emerged. The single most important thing you can do for your family may be the simplest of all: develop a family narrative."

Do You Know?

In doing research on this subject, Dr. Marshall Duke and a colleague, Dr. Robyn Fivush, created a "Do You Know" list of twenty questions for children to investigate what they know about their families.[2] Children were given this test and asked to circle Y for yes and N for no. It was suggested that we might adjust the list by adding questions to fit our own families. (You might find it interesting to answer the questions yourself before trying it out on your children and grandchildren.)

Here is a list of the "Do You Know" questions created by Dr. Duke and Dr. Fivush:

1. Do you know how your parents met? Y N
2. Do you know where your mother grew up? Y N
3. Do you know where your father grew up? Y N
4. Do you know where some of your grandparents grew up? Y N

5. Do you know where some of your grandparents met? Y N
6. Do you know where your parents were married? Y N
7. Do you know what went on when you were being born? Y N
8. Do you know the source of your name? Y N
9. Do you know some things about what happened when your brothers or sisters were being born? Y N
10. Do you know which person in your family you look most like? Y N
11. Do you know which person in the family you act most like? Y N
12. Do you know some of the illnesses and injuries that your parents experienced when they were younger? Y N
13. Do you know some of the lessons that your parents learned from good or bad experiences? Y N
14. Do you know some things that happened to your mom or dad when they were in school? Y N
15. Do you know the national background of your family (such as English, German, Russian, etc.)? Y N
16. Do you know some of the jobs that your parents had when they were young? Y N
17. Do you know some awards that your parents received when they were young? Y N
18. Do you know the names of the schools that your mom went to? Y N
19. Do you know the names of the schools that your dad went to? Y N
20. Do you know about a relative whose face "froze" in a grumpy position because he or she did not smile enough? Y N

Four dozen families in the NYC area were asked the twenty questions in the summer of 2001. They compared results with several psychological tests that the children took and then reached a surprising conclusion: "The more children knew about their family's history, the stronger their sense of control over their lives, the higher their self-esteem, and the more successfully they believed their families functioned."

Then Mr. Feiler says, "An unexpected thing happened. Two months later was September 11, 2001. All those families had experienced the same horrific terrorist attack! The researchers went back to the same children of those families and found that the children who knew more about their families handled the stress of that event better. They were more resilient in processing the effects of the stress created by that event."

Psychologists have found that every family has three different kinds of narratives: An ascending narrative, a descending narrative, and the one that makes the best stories, the oscillating narrative.

Here is a story to illustrate: While caring for our eleven-year-old identical twin grandsons last year, I decided to try that progression out on them with our own family story and see what happened.

First, the ascending narrative: The twins' family had named their house Ida (we have this weird tradition of naming our houses in this family), at the suggestion of their mother, but they didn't know why. I explained that, long ago, they had a wonderful grandmother named Ida. She and her husband had ten children by the time she was thirty-eight years old. They all worked amazingly hard together on their very large farm in Star Valley, Wyoming, milking cows, making their own clothes, cooking from scratch, and planting and harvesting crops, but they also had a lot of fun sledding in the winter and swimming in the creeks in the summer.

Next, the descending narrative: I explained that one day, something awful happened. The flu, which was a deadly disease at that time, began sweeping through the valley where they lived. Many, many people died, and Ida allowed many people who were stricken by the disease to lie on cots in her living room while they recovered or until they passed away. One day Ida became ill, too, and within a week, the worst happened . . . she died. But that wasn't the end of the family's sorrow. Ida's two youngest sons died the same week. One was two-and-a-half, and the baby was nine months old.

Finally, the oscillating narrative: I said that somehow, through many years of struggle, the dad, our Grandpa Ray, and the older children (one of whom was their Grandma Hazel) stepped up and helped raise the smaller children. They found help in a woman who had also lost her husband and had five children of her own. The two families joined together to create a mighty force of good children doing exceptional things. The girls all became great teachers, and the boys became successful farmers and businessmen who were a great force for good in Star Valley.

The twins couldn't believe that incredible story! Their house was *named* Ida, for crying out loud, and they loved knowing the story behind the name. They were excited to see pictures of her family on their "ancestor wall" downstairs that they had been walking by for a couple of years knowing only vaguely who those people were. Now they knew!

Interestingly, our son Talmadge, while studying for a graduate degree in Positive Psychology at the University of Pennsylvania, became enamored with Bruce Feiler and his studies. Tal was interested in writing a book about the important influence of fathers in the lives of their children and knew that Mr. Feiler had written a book called *The Council of Dads*. Tal was dying to pick his brain for a few minutes, and most fortunately, we were able to contact Bruce. We met at a restaurant in NYC for a brief brunch because he was off to catch a flight to visit his own father. Practicing what he had been preaching about the importance of family narratives, he was going to see his dad, who was aging. He was excited to record stories of his dad's life history for his children's use as well as future generations.

The stories of our family narrative have become even more important to me since I have been studying the amazing effect that knowing about our parents, grandparents, and ancestors back through time has on our children and grandchildren. So many of my friends and relatives are champions when it comes to genealogy. I have done quite a lot of research myself, but for me, the stories are even more important than the dates. That dash between the birth and death dates holds so many valuable stories for our children and grandchildren to digest. According to Mr. Feiler's research, knowing the hard times as well as the good times of their parents and grandparents can make our children and grandchildren more resilient and more self-confident and help them to have more grit as they work through their own hard times.

So, grandmothers: start telling ancestor stories! Instead of getting out your grandchildren's favorite books at bedtime, tell them family stories. Tell them at the dinner table when you are with them. Email them a story or tell them a story on the phone. Engage them if you're driving a carpool for them or when you're with them on a family trip. And don't forget to tell them stories about yourself. Tell them about the good things that have happened to you as well as the hard things. You never know how much they might appreciate it at the time, but it is a great way to reveal a bit of yourself and give them true grit!

Instead of getting out your grandchildren's favorite books at bedtime, tell them family stories.

When our children were young, we bought a big leather-bound journal and started recording the stories that Richard and I knew about our ancestors, which we translated into children's language. We had the kids illustrate the stories. We found that drawing pictures of stories make them memorable and easier to recall. Our uninhibited young children came up with some memorable pictures of the lives of our ancestors.

In order to tell the stories, you have to know the stories. I thought it would be worthwhile to spend the rest of this chapter telling snippets of the stories of my mother and six of my heroic grandmothers who came before me! I hope these stories will inspire you to learn, record, and tell the stories of your own mothers and grandmothers who came before you. Entice your parents or other older relatives to help you write or record stories that may never have been written.

As you read the stories that follow in the chapter of my wonderful mother and valiant grandmothers, keep in mind that stories that aren't so positive are equally important for your children and grandchildren to know. I have a kind and gentle half-brother whose path in life led him to alcoholism. His wife was also an alcoholic, and though she tried to be a good wife and mother, she was physically and emotionally abusive. They adored their children, but their two girls have a different life story to tell. One was in and out of correctional facilities as a teenager. The other has dealt with a fetal alcohol syndrome her whole life and is now struggling with her health because of lifelong excessive smoking habits. But two finer people you could not find in the world. The older daughter (sixty-two) never married but spends her life valiantly serving others. The younger daughter (sixty) is a nurse and is doing all she can to help her grandchildren thrive. These stories and my mother's and grandmother's stories require a lot of courage and grit!

Thoughts?

- How much do your children know about your family narrative? Ask them these "Do You Know" questions and find out!
- How often do you tell your grandchildren stories about your life or the story of your grandparents' lives? Think of using those stories in the car or at bedtime instead of reading a book they've heard a hundred times.

My Mother, My Hero

Too bad, so sad that we can't appreciate our mothers as much as we should while we're living with them! I vividly remember tears running down my cheeks and on to the piano keys while saying, "I hate practicing!" as my mother stood over me, with arms firmly folded across her chest, saying, "Someday, you'll thank me for this!" And I do!

I adore my mother. She would be 113 if she were still alive today. She gave birth to me when she was 41 and to my sister Lenna at 42. We are lucky to be alive! This quote makes me think of her face:

> *"When she smiles, the lines in her face become epic narratives that trace the stories of generations that no book can replace." —Curtis Jones*

Here is her story:

My mother, Hazel Clark Jacobson, was born in Star Valley, Wyoming in 1905. She was type A, strong willed, and a competitive athlete. Basketball was her greatest love, and the fact that she was the only girl on the floor didn't bother her for a minute! She honed her broad-jumping and high-jumping skills incessantly when she was young, and well into her eighties, she still bowled and played volleyball. In fact, in one volleyball game in her early eighties, she hit the ball so hard that her wig fell off! She scooped it up, hung it on the volleyball post, and, without missing a beat, made the winning point!

Music also became a passion, but only after her father commandeered her to play in a dance band. He played the fiddle, her brother played the banjo, and a friend played the sax, but they really needed a piano player. When she was a young teenager, her father taught her a few chords, sat her down on the

By the end of her life, she had taught at least a thousand piano students.

piano bench at her first practice with the band, and said, "We're playing 'Let Me Call You Sweetheart' in the key of G. Go!"

And away they went. After a few practices and with her natural ability to know when to change the chords, she started playing for dances, which was pretty much the only form of entertainment in Star Valley and through most of the pioneer settlements in those days. Huge crowds loved the music and danced the night away every weekend. Some dance halls even had springs made for the floor so that it would be easier on the feet. It must have been the forerunner of Dick Clark's *American Bandstand*!

When she went to college, she took piano lessons from a demanding professor and made an excruciating effort to learn to read notes. By the end of her life, she had taught at least a thousand piano students and prepared about forty to fifty students a year for biannual recitals. She accompanied innumerable people on the piano as they sang or played a musical instrument for funerals, weddings, church meetings, operettas, and gala parties. When she was older, she had a little organ that she loved to play in her home transferred to the rest home, or "old folks' home," as she called it. Even though she was older than many of the residents, she thrilled those who were "still in the world" when they heard the old songs they had grown to love.

Bursting with energy, she grew up in a family of ten children on a big farm where they milked about fifty cows twice a day and plowed, harrowed, planted, and harvested fields from the time those kids were tiny. Fortunately, she took the time to record some of the fascinating stories of her childhood. Try to imagine your own children or grandchildren doing this as you read the following excerpts from her journal, recorded in 2003:

I was born at Freedom, Wyoming, on October 13, 1905, so they tell me. I remember the four-room house we lived in there. One of the earliest things I can remember is working in the fields with Hilda and Wilford on the disk [this was a machine to plant wheat and barley with little round metal disks attached to an iron machine]. Our dad built a box on the disk and we stood up in it driving the horses. Hilda was eight, Wilford was six, and I was five. That's what they said, anyway. We drove the horses round and round the fields. Our chins just fit over the top of the box.

Another thing I remember well . . . Mother left my sister Florence and I home to do the work. We hated cleaning up that dirty house. We had an argument about who should do what. We got so mad that I slapped her hard right in the face. She slapped me just as hard right back, and at that, we went right into the house madder than two hornets and flew into the work. In about forty-five minutes to an hour, we were all done. We came outside about the same time, one from the front door and one from the back. We met by the side of the house and had such a good feeling realizing it was all done that we ran into each other's arms. She was eight. I was nine.

We always worked hard. During hay season, we came in from the hay field at noon for lunch and would ask our dad if we could run down to the canal, a quarter of a mile away, for a swim, and he would say, "Yes, if you can do that, eat and get the horses ready to go in one hour." That was easy, so away we ran. In this same canal during irrigation times, we would catch whitefish. When the head gate was shut off, there was quite a deep gulley in front of it filled with fish. I remember Florence suggested we wade in and catch them with our hands. I didn't want those slimy things around my legs, but she went in first and I didn't want her being braver than me. Quite a sport, once we got into it. We caught forty and cleaned them and took them home to Mother. She was very glad to have something different for dinner. We were nine and ten then.

We went to school by crossing two sloughs and a river on horses . . . summer and winter. Hilda, Wilford, and I rode this little trusty pony. We were nine-and-a-half, seven-and-a-half, and six years old. When we went through the deep waters of the river, especially in the spring, we held each other's feet up so we wouldn't get wet. In the winter, we chopped the ice so the horses would dare to go in the water. Wilford dropped his ice skates in one morning. We tried to fish them out but couldn't, so we left them there until night.

One day, Dad told me to take his sweep rake up to this field to buck some hay. In order to get into the field, I had to go along this route with the fence on one side and a deep gully on the other side. I had two trusty Belgian mares. As I went along, I could see that we barely could make it . . . the spread between horses being about twenty to twenty-five feet. No possible way to crowd in any farther. As I was going along and holding my breath, I thought to myself, I wonder if Papa has been up here and measured the distance between the fence and the deep ravine, as he seemed so sure I could make it. I'm still wondering. Then when I got to the gate, I was supposed to undo one horse from the sweep and rake and swing her around to pull the rake sideways through the gate, keeping a light rein on the other mare so she would come sideways. Made it! Now that was a sample of many, many nearly impossible things we all did all the time. **But when you master the seemingly impossible, it does something for you that fits into your very character for a lifetime and makes the next impossible thing seem that much easier.**

These delightful and quite incredible stories go on and on. It was wildly different world for farm kids in the early 1900s. Our children and grandchildren treasure these stories! That last sentence in bold has often been quoted to our grandchildren by their mothers when they are required to do hard things. Our darling seven-year-old Cubby has just moved to a new state and into a Chinese immersion school, where his teacher speaks only in Chinese for half the day. He has a tutor, since he is a year behind in Chinese. After a tutoring session, his mother acknowledged that what he was doing was really hard! To her surprise, he repeated Grandma Hazel's now-famous quote exactly: "But when you master the seemingly impossible, it does something for you that fits into your very character for a lifetime and makes the next impossible thing seem that much easier." That boy has a lot of grit! I think Cubby's going to do just fine!

Mother became an incredible schoolteacher. Her career began in 1924 at age nineteen. As soon as she graduated from high school, she went to what they called "normal school," which was an intensive teacher-training school for high school students so that they could become teachers. *Wikipedia* defines "normal schools" as "teacher training schools, which were tasked with both developing this new curriculum and developing the techniques through which teachers would instill . . . ideas, behaviors, and values in the minds of their students."[3]

In the end, we figured that she taught at least a thousand schoolchildren and imprinted ideas, behaviors, and values even beyond what was in the instruction manuals on the minds of those children that would last them a lifetime. I often meet her students when I go back to my hometown, where she taught for many years. They are now grandparents, and all seem to have the same memory of her: "When I was a struggling child, your mother believed in me and thought I could do anything! It made all the difference in my life!"

Saydi's family has an annual "Grandma Hazel Day." Over the years, she and her four children have had many happy days remembering what Grandma Hazel would want them to do and enjoy!

Perhaps her finest role, though, was that of grandmother! My children remember her teaching them how to pick beans without pulling up the whole plant, shelling peas, and pulling weeds. They knew that she loved them, but she made them toe the line and expected perfect obedience!

Our daughter Shawni now has a daughter with the middle name Hazel, and our daughter Saydi's oldest is named Hazel. Saydi's family has an annual "Grandma Hazel Day." Over the years, she and her four children have had many happy days remembering what Grandma Hazel would want them to do and enjoy! With the guidance of their smart mother, they always start with a challenging work project. They also enjoy her favorite pastimes, like bowling and watching football on TV. They might even make the food she loved to prepare, like creamed peas and potatoes, and have a Hershey's chocolate bar. Some years, they do a special service project, which Grandma Hazel was so good at doing. How blessed I am to have had a mother who taught our children and grandchilren so skillfully without realizing how far her teaching would go!

Writing and Telling the Family Narrative

As I launch into this next section, I do so knowing that many of you may be new to thinking about genealogy. You may have never given much thought to your ancestors. In addition, your history may be fraught with the complications of divorce or dysfunction. For some of our children and grandchildren, who live in a world of temporary relationships and cohabitation, family history is going to become more and more difficult to document. On the other hand, many of you may be far ahead of me in researching your family history and finding the stories of your ancestors. Some of you have published books about their lives! Hats off to you!

The rest of this chapter is dedicated to women who, without knowing it at the time, have changed my life because of the good and hard things they have done. All but one of these women I never knew. Thankfully, some did write journals, and those who knew them have left behind stories and dates and fragments of their lives to help piece together their remarkable lives.

None were famous. They were just ordinary women doing extraordinary things! They faced hard times and sometimes excruciating loses with exceptional valor. Most of these women didn't leave detailed journal entries. But I'm sure there were days of sorrow and anguish and, often, their longings to turn back or quit trying. One thing they all had, though, was *grit*! Their stories are strong and empowering. I am thrilled that I share their genes. When I have encountered hard times in my life, I have thought, *If Grandma Elizabeth could do that, I can do this!* I have loved sharing these stories with my grandchildren.

I call each of these ancestors my "right-angle" grandmothers. You will see that each was converted to the Mormon church in different countries and under different circumstances. Their decision to join a new religion and immigrate to America sharply changed the trajectory of my life and the lives of their progeny forever. Perhaps you have come from a difficult or even dysfunctional family, and *you* are the right-angle ancestor for your progeny; you are the hero that your grandchildren need. Maybe you are "the change" that will affect generations to come. If so, record *your* story! It will be all the more valuable to your grand-children as they look to your example for inspiration in making a difference in their own lives.

A good friend had a great idea as she was researching the lives of her ancestors. She had found long stories of their everyday lives that she really wanted her children and grandchildren to know. But she was also realistic! She knew most of her progeny were probably not going to read about their ancestors via long treatises on their lives. She suggested writing short vignettes of these fascinating lives in four hundred words.

I loved that idea and have set out here to give you just a taste of the remarkable things these grandmothers have done in four hundred words (plus a little commentary). That is hard! There is so much to tell! But it was a great way to consolidate the events of their lives to include only the most important values they taught as they dealt with hard things and carried on. I have been blessed to have found a way to get to the home countries and birthplace of many of these grandmothers and, in one case, the actual homes where these grandmothers lived, which filled me with joy and wonder!

If you are interested in finding your own ancestors, go to *familysearch.org* and sign in as a guest. It is totally free, and all you need is names, birthplaces, and any dates that you have (birth, death, marriage, etc.). You might be amazed at what you find. If anyone in your family, including a distant cousin or aunt, has posted about your ancestor, you will find documents, pic-tures, and some memories recorded by those who knew them. *Ancestry.com* also has a wealth of information.

Before I start on these narratives of valor and endurance, I have to add a little note about my wonderful great-grandmother Sarah Ann Holmes Aland (July 2, 1852–December 17, 1914), who was my Grandma Nellie's mother. Very little is written about her life, which also included a plethora of hardships. She showed a side of discouragement that we rarely find in journals along with a good sense of humor when she wrote a few sentences here and there in her diary. She had a plethora of physical trials that seem to pile on, one after the other. After her husband died, she was sick and lonely and miserable. One day, at the height of her troubles, she bumped her head really hard coming down the stairs and declared, *There now, I've broke my bloomin' head & I'm dam glad of it!* Don't we all feel that way some days? With compassion, it was easy to read between the lines and often feel those kinds of emotions as I have researched these stories.

If you decide to write stories about your own ancestors for the benefit of your children and grandchildren, give each story a compelling title, just a few short words that encapsulate the story, captures their interest, and urges them to read on. And at the end of the story, think of the value that person taught as you ask yourself, *Therefore, what?* Passing those values on to our grandchildren is one of the most important things we can do. If you have good people who have survived difficult circumstances in your family tree, knowing that their blood is in their veins will do remarkable things for self-confidence and just plain grit, for you as well as your grandchildren.

As I prepared these stories, I thought of one of my favorite quotes from Anna Quindlen that so perfectly applies to the lives of these wondrous women. As I have researched the lives of my grandmothers, I realized that they couldn't have known at the time how much influence their valiant lives would have on their progeny. This also applies to our lives as we leave a legacy for our own grandchildren:

"We are building for the centuries. We are building character, and tradition, and values, which meander like a river into the distance and out of our sight, but on and on and on." —Anna Quindlen[4]

So here we go with a glimpse of the lives my courageous grandmothers. After researching their stories, my life will never be the same!

The Grandmothers Who Gave Me Grit

Grandmother Ida: Tragic Loss of a Champion of Work, Family, and Education

Ida Emma Weber Clark (January 21, 1882–January 25, 1920) was my mother's mother and was born in Freedom, Wyoming.

> *You already know part of Ida's story from the example earlier in the chapter. How I wish I could have known Ida when she was alive! I wish I would have thought to ask my mother and her siblings who knew her more questions about her character, her goals, and her fondest dreams before she died!*

Ida was born in Schmiedrued, Aargau, Switzerland. Several years after her parents joined the Mormon church, the family decided to immigrate to America. On the journey, Ida, age six, was literally blown overboard on the ship during a ferocious storm. A heroic man standing nearby grabbed the back of her dress and pulled her to safety! Hooray for that good man. Otherwise, none of her posterity, including me, would be here!

She married Arthur Raymond Clark, and they were pioneers who helped to settle Star Valley, Wyoming. Extremely hardworking in the home as well as on the farm, Ida was not only a wonderful cook for her family but she also fed twenty to twenty-five ranch hands three meals a day for two weeks during the harvest. Her children can never remember seeing her wear anything except a black skirt and yellow blouse. A beautiful alto singing voice provided many fun hours harmonizing with her siblings. Being the mental, emotional, and financial force behind her determination to build a new home for their ten children in a nearby town called Etna, she drove a team many miles back and forth through narrow canyons to get building supplies while her husband worked on the house and the farm.

When it was time for her oldest daughter, Hilda, to go to high school, the school was thirty miles away. The only way to get there was by horse and buggy or a "one-horse open sleigh" in the winter. That meant the kids had to board there for long periods during the school year. Hilda declared that she was not going to high school and was determined to stay home rather than leave her mother to care for the house, the farm, and the children. Ida looked her oldest daughter straight in the eye and said, "Hilda, twenty years from now, no one will remember if this floor was mopped or the crops were gathered, but they will remember if you go away and get a good education!"

In 1920, the dreaded worldwide influenza pandemic (which killed more people than the plague, World War I, and World War II combined), came to Star Valley. She was the bishop's wife, so dear Ida took care of not only her family but others stricken in the community.

The sick lay in cots in the family's parlor. She cared for them until she was also stricken. She died just as she turned thirty-eight. Her two youngest sons, Gerald, two-and-a-half, and Byron, nine months, died the same week and were buried in the night without a funeral to prevent further infection. It is a tribute to her that all her remaining children (including my mother) were well taught in the important values of life. All five of her daughters became wonderful mothers and outstanding teachers and changed many lives for good. Her surviving sons became excellent fathers, farmers, and friends as well as successful businessmen who contributed much to their families and communities!

Grandmother Verena: Immovable in Her Faith Because of a Miracle

Verena Goldenberger Weber (September 22, 1855–May 9, 1917) was Ida's mother and was also born in Schmiedrued, Aargau, Switzerland. She was married at age twenty-one to Samuel Weber, probably in part because of his serenades to her, since he had beautiful singing voice!

> *I have now visited the beautiful little village of Schmiedrued three times. It was such a delight. Each time I knew a little more about their history and grew to love them more dearly.*

Verena came from a wealthy family and had been well trained in sewing. She was an expert in tailoring men's clothing and made more money than her husband, who worked in the local mill.

Verena was empowered by her faith in the gospel of Jesus Christ after the Mormon missionaries blessed her little four-year-old son Erwin, who was besieged with a horrible skin disease that the doctors called incurable. He was miraculously healed. Her faith remained powerful and potent, even when that little son was killed by a lumber wagon when he was seven. Adding salt to her wounds, another baby was born the year after Ida was born and he too perished! She remained valiant in her beliefs through her losses, despite the fact that her friends and her rather wealthy family disowned her and that her best customers left her when she joined the church. Even when she was near death with typhoid fever and everyone thought she would die, she summoned her faith and recovered.

When they entered the sailing ship to immigrate to America, Verena was pregnant with their eighth child. Even though she was proud of the fact that it never took her more than three days after the birth of a child to return to her sewing, what a brave soul she was as she boarded that ship with all those little children for the long journey. The smells on the ship in those first months of pregnancy must have been wretched! The family survived the voyage, but sadly, the baby she gave birth to after their arrival passed away before his first birthday, and another baby born the next year survived for only six months! In all, she bore thirteen children and lost four. I can only imagine her grief!

While Samuel was outgoing and loved social interactions, Verena was shy and retiring. But her judgement and ability to sort out a problem was impeccable, and Samuel depended on her for important decisions. Her inability to fully learn English when she got to America was very difficult for her! Her daughter Martha often heard her say, "I would have liked to have said something about that question if I could have expressed myself a little better."

Nevertheless, Verena became a community leader, and a beautiful stone monument at a park in Freedom honors her with a plaque that says *Dedicated to Verena Weber for Her Generosity.* That miracle early in her life remained a beacon of light and supported her faith. Her tragedies seemed to become pillars of strength!

Grandmother Elizabeth Clark: Lover of Religion, Family, and Bluebells

Elizabeth Gower Clark (February 20, 1819–October 28, 1882) was my mother's great-grandmother on her father's side. She was born in Little Baddow [love that name], Essex, England.

What a thrill it was to stand in a forest of Bluebells near Little Baddow, where I knew Elizabeth must have played as a child! One year, our daughter Saydi happened to be living in England for six months with her family, and Little Baddow was about forty-five minutes away from her home. We gloried in walking through that carpet of bluebells, and then we traveled to the church where she had married Daniel Clark in Colchester, Essex, England, which was only a little farther. That day, Saydi's children Hazel and Charlie stood hand in hand at that church's ancient wooden front door pretending to be the Elizabeth and Daniel as they left the chapel on their wedding day.

Just before the birth of their seventh child, Elizabeth and Daniel heard the message of the Mormon missionaries and were converted. After the word got around that they had joined this "strange religion," friends and neighbors not only turned against them but began to persecute them. As rumors spread, the schools refused to let their children attend, and they had to do their best to teach their children at home as the persecution continued.

To add to their trials, the Crimean War was raging, with Russian troops assigned to Colchester where troops commandeered homes for their quarters. The Clarks' home was one of them. Life became so difficult that Elizabeth and Samuel decided to escape with their children in the middle of the night. They fled to Barking, six miles outside of London, and soon decided that they would emigrate and join other Mormons who were leaving for America in droves. In 1861, their three oldest daughters were sent ahead with the funds the family could scrape together to prepare a way for the rest of the family to join them. Their oldest daughter, Elizabeth (twenty), married soon after she arrived and was determined to find a way to get her family to Utah. She was able to sell bushels of wheat for five dollars each and worked diligently to raised $100 to get her family to America!

When the rest of the family arrived in New York in 1862, the distance to their daughters lengthened as they had to travel through Canada to avoid the horrors of the Civil War. The family finally reached Nebraska and joined a wagon train to the West. One night, while Daniel was taking his turn to watch the horses overnight, he drank some bad water from the creek; he sickened, and within a few days, Elizabeth's beloved and devoted husband was gone!

Elizabeth must have been devastated! It was up to her to get her six children to "Zion." There is no journal or record of the hardships that she endured, but they must have been terrible! I can also conjure up the rejoicing that occurred when she joined her daughters along with the profound sadness at the new she bore that their father had not survived the journey. When they arrived in the "promised land," Elizabeth's hardships didn't end. She faced more trials with a second husband, more losses, and heartbreak, but she never gave up. Her children cared for her lovingly, and she died knowing the most important part of faith is to move on and never give up!

Grandmother Nellie: Stalwart Wife, Mother, and Community Builder

Elizabeth Ellen Aland (aka Nellie) (October 21, 1869–December 17, 1957) was my father's mother.

In my lifetime, I have looked into the eyes of only one of my grandmothers. It was Grandma Nellie. How I wish I had been smart enough to ask her a thousand questions. But I was only nine when she died, and I was in a childhood fog when it came to learning about my ancestors. I remember the little room where she slept with an old-fashioned piano at her side. She had cataracts, and she couldn't see my sister or me; still, every time we went to see her, she requested that we sing

"When It's Springtime in the Rockies" while my mother played the piano by ear. By then, she was heavyset, with beautiful eyes and a twisted bun in her gray hair. She sat on the side of her bed and smiled and offered us love and ginger snaps when we finished.

A beautiful young woman, Nellie was courted by many young men, but she was taken by the handsome Frederick Jacobson, and they were married when Nellie was twenty and he was twenty-two. She bravely moved in with her mother-in-law to a household full of small children, where she became a generous helper and a well-loved daughter-in-law.

Nellie gave birth to ten children, one of whom was my dad, who was born in 1892. She was a domestic expert and was said to be able to make a lovely meal out of almost nothing! She learned to play the piano, organ, accordion, and Jew's harp and had a beautiful singing voice. Her health deteriorated after the birth of her seventh child, but she carried on, bearing three more children.

Indians often roamed through the valley, begging for "biscuit-ee-wino," meaning bread and wine. All the settlers were happy to share their bread, but they didn't drink wine, and the Indians had to settle for a drink of water. At the Jacobsons' house one day while Nellie and Frederick weren't home and a small group of Indians were roaming through the town, one of the "big bucks" decided to grab baby Cyril and take him along with them. Five-year-old Maude ran screaming to the neighbor's home, and the father there quickly returned to rescue the baby before the Indians got away.

Nellie's husband Freddie died suddenly of a stroke when he was fifty-eight. Even though she was crushed to lose the love of her life, Nellie gathered herself together and carried on. She was a widow for twenty-eight years, years that she filled with good works, as she lived a life full of enormous contributions to Bloomington and the Bear Lake Valley. She was the president of the community Booster Club, which sponsored dances, dinners, and entertainment and raised funds to build a new Amusement Hall.

My dad and his brothers hauled the lumber for the building, and Nellie helped to raise funds, not only for the building but also to buy a much-needed piano for the facility. Later, she was instrumental in getting the National Forest Service to harness springs for public use and to provide picnic areas for the gorgeous Bloomington Lake as well as to build a road to that beautiful place and other nearby areas of beauty, which, until that time, was only accessible by horse and wagon. Nellie died with her loved ones around her, who will always pay tribute to her for her wonderful life!

Grandmother Elizabeth Jacobson: A Mountain-Moving Mother Despite Horrendous Trials

Elizabeth Pedersen Jacobson (December 3, 1825–February 11, 1899) was my father's great-grandmother. She was born in Noreborn, Elling, Denmark, the fourth child of eleven children.

One summer, Shawni and I visited this beautiful little town in Denmark. We had rented a car in London and dropped off Charity, who was going into her senior year of high school, at a summer program at Oxford University. We had a fabulous experience in an old-time museum in the village where they lived, seeing the farm instruments and household items from our ancestors' time. Last year, our son Talmadge, who lives in Switzerland, visited the same town and even found the village historian, who took him directly to the house where the Jacobson family had lived for many generations.

When she was twenty years old, Elizabeth married Frederick Jacobson, and they began their family. As a couple, they listened to the message of the Mormon missionaries and believed that their message was true. They were baptized in 1853. Elizabeth's parents were kind, but her father was strict and unbending, and when she joined the church, her parents disowned her and never forgave her.

By the time Elizabeth gave birth to their sixth child, she and Frederick were eager to emigrate and join fellow members of the church in Utah. Little did she know the trials that lay ahead. Tragically, their oldest daughter, Anna Christiana, thirteen, passed away just before they were about to leave. They forged on, made their way to Hamburg, Germany, and along with 1,556 other passengers, including four companies of newly converted Mormons, they sailed for America. Two weeks into their journey, they discovered that someone had boarded the ship with measles! It spread quickly, and the unthinkable happened. Their six-year-old daughter, Sarah Marie, succumbed, then two days later, nine-year-old Engerline, then their darling baby two-year-old, Elizabeth. All three little girls were buried in a watery grave.

Altogether on the ship, fifty-four children died with measles. To add to the misery, Elizabeth was sick with a pregnancy, and then the to complete their sorrows, their son Jens, eleven, became ill. On arrival in NYC, they carried him to a hospital, where he died. I cannot fathom the grief! Instead of seeing their dreams fulfilled to have their family together in America, they arrived with only their oldest son Peter.

Somehow, this mountain-moving mother went on. Frederick, Elizabeth, and Peter made their way by train and by steamboat to Florence, Nebraska. From there, they joined a company of covered wagons, and Elizabeth walked one thousand miles to their destination in Utah . . . pregnant. She gave birth to baby Amelia (who, by the way, was Donny and Marie Osmond's great-great-grandmother). In 1863, Elizabeth and Frederick were asked by Brigham Young to move on and colonize the Bear Lake Valley, where two more babies were born in a tiny log cabin in Bloomington, Idaho. The youngest was my grandfather, Frederick Jacobson. (I am so grateful that she was brave enough to have that last child. Otherwise, I wouldn't be here!)

In the end, her husband left her for another woman. Cataclysmic! Resolute, she remained true and faithful to her family and her God.

Grandmother Ellen: Heroic Despite the Grueling Loss of Ten of Her Thirteen Children

Ellen Sarah Harding Aland (April 14, 1811–May 18, 1880), my father's great-grandmother, has just been added to my list of grandmother heroes! The best information I could find about her was from her family group sheet containing her birth and marriage dates and the birth and death dates of her children. But what a story that tells! She was born in Ramsbury, Wiltshire, England in 1811. Ellen married John Sparrow Aland and moved to Batheaston, Wiltshire, England, where she gave birth to thirteen children (that is not a typo), six of whom died before she left Batheaston, and two more were lost along the way. When I think of my own grandchildren at the ages of those children she lost, my heart hurts. She lost William at five months, Thomas at eight years, Sarah Ellen at six months, Hugh at nine months, Kate at three days, and her last child, Harvey, on the day he was born.

Again, the story goes that Ellen embraced the message of the Mormon missionaries; perhaps the Mormon belief that families are eternal and that she would someday be able rejoin those children in heaven was a compelling factor in her conversion. She joined the church and emigrated in 1854 at age forty-three. For unknown reasons, her husband did not join the church and sadly did not join her on the arduous journey to America.

Courageously, she set out to join fellow Saints in America on her own with seven children. Tragically, her two oldest daughters Elizabeth (twenty) and Ann (eighteen) died somewhere along their arduous journey. To heap on the sorrow, after finally arriving in Bloomington with her five remaining children, her son Francis (twenty-one) was having fun wrestling with a friend when his neck was broken and he also passed away. Tragically, her darling daughter Emily Kate (twenty-five) died in childbirth, leaving four little children for Ellen to care for. Just imagine the searing sorrow of going through thirteen pregnancies and then losing ten of those precious children one by one. Ellen had only three surviving children when she passed on to greet the others in the next life. She remained strong and true to the faith to the end!

Serendipitously, a few years ago, our youngest daughter, Charity, had moved to London with her husband Ian and lived only about two-and-a-half hours from Batheaston. As we drove along, we had no idea what we would find. We were hoping for a small, quaint village and not a large, sprawling city, and we got our wish. We drove into the little village via a truly breathtaking road barely wide enough for one car with steep ivy-covered banks rising almost straight up on both sides.

We were dazzled to see the charming village of Batheaston emerge at the end of the path, and we were thrilled to have lunch at an old rock monastery from the fifteenth century, which was surely there when the Alands were there 185 years ago. The countryside surrounding the village couldn't have been more picturesque. What an empowering experience to be in the very place where this grandmother lost and gained so much. She couldn't have known how much her difficult life would be "building character, and tradition, and values, which meander like a river into the distance and out of our sight, but on and on and on . . ."

Therefore, What?

Knowing these magnificent women's life stories is not only inspiring—it is life changing! They were ordinary women who became great because of what they believed was most important in life (which, in most cases, was their faith). Their ability to do really hard things with determination and grit is beyond remarkable. What they did is rooted in their faith, hope, and charity! They had the ability not only to survive but to thrive, which has always been such an inspiration to me. Their faith in God has empowered me to accomplish hard things.

I can't help but think that their genes play a part in all our family's lives. Of course there are thousands of combinations of genes that exhibit themselves in different people in different ways, but I really believe that because I come from a long line of hardworking pioneers and generations of farmers on both sides of my family. Because of them, I feel that I've been granted some extra grit.

For starters, I love to work! I love working with my hands and with the earth. I have to admit that I really like pulling out weeds! I love the sense of accomplishment that comes with cleaning things up and making things grow. Interestingly, Richard, who comes from a long line of writers and has an aunt who was a famous poet, loves working with his brain and has authored or coauthored over fifty books.

Our children have felt the faith and the strength of their ancestors. As destiny would have it, our son Talmadge has moved to Switzerland with his wife, who was born in a town not far from where our Swiss ancestors lived. Who knew? And our youngest daughter Charity has moved to England, where so many of

> **Their ability to do really hard things with determination and grit is beyond remarkable. What they did is rooted in their faith, hope, and charity! They had the ability not only to survive but to thrive.**

our ancestors lived and loved before they sacrificed their home-land for a new adventure.

Just like their ancestors, some of our children have left for a foreign country, not knowing what the future would hold or who would be there to embrace them when they got there but with faith and determination to accomplish their dreams. Their path is certainly not as dangerous as those of our ancestors, but I really believe that their belief that they should follow their dreams comes from the same source . . . the belief that they are watched over by a higher power who will guide them.

Our plucky daughter Saydi, who is a glutton for adventure, became a "pioneer" in her own right. She and her husband and four children decided to uproot their lovely lifestyle after living in Boston for twenty years for a year of adventure on a farm in California. They managed a one-hundred-acre farm near Half Moon Bay in California for a friend. While her husband, Jeff, set up an office for his company in Silicon Valley during the week, Saydi and the kids learned how to work a big farm, including learning how to milk goats twice a day, make goat cheese and goat yogurt, hatch chicks, create new recipes for eggs, plant a plethora of trees and vegetables, and deal with a mountain lion killing their sheep. They survived torrential rain and the woes of planting crops that were eventually eaten by gophers. Their kids became beekeepers, and they learned how to deal with the life and death that always occurs on a farm. Our ancestors would be so proud of them!

Our oldest grandchildren are doing really hard things as well! Shawni and David, with their family of five kids under seventeen, spent a semester in China. That was hard stuff for everyone! Our oldest grandson is a missionary in Taiwan, where he is rejected many times every day. That's even harder!

Those timeless values of courage, determination, and the faith and grit to survive hard times are part of the fiber of these heroic grandmothers, which they unknowingly have passed on to our children and grandchildren.

This is my all-time favorite poem about the importance of those who came before us. It is from a gifted Mormon pioneer who captures in just a few words the faith and strength and valor which our ancestors, whether they were pioneers or not, have passed on to us:

> *They cut desire into short lengths*
> *And fed it to the hungry fires of courage.*
> *Long after, when the flames had died,*
> ***Molten gold** gleamed in the ashes.*
> *They gathered it into bruised palms*
> *And handed it to their children*
> *And their children's children*
> *Forever.*
>
> —Vilate Raile

I am forever grateful for the amazing lives of these stalwart grandmothers of faith and courage. They truly shortened their own desires and went forth with determination and courage. The "molten gold" they handed us from their bruised palms is priceless. We see the glint of gold in ourselves, our children, and our grandchildren when dealing with hard times.

Because I firmly believe that there is a life after death and that these women live on in a different realm, I also believe that they could be the angels who comfort us when we are experiencing difficulties in our lives. We'll never know for sure until we get there, but I think I will know them

These narratives will give your grandchildren grit to get through the hard things and resilience to bounce back in troubled times.

when I see them and will certainly be able to thank them for their sacrifices on our behalf!

The challenge, then, for this chapter is not only to tell your grandparents' stories but also to write the stories for your children and grandchildren and those who "go on and on and out of sight." (Suggestions for "how to" are coming in the next chapter.) The same goes for the stories of your parents as well as the stories of your own life. These narratives will give your grandchildren grit to get through the hard things and resilience to bounce back in troubled times. I can almost promise that it will make a difference in their lives and in yours too!

Thoughts?

- You have ancestors with fascinating stories! Remember that if you don't already know about them, you may be able to find their stories at *familysearch.org* and *ancestry.com*. You might be amazed at the stories that relatives (aunts and uncles; second, third, and fourth cousins) have submitted as memories and records of your ancestors for you to enjoy—and share with your grandchildren!

- If you can't find anything there on these websites, you can post the interesting stories that *you* know about your parents, grandparents, and ancestors that are not known by others in your family. The stories, pictures, and documents that you record will then be available to many extended family members who don't know those stories and would love to have them!

- Some of your stories may not be happy ones. You may even have a horse thief or a bank robber in the ancestry. Embrace those stories and make them a part of your "folklore." As you share them with your grandchildren, emphasize the importance of those who were "the change," especially if that person is you.

- A big hug to those of you who are already far ahead of me on this and are the champion researchers of family history that we all wish we were!

Notes

1. Feiler, Bruce. "The Stories That Bind Us." The *New York Times*, March 15, 2013. http://www.nytimes.com/2013/03/17/fashion/the-family-stories-that-bind-us-this-life.html.

2. Duke, Marshall P. "The Stories That Bind Us: What Are the Twenty Questions?" *The Huffington Post*, March 23, 2013. Updated May 23, 2013. https://www.huffingtonpost.com/marshall-p-duke/the-stories-that-bind-us-_b_2918975.html.

3. "Normal School." *Wikipedia*. https://en.wikipedia.org/wiki/Normal_school.

4. Quindlen, Anna. *Living Out Loud*. New York: Random House, 1988.

CHAPTER 8

What about YOU?

Taking Care of #1

Those wonderful daydreams of having luxurious time to take care of ourselves when our children fly from the nest are often replaced with increased demands of caring for adult children who still need our attention. In reality, we are also often sandwiched between caring for our beautiful grandchildren, fresh from heaven, and our parents, who are struggling with their health, and even our aged parents who desperately need help in moving back to heaven.

But let's face it: in order to have the best quality of life with our grandchildren, we have to take care of ourselves. One of the things that Richard and I have always suggested when speaking to parents is to have a regular *five-facet review,* which was discussed earlier. It is a way to evaluate their children's lives as

Take notes in a journal or in the "Thoughts" section about how you are doing right now physically, mentally, emotionally, socially, and spiritually.

they grew. We challenge parents to have a meeting with each other once a month and spend a few minutes talking together about how each child is doing physically, mentally, emotionally, socially, and spiritually.

As we begin the journey through this chapter, I'd like to challenge you to do the same, but do it for yourself. Have a meeting with yourself. Take some time to think. Take notes in a journal or in the "Thoughts" section about how you are doing right now physically, mentally, emotionally, socially, and spiritually. Then challenge yourself to do better in areas that need improvement. For those of you who are young grandmothers in your forties and fifties, your physical assessments may be different than those of you who are in your sixties, seventies, and eighties, as will the other facets of your life. Whatever your situation is, there will be room to improve in one or more of these areas. It's a great way to think about how balanced you are.

Below I provide an example of my own evaluation of how I'm doing physically, and it is bound to make you feel better about yourself and will hopefully stimulate your thoughts about the other facets of your life.

How am I doing physically? Even though my mother was an athlete and adored participating in sports, I am a slug! To be honest, I have to force myself to exercise. I can sit for days writing a book without feeling any need to go anywhere but the bathroom. I have to force myself to get up and do something. When all our children were home, I claimed that I was in constant motion all day every day, running up and down and stairs, and was increasing my flexibility by incessantly picking up toys and discarded art projects. I was pretty much right!

Now that I'm older, I am trying to do better. I bought a fitness tracker and started counting steps. When we visited our children in New York and London, I walked 10,000 steps on several different days. (Several friends I know do that every day.) Once I even walked 23,000 steps, but I have to admit that it was counting the steps of my horse on a half-day ride through the mountains. To be honest, those days are rare. Luckily, I have a bad knee, which is a really good excuse for not exercising. Still, I force myself to get on the elliptical a couple of times a week, and sometimes, much to my chagrin, I find myself in the exercise rooms of hotels where we are staying.

A couple of years ago, I found my sport! Biking. Electric biking, that is! For my birthday, Richard bought me a great little bike with a battery, and I love that little knob that I can turn when the going gets tough on the spectacular paths through Zion's Canyon and Snow Canyon in Southern Utah. I don't even have to sweat, but I do get my heart rate up, and the scenery is matchless!

This year, I finally hit the incredibly old age of seventy and started to turn over a new leaf with my health. Not so much with exercise, although I'm doing better, but after saying I was going to do it for too many years, I have finally lost some weight! My knee is feeling better, and I am committed to eating less and drinking more water. I have come a short way, but there is a long way to go!

I laugh about my physical inabilities, but in all seriousness, staying healthy, doing a little better than we have been in all five of the facets of our lives as we get older, is the key to our succes.

I laugh about my physical inabilities, but in all seriousness, staying healthy, doing a little better than we have been in all five of the facets of our lives as we get older, is the key to our success in not only feeling better about our health but in being more vibrant in our relationships with our grandchildren, our spouse, and our extended family.

Many of our ailments, both physical and mental, come from the inevitability of aging and health issues beyond our control. When I asked my dear friend Margaret what she thought was the best part of growing old, her answer was stunning. The best part, she said, was just being alive and grasping the joy of every day. Several years earlier, she had been diagnosed with breast cancer and had gone through the horrific experiences that many of you have probably endured with chemo and radiation. Just when she started to feel normal again, the cancer was back. Dealing with the fact that it was a very aggressive cancer and if one cell got loose, it would spread very quickly, she and her team of doctors decided to go with a double mastectomy as well as reconstructive surgery. In hindsight, she said it was a more serious surgery than a quadruple bypass heart surgery. The grueling recovery can only be appreciated fully by those who have experienced it.

I have never known a happier grandmother; even after many years after being declared cancer-free, she has never lost the wonder of living as she continues to seize the day, relishing every day she lives, especially as she treasures the dearest relationships in her life.

Good luck with this challenge and in considering the five facets of your life. My journey through the important components of my life has been an eye-opening and soul-searching experience!

Thoughts?

- How healthy are you? What do you need to do to improve your health?
- How does your health compare with the heath of your mother?
- Have fun contemplating the five facets of your life: physical, mental, social, emotional, and spiritual. Don't just trust your thoughts and goals to your memory. Write them down below! Our memory systems may not be what they used to be. :)

Writing Our Stories

Most of us know our grandchildren pretty well, but the question is, how much do they know about us and about the things we love? Our relationship with them needs to be a two-way street. The older my grandchildren and I get, the more precious our relationships become. Life seasons us and makes the future more delicious as we develop relationships with our spouses, our families, and especially our grandchildren. Most of us don't think much about being rich and famous anymore! High school reunions, if they are still happening, have become a joy instead of a comparison-fest. What's more, we now have the luxury of sharing our joys and our passions with our grandchildren!

If you are wondering just how much they *do* know, you might be surprised at what they *don't* know! As Erma Bombeck said:

"When a grandchild says, 'Grandma, how come you didn't have any children?' a grandparent holds back the tears."

In the last chapter, we discussed the importance of children knowing your family narrative. *You* are a big part of that! Some of the things that your grandchildren will cherish as they get older are tales that you tell them about your life. Have you shared some funny stories from your childhood? Do they know what you love? Do your older grandkids know that you were the editor of the high school newspaper and what a favorite professor in college taught you? Do they know about your service to your neighbor in need, your involvement in the community, and your responsibilities at church? As

Some of the things that your grandchildren will cherish as they get older are tales that you tell them about your life.

a friend said, "I don't want my grandchildren to learn about me from my obituary."

My mother's youngest sister, Wanda, born in 1915, completed a questionnaire with several pages of questions about her childhood and her beliefs when she was about seventy-five years old. That document is one of the most treasured bits of our family history. One of the requests was "Share an experience with an outhouse." She wrote the following:

> One night when I was about nine, I was really mad at somebody. I went out after dark and went to the outhouse to make them worry. On the way out, I could see this still, dark form that looked just like a bear on the side of the path. Ordinarily, I would have been scared to death, but I was so angry that I went right up to it and touched it. I thought that if it ate me, they'd be sorry! It turned out to be a sawhorse with a blanket thrown over it. That was the end of that ornery streak.
>
> We used to go out to the outhouse when the dishes were being done and look at the catalogue which was used for toilet paper. We usually got yelled at to "get in here and help with the dishes."

Day-by-day journals of our predecessors are wonderful to have, but Aunt Wanda's document is concise and hilarious because she just answered questions about her childhood that no one would have otherwise known. Because she lived with my mother much of her life, her answers also told us about the life of my mother! Her wonderful sense of humor adds much to the commentary.

A friend directed me to a "totally awesome" webpage that will help you think of things about your life that you can share in writing. Simply go to *familysearch.org/blog/en/52stories/*. It's a simple, easy, non-threatening way to write about your life. You don't have to be a great writer, but it will be a piece of you that will be treasured forever by your progeny. There are fifty-two questions, one for each week of the year that you can answer in one sentence, a paragraph, or a long story. At a set time each week, perhaps every Sunday afternoon, you can write your memories prompted by that week's question. It is brilliant! Here are the categories:

- Goals and Achievements
- Love and Friendship
- Occupations and Hobbies
- Home and Hearth
- Mothers and Motherhood
- Fathers and Fatherhood
- Events and Milestones
- Travels and Vacation
- Education and School
- Values and Beliefs
- Causes and Convictions
- Holidays and Traditions

You can add or substitute other categories as they apply to your life. I think I would add "Trials and Tribulations," because no life is complete without those, and they teach you so much about life. I am extending a challenge to you to do this, this year. I am challenging myself to do the same. I have spent so much time researching ancestors and not nearly enough time documenting my own life! Even though I have been writing books for most of my life, I have never really written many personal stories, worries, and achievements that probably no one would care about but my posterity.

For example, one of the questions in the "Occupations" category is "What was your first job and what did it teach you?"

I don't think many of my children and none of my grandchildren know that I was a carhop at the local A&W when the local drive-in hamburger stand in our tiny town (population of 2,756) was on the direct path to the World's Fair in Seattle in

It's just a fun way to conjure memories and produce a document that will engage your children and grandchildren.

1962. I almost killed myself every day of that sweltering summer waiting on hundreds of people from all over the world as they passed through. Up until that point in my secluded little life in Southeastern Idaho, I had never seen an African-American person or an Asian person face to face!

In the questionnaire, you can skip questions that don't apply and add things that aren't asked. The important thing is that you can get your own history written without the painstaking effort of doing your life story chronologically. It's just a fun way to conjure memories and produce a document that will engage your children and grandchildren with the fun and interesting details of your life. Don't wait until you are gone and have others try to remember or recreate a story. Share them now. Talk about them as you engage with your grandchildren. Use your stories as bedtime stories. It will give you both some joy!

When I asked a friend what she thought her grandchildren knew about her, she showed me a book that her grandchildren (with the help of their mothers) had given her on her seventieth birthday. Her daughters and daughters-in-law asked each of their children to write just one word on a small chalkboard that described their grandmother best. Then a picture was taken of each child smiling and holding their "word" for Grandma. A little book was produced online, printed, and presented to her on her milestone birthday! It was so delightful and revealing to see her book with those darling grinning grandchildren, holding that one special word that personified their grandmother.

Thoughts?

- Will you join me in setting a goal for writing some stories about your life? I don't do well without deadlines. That said, there are no "start" or "stop" parameters. Do what works for you. The important thin is to start writing!
- What do you want your grandchildren to remember about you? Jot some notes and stories that come to mind in the space below.

Ideas for Sharing What You Love

I have been pestering my friends who are grandmothers to re-member how they taught their grandchildren what they value and what gives them joy. I also asked them how they helped their grandchildren know them not just as "Grandma" but also a person who feels passion for the things they love in life. I asked them how they have strengthened their bonds with their grandchildren as they shared their love for the good things of life.

As your read on, be thinking of the things that you love and how you have shared them with your grandchildren. In the dis-tant future, as your grandchildren think back on their time with you, your love for the good things in your life will inspire them to develop passions of their own.

I love this quote by Maya Angelou:

> *"My mission in life is not merely to survive,*
> *but to thrive; and to do so with some passion,*
> *some compassion, some humor . . ."*

Here are some ideas:

"My grandchildren know my passions well. They know I love reading because I take them to the library wherever we are and I read to them from my favorite books. Before we went blueberry picking, I read *Blueberries for Sal*. And when one of them lost a tooth, I read *One Morning in Maine*. Because I heard about one of my sons taking his daughters camping recently, I sent them *Do Princesses Make Happy Campers?*

A dear friend with a grundle of grandchildren under eight says, "All my

Be thinking of the things that you love and how you have shared them with your grandchildren.

grandchildren know how much I love nature. We go on special hikes, and during the summer, we always take a nature walk
every Sunday afternoon, with Grandma getting so excited about
every acorn and pinecone. One Sunday afternoon, when I was
with the grandchildren of one of our families, we decided to do
a nature hike and gather special things to make fairy homes. The
hike was so much fun as we found specific things they wanted to
bring back. Then for the next hour or two, I helped them make
fairy homes in the backyard. It was so memorable and helped me
feel close to each of the children and their distinct personalities."

A friend who has just lost her husband wrote his biography as
well as her autobiography and gave a copy to each of her families
for Christmas. She wanted them to know about her life from a
document that could be referred to again and again. Her children and grandchildren were passionate about their grandfather
before he died, and she knew that by the time the grandkids finished reading her memories of him in it, they would know that
she adored him too!

"One year, with school just starting and all the feelings of fall
in the air, I was flooded with memories of school. So I sat down
and wrote a letter to all my grandkids who were going to school
that year and told them about how I always loved the feeling of
school starting. I mentioned my long bus rides, how I appreciated
good teachers, and that I was serious about homework (because I
had to be to keep up). Then I put a new pencil in the letter before
sending it off to them. They thought it was pretty cool."

"Years ago, I remember reading a book by a mother who
talked about the things she would do when she graduated from
motherhood to grandmotherhood. She said she would always
keep a basket of fabric scraps for girls to make doll clothes with.
I guess, from that seed planted, I have a large sturdy bag by

my sewing machine where I throw scraps too small to keep for quilts and have told grandkids they are always welcome to do whatever they want with those scraps. From those small scraps and strips, collages, toy dog leashes, and braids have evolved, and then

Another creative grandmother has engaged her grandchildren in her passion for reading by creating Nana's Reading Club.

the next thing, they are asking me, 'Grandma, I want to sew something; will you teach me?' Then we make snakes and little pillows and blankets for dolls and are even graduating now to a few doll clothes. Now they bring me their mending."

Another creative grandmother has engaged her grandchildren in her passion for reading by creating Nana's Reading Club. Every summer, she challenges her grandchildren to read books by offering rewards for the number of pages they have read. She likes to read all the Newbery Award books so she can suggest them if kids or moms ask for suggestions.

"We start the reading club right after school is out and end before school starts. This year, the awards (gift card amounts) were based on how many pages they read. It was X amount for 300 pages, more for 500 pages, and more for 1,000 pages. The little ones count the pages read to them. Older children can also count pages they read to little ones. The rewards started with a sleepover at Nana's, but now that I have seventeen grandkids, a gift card is just easier. At the first of summer, I give them a sheet with the rules, a sheet to keep track of their pages, and a $15 gift card to Amazon to buy a book to get started. I have been doing it for years. When they were all much littler, I had them keep track with stickers. Some kids do it, and others don't. The kids keep track of their own number of pages read, and extra points are given for reading the scriptures. The rewards are presented at the end of the summer."

A friend who is a fun and creative writer said, "About ten years ago, I wrote about twenty-five stories from my childhood telling of different incidents and then drawing conclusions at the end to make a teaching point. I gave each family a binder with the stories (written at a child's level) so they could read them. Some of the titles of the little stories are "The Green Bean Gravy," "A Trip to Mead's Peak," "The Big Snake," and "The Brown Gloves."

"I love to go fishing, so I take the grandkids whenever possible. This has become more difficult the last year or two, but we went several times this summer. I think those grandkids will never forget how much I loved those lazy afternoons fishing with them."

"I also love to paint with acrylics. I let the kids sit with me and use my paints to make themselves a picture. I want them to learn to love these things, too. When our kids were growing up, one of my kitchen walls was the gallery wall where all their pictures and drawings could hang. Now with grandkids, it's even more fun. I think when we make a positive fuss over their artistic attempts, we stir in them a desire to push it further, create more, stretch the possibilities they can imagine."

An elegant friend, who loves to cook and always sets a spectacular table, sent this: "You asked how I communicate things I love to my grandchildren. As our granddaughters have each turned 17, I begin giving them place settings of beautiful red dishes for birthdays, graduations, Christmas, etc.

"Duty makes us do things well, but love makes us do things beautifully."

By the time they marry or set up a home of their own, they should have a fun secondary, celebratory way to do holidays and special occasions.

"But the real communicator is a small book I created titled *Love Makes Us Do Things Beautifully*. This comes from a saying I've used for years: 'Duty makes us do things well, but love makes us do things beautifully.' The book is organized by months with colorful photos of how to set a table with their red dishes for each month's special occasions. I add just one seasonal recipe each month to suggest a taste for, such as, 'September, with Your Red Plates,' etc. *But* this book really gives me an avenue to share how I feel about our opportunities as mothers and homemakers to gather loved ones and honor who we are and what we hope for. Something happens at a beautiful table that is far more important than food.

At the end of the book, I added the section called 'My Grandmothers' Plates.' Here I put photos, pattern names, and dates of my own plates (my wedding Lenox, etc.) and of the patterns of plates that were my mother's and my grandmothers'. It was a lovely sight to see these photos together. Hopefully, this little book will be kept and valued until each seventeen-year-old girl grows to more fully understand the message and measure of love with which it was given. So far the gift has delighted our girls."

A friend said that she lets her grandchildren know that poetry is very important to her by telling them that all she wants for her birthday is for them to memorize a poem and recite it to her on her special day! She laughed when she told me that once, when her grandchild who lived in Paris was reciting a poem over the phone to her, her eyes got bigger and bigger as the poem went on and on until the mom and grandchild on the other end began to giggle and had to admit that they were reading it!

When you have the grandchildren with you, perhaps for a Sunday dinner, take ten minutes to tell story about an ancestor.

I have a friend who is a champion when it comes to the importance of family history and teaching her grandchildren about their ancestors. Her passion has led to many, many creative ideas. Her children and grandchildren make no mistake about the fact that family history is enormously important to her! Here is her fun idea for having Ancestor Sundays. She suggests that you start with stories about your parents and then move back on your family tree:

"When you have the grandchildren with you, perhaps for a Sunday dinner, take ten minutes to tell story about an ancestor. Have a photo of the ancestor and/or a picture of the place where they were born. If available, wear and dress the grandchildren up in clothes you may have from that era or a favorite hat. Use a memory item like a yearbook picture, a dance card, or anything that reflects that ancestor. Encourage everyone present to ask questions about that ancestor. You could serve a favorite dessert of the person you'll be talking about, maybe something that the children may never have ever heard of, like tapioca pudding. You could even sing an old-time song."

Another of her terrific ideas is that when her grandchildren are together, she has them play a fun game that many of you will recognize from your childhood called "Who Stole the Cookie from the Cookie Jar?" But instead of using random numbers or their own names, give each child the name of an ancestor that they have to remember when they are called on to insert a name. They laugh at the old-fashioned names, and it is a good way to get those names registered in their memories!

Thoughts?

- What ideas have used to teach your grandchildren about the things you love?
- What things do you remember your grandmother being passionate about, and how did she teach you about them (whether she did it purposely or not)?

A Passion for Grandchildren

"Few things are more delightful than grandchildren fighting over your lap." —Dory Larson

Something we can all agree on is our passions for our grandchildren. From the moment they are born, there is a love affair, which, like all love affairs, has its worries, it eras of ups and downs, but mostly a passionate love for another person. And in this case, it is a passion that lasts forever!

An adoring grandmother writes, "My grandchildren know how much I love each of them. I take lots and lots of pictures to remember every special thing they do. I get so excited about their interests, whether it's fishing, playing soccer, dancing, finding bugs and butterflies, or their artwork."

As for me, I love observing them. I love their sweet, chubby feet when they just beginning to toddle. I love their waves hello and goodbye on FaceTime, I love to hear them breathing into the phone when they can't think of what to say, I love their horrible spelling in handwritten notes, I love bolstering them when they have worries, and I love that that they love me back!

> I love their sweet, chubby feet when they just beginning to toddle. I love their waves hello and goodbye on FaceTime, I love to hear them breathing into the phone when they can't think of what to say.

I know that you have your own love stories and passions for your grandchildren, and I hope they will be called to mind as I share my passion for our grandchildren with some of my fondest memories and experiences with my grandchildren to close this chapter.

I love the way their minds think in ways that catch you by surprise. When my grandson Max was four years old, he kept saying "Sure!" whenever anyone asked him a question that could be answered affirmatively. After I had asked him several questions and his reply was always "Sure!" his dad said, "Just say 'Yes,' Max!"

To which Max replied, "You know, Dad, 'sure' *means* 'yes' in Spanish!"

Ashton's mother had a hard time keeping him on task when he was five years old. One day, she made him a peanut butter sandwich, and knowing that he would dawdle while eating it, she placed a cookie by his sandwich and told him that he could have it only after he ate his sandwich. Twenty minutes later, he was still sitting there with a half-eaten sandwich, just playing with his fingers. So his mother urged him on by saying, "Ashton, I'm going to be really tempted to eat your cookie if you don't hurry and finish your sandwich!"

After a second warning about being tempted to eat his cookie from his mother, Ashton confidently said, "You won't eat my cookie, Mommy. Just believe in yourself!"

Love notes from kids are always treasures. A sweet note from seven-year-old Grace in bright red-and-green magic marker at Christmas time says . . .

> *MERRY CHRISTMAS GRAMMIE! I am very sorry that I did not give you a present. But . . . .I will give you a foot rub for 15 minits. Can I? I would love it if I could!*
> *Your Grand douter, Grace.*

Here is another one scrawled in large letters in pencil.

> *I can rememder that wen you come over you always did awr chors* [our chores] *for us. I am so glad I have such a nice grammy. I love you!*
> *Love, Hazel*

One of my most treasured gifts is from a five-year-old grand-daughter to both Richard and me. It was a flat rock about the size of a small Post-it note that stands on its own. It has her picture about the size of a penny glued to each side of the rock.

This was the message she dictated to her mother:

Grammie, this is a Swiss rock that we found while hiking. I hope you like/love the present. The side that has sparkles is for you. Grandfather, the side that you get is the rock only. Both are pretty. Please put it on your "partner's desk" [a desk in our study that has two sides] *so grammie can see her side and grandfather can see his side.*

Love, Annina

I found this message from an anonymous source posted on my refrigerator with a magnet:

Grammie, whatever you are doing right now, sit down and take a break!

On a crumpled-up piece of paper folded in fourths was writ-ten an unsigned note from a grandchild who apparently was struggling to write as he scratched out this message:

gramy, Don't' wrap this present be cause in side this pack-age from me to you is love!

Of course there is an indescribable, almost searing love for grandchildren with disabilities. I have a passion for our eleven-year-old granddaughter Lucy. In fact, everyone loves Lucy!

As mentioned in earlier chapters, she has Bardet-Biedl Syndrome (BBS), named for the scientists who discovered it. BBS kids usually lose their eyesight between the ages of ten and fourteen. Lucy is eleven, has no peripheral vision, and is already learning to use a white cane. In addition, she will always struggle with her weight (among other things). She is missing a hormone called leptin in her pituitary gland, which suppresses appetite and tells her when she is full and also speeds up her metabolism. Lucy is always hungry!

Before her vison began to seriously deteriorate, her parents, Shawni and David, were blessed to be able to provide her with some marvelous experiences that she can store in her brain for when the time comes that she won't be able to see any more. They have taken Lucy (along with her siblings) to see the world, including living in China for six months. They encouraged her to do a lot of extra walking and climbing stairs before the family left for Europe a few years ago because Lucy's greatest desire was to climb the Eiffel Tower. Even with her extra weight, she made the climb . . . every step! Lucy has also been able to see the breathtaking beauties of Switzerland and the wonders of London, along with so many other beautiful sights which she will treasure in her memory when her eyes go dark!

Last Christmas, Lucy (and her parents) showed a lot of grit when the family went to serve in an orphanage of profoundly handicapped individuals in Ecuador. At first she was unsure of her ability or desire to help the "kids" as the majority were in their twenties with the minds of three- to six-year-olds. But by the end of the week, she had read to them, played soccer with them (many in wheelchairs), brushed their teeth, and fed them.

On their days off at the orphanage, they explored the jungles of Ecuador where Lucy worked up the courage to go on a Super Man–style tandem zip line, holding hands with her mom, and had that marvelous feeling of flying along, using her tunnel vision to see the wonders of the forest. Her heroic mom and dad struggled mightily to get her through the rugged terrain to see waterfalls and play with monkeys, experiences which she will always treasure!

If you want to take a look at their adventure go to *71toes. com/lucy* and scroll down several pictures to find Lucy. Warning: there are a lot of pictures! :)

Along with disabilities that come with syndromes also come extraordinary abilities. Lucy is an incredibly talented artist with a style unlike anything any of us has ever seen. As a little child, she spent hours each day creating astonishing pieces of unique, bold, and colorful art.

She also has a gift with words. Here is a note from Lucy when she was about nine. She is the best note-writer in the world and is now writing her own book, which tugs at my heart when I realize that she is losing her sight (though she is getting really good at braille). This is her thank-you note for a birthday present we sent to her, after years of her yearning for a dog.

Dear Grammie and Grandfather,
　Thank you for the big, fluffy dog. He almost feels real,
but at the same time, I know he's a stuffed animal!
　Love, Your Granddaughter Lucy.

(She got a real dog the very next year.)

Lucy has spectacular relationships with her siblings and unique bonds with her cousins. Richard and I like to think that cousins are somewhere between a sibling and a trusted friend. Friends often come and go, but cousins are forever. There can be special, deep, supportive, comforting, and nourishing relationships between cousins.

With her unique ability to perceive kindness and give love, Lucy left this message for her cousin Isaac on the day he turned fifteen while we were together at Bear Lake. Isaac loves kids, and Lucy has a soft spot in his heart. She had decorated a piece of printer paper with her remarkable artwork, including a brilliantly colored rainbow, a yellow star, some red hearts with smiley faces, and his name, artistically colored in block letters. It says:

ISAAC. You re so nice and kind! You are the perfect boy to have a birthday on July 19th!!! You always are looking for kids that are sad and chearing them up! Love, your favorite cousin . . . (please turn over to guess who it is . . .
Lucy Pothier, Lulu, Lu, LP! LUCY Eyre POTHIER.

When Lucy was about eight, the family happened to be with us for Christmas. We found this adorable letter to Santa, written with a black sharpie in letter almost an inch tall, left next to the cookies:

DEAR SANTA,
I'M SO SORRY ABOUT CRYING ABOUT GETTING WHAT I WANT.
I WISH I COULD BE BETTER NEXT YEAR.
I WISH YOU COULD FORGIVE ME, I'M SO, SO, SO, SO, SORRY.
I HOPE YOU LIKE THE COOKIES AND MILK ON THE TABLE!
LOVE,
LUCY

And this was Santa's reply:

No problem, Lucy. You are the best at repenting!
Love, Santa
P.S. Yummy cookies!

Lucy is a conscientious and excellent student and is full of passion and love for the world around her. She has brought our family so much delight.

In conclusion, the challenge for this chapter is to survey your own life. I am speaking to myself, too, as I challenge you to consider what you are doing for yourself and how you can improve. Those pipe dreams of living a life of leisure and bliss so that you could take care of yourself when your children were old enough to take care of themselves have vanished. The real world keeps demanding your time, your energy, and your thought. But it's also time to take care of yourself. Consider your five facets. If you haven't done well, try again with renewed resolve. If you are going great, congratulations! Keep going!

In addition, it is time to record the interesting stories of your life for your grandchildren and those who will come beyond. And it just as important is to have fun with your grandchildren as you teach them about the things that you love about life; most importantly . . . them!

One of the most imporatnt things about *you* as you look back on your life with your grandchildren will be the memories of their sweet stories, along with the fervent worries you've had about them. Remember to record not only the stories but also the feelings.

Thoughts?

- What are the things you love most about being a grandmother?
- What are your favorite stories from moments with your grandchildren?
- Do you have a specific place to record your memories and keep your "grandchildren treasures"? Keep the thank-you notes and love notes they give you. They will increase in value as time goes on!

Chapter 9

The Entitlement Problem

Entitlement

So much of our world has been sucked into the entitlement mentality. About seven years ago, Richard and I wrote a book called *The Entitlement Trap*. Since then, we have been giving speeches all over the world to groups of highly affluent parents who are concerned about the entitlement attitudes in their children. These are families whose kids are essentially saying, "I deserve to have everything, and I want it right now, and I don't want to have to work for it." We spend our time with these parents helping them create systems for dealing with money that involves the kids earning the money through family responsibilities as well as a system for saving and giving and budgeting.

We also speak often to middle- and lower-income families and find that entitlement attitudes are endemic everywhere, including among families who receive welfare or government assistance. When I went back to my great little hometown in Idaho, I was excited for the parents there to tell us that their hardworking farm kids were not in the "I deserve stuff and don't want to work for it" mentality. But no! The entitlement issues were alive and well there too.

During our opening remarks in speeches across a wide spectrum of economic levels, we often ask the audience to show by raising their hands how many of them had jobs outside their homes while they were growing up. Almost every hand goes up, and they report with pride that they mowed lawns, babysat, or worked in the pizza-delivery business. Then we ask how many of their children have jobs like that now. Hardly anyone raises their hand.

We concede that there are reasons for kids not having jobs nowadays. They are often busier than their parents, with homework, athletics, music, and extracurricular activities, but we think together about ways they can raise responsible kids and avoid the entitlement attitudes. One of the things we talk about is the importance of telling children that the money used by the family doesn't just come from nowhere. Whether it comes from a grandfather who worked hard to start a business generations ago which was turned over to his son, a father who started with nothing and built a company with sheer grit, or from a mother who opened a new restaurant with determination and hard work, the things the family enjoys today are a result of a lot of hard work over many years.

Interestingly, at the end of our presentations, someone almost inevitably says something like, "But what about the grandparents? Just when we have succeeded in setting up a system where our kids can earn their own money and pay the consequences when they don't follow through on responsibilities, along come the grandparents who dump a bunch of money and a lot of 'stuff' on them. They do it for their birthdays, or for holidays, or sometimes just because they want to be generous and give kids what they want, or what they wished they had when they were that age, or maybe even because they want to become the 'favorite' grandparent. And our plan to get them past entitlement and make them self-reliant is destroyed! What can we do?"

It is essential in all situations to have parents and grandparents who communicate effectively with each other about the needs of the kids.

As mentioned so often in this book, every grandparent is different. And every parent is different. We all come from a different place, a different childhood with different baggage concerning the use of money. But it is essential in all situations to have parents and grandparents who communicate effectively with each other about the needs of the kids. It's a way to team up and work together to meet those needs in order to avoid entitlement attitudes.

Maybe your children are happy to have help with things they can't afford. They may want their children to have something you can provide. The important thing is to talk about it! I know that it is one of the great delights for grandparents to "spoil their grandchildren," but I think that means sharing fun experiences rather than just giving them money. If there is some kind of a family economy set up for kids to earn their own way, it is a good idea to check with the parents before you surprise them with the very game or gadget that a child may have been saving his or her money for.

We had a very interesting rabbi who attended one of our presentations in New York City. He loved his congregation and loved the concepts in *The Entitlement Trap*. He had even had meetings with members of his congregation, fabulously wealthy fathers from Russia, who he felt were ruining their children by giving them access to too many things, too much time on the internet, and way too much money. He strongly advised them to think of ways to have their children earn the things they wanted so they would feel the pleasure of owning something that they had worked for.

He was disappointed in their response. Not all but most of the parents said that they had been deprived as children of every-thing they had wanted in their early lives. Some had been hungry and cold. They had promised themselves that they were going to find a way to make a lot of money so that their kids and grandkids could have anything and everything they wanted. They didn't want to face the fact that giving kids too much was a disservice to them and would create entitlement attitudes that would plague them throughout their lives.

We understand the desire to give children and grandchil-dren more than what we had as kids. Both Richard and I grew up in families that I'm sure would have been considered below the poverty level during our childhood. Richard's father died at thirty-nine, when his mother was thirty-eight. She somehow raised five children on her own and was a widow for fifty-two years before she passed at ninety-one. Each child in that family was allowed five ounces of orange juice with their breakfast of a bowl of cereal. Grandma made milk from powder every night before she went to bed.

I was raised on a farm with a father who was needed on the family farm as as child and was only able to finish the eighth grade. In addition to running our farm, he brought in extra money working for the highway department, building and repairing roads and plowing snow in the winter. My mom was a school-teacher with minimal pay.

Still, as children, neither Richard nor I felt that we were poor. We were living at about the same economic level as many of our friends who lived in our neighborhoods. Richard had a paper route, and I earned money for my own clothes by practicing the violin and piano (my mother's plan to encourage me to practice). Later, I worked as a carhop and a cook at the A&W drive-in in our little town. We liked what we learned from working for what we got and passed that ethic on to our children.

> Our kids got their money the old-fashioned way. They earned it! They did it by doing assigned chores and fulfilling responsibilities.

When our children grew old enough to add and subtract, we felt it was crucial to raise responsible kids by teaching them how to earn and save money. There were no "allowances" or handouts in our family economy! Our kids got their money the old-fashioned way. They earned it! They did it by doing assigned chores and fulfilling responsibilities that required their initiative, like getting up and out the door on time for school and doing homework and music practice without being told. It was their responsibility to report what they had done every night on a Post-it note and put it in the Family Bank. On Saturday, they could take money out of the bank according to their earnings. They were expected to buy their own clothes and their own "I wants" with what they had earned. In addition, we had a 10/20/70 rule. Our kids were required to "give" 10 percent, save 20 percent, and use the other 70 percent for what they needed.

The idea was that if they had actual "earned ownership" of the money they received on payday each Saturday, rather than being handed an allowance each week, they would be much more likely to think carefully about what they bought and then take care of their purchases afterward. Some of our kids were wildly successful with this system. Some were often less successful and had to do their school shopping at Goodwill. Others weren't interested until they desperately wanted a new electronic gadget and needed the money.

---

*If your children are looking for a way to start a workable "family economy" with your grandkids, send them to **valuesparenting .com/family-economy** to find specific ideas. Or refer to our book* The Entitlement Trap.[1]

Jumping ahead to grandparenthood: Some of our children who bought into this Family Bank system were able to carry it forward as they left home. In many families we worked with, it morphed into an LLC (limited liability company) where parents deposited money which could be drawn by the kids as interest-free loans for college and down payments for a first home—giving them a greater feeling of independence than outright gifts would have done.

It has been so fun though to watch our children deal with money as they have matured. One daughter who couldn't keep a nickel in her pocket for an hour without finding something to spend it on has become extremely frugal—partly due to a husband who is an economist and whose business is making numbers work. And one son who was a real miser has now learned that hard-earned money is also meant to be spent on quality things that you really love. As parents, our children have carried on the tradition of having their children work for things that they want, adapting our system to what works for them and their kids.

One of our sets of parents has gone "whole hog" and had their kids figure out a way to earn money outside the home for everything they want. The oldest daughter in that family was determined to have her own horse when they lived in rural Washington state. By the time she was nine years old, she had earned enough money to buy a horse by running lemonade stands, selling things she didn't want, and even going door to door in their quiet little neighborhood armed with a toilet brush and bottle of cleaner, offering to clean toilets for a dollar. (We definitely thought she should raise her price!) The horse cost $100. But she also had to pay for the hay and feed and take care of it. That old horse lived in their backyard, and we watched her drag that hay and water out to him every day when we visited. She was thrilled about having her own horse, but I think she was also secretly very happy when they moved and she had to sell the old guy! This particular granddaughter is exceptional, but it taught us that kids really can work for what they want and can escape the entitlement attitude that affects so many.

If parents are unable to help much with special financial needs, then grandparents, especially those who live near their grandchildren, can (with the approval of the parents) help by hiring the grandchildren to do work for them. Two of our teenage grandsons, who were desperate for money to join the football team and to buy car parts, pulled weeds for me and hung new blinds to earn some of the money they needed.

With that bit of personal recollection as a background, let's go on to what grandparents generally can do in order not to add to the problem of entitlement in their grandchildren.

Thoughts?

- Think back at how you earned, spent, saved or gave money when you were young. Did you always wish for more? Did you feel entitled?
- Did your childhood and youth experiences affect how you managed money with your kids? What about now with your grandkids?

- How did your kids get money when they were in your home, and how has that affected how they handled money later?

Gifts for Holidays, Birthdays, and Anniversaries

At no time are entitlement issues more exposed than at Christmas and on birthdays. There is so much excess in asking as well as in giving.

But it can be tricky! Children love gifts, and there is special delight in giving them things that they really want. My learning curve was a bit slow, though, as I started trying to pick out gifts that I thought my grandchildren would like to have. Even if I got it right, there was always the danger of giving the things that the parents don't want them to have. And the last thing we want is for our grandkids to love us mostly for what gifts we give them or to start measuring how much we love them by how many gifts they get from us.

It's always fun to buy gifts for those new babies and especially good to shop with the mothers so you know what they *really* need instead of having them wonder how to take it back. It didn't take me too long to recognize that look in the mother's eyes at gift-opening time that told me the grandchild would never be wearing what I thought was adorable! I quickly learned that the mother would much rather be asked what the child needed than for me to try to figure it out and get it wrong!

The last thing we want is for our grandkids to love us mostly for what gifts we give them.

There is also the issue of what the parent *wants* their children to have! I was pretty slow to realize that one of our daughters-in-law was very careful about her little children having access to the world of electronics. I was gladly handing her four-and six-year-olds my phone, which they begged me for the moment I stepped in the door. They knew I would hand that phone over to them with pleasure when I saw the sheer delight they got from having that precious thing in their hands to play Minecraft or Pokémon. They immediately disappeared with my phone, which I learned later was because if their mother caught them with it, they would immediately be asked to give it back!

You'd think I would have started being more careful when one of our four-year-old twin grandsons from a different family handed me my phone after playing on it for a while and said, "Sorry Gwammie, I think I duweeded something." Indeed. He had deleted several things! After that, I didn't give my phone to a four-year-old without me holding them in my lap and without the permission of his mother.

Slowly, I started to realize that usually handing a child of any age a phone was not really wise. Screen time for young children is becoming a serious problem. But I do have to say that an app called "Peekaboo Barn" (or others that you may know) is a lifesaver in a restaurant or on a plane with a screaming baby or toddler! :)

Getting Christmas gifts for the grandchildren is a big job! Richard takes care of the gifts for our children and their spouses, and I make sure the grandchildren are covered. We don't give big gifts, but I do love to get them something that they really want! One year, a month before Christmas, I was in the home of one of our families in California. I realized that I could solve the dilemma of what to get them for Christmas online by asking the actual kids what they wanted instead of bothering their mom, who has so many little kids. I sat down with a seven-year-old and a computer and went to Amazon. He was perfectly delighted that I would ask what he wanted. I gave him a dollar amount, and he immediately knew *exactly* what he wanted: an electronic game and some

Pokémon cards. They were ordered, and I was thrilled to check this kid off my list!

Then the mom, in the kindest possible way, wanted to help me decide on gifts for the other kids. Until then, I still hadn't figured out that she really didn't want her kids to have electronic gadgets. They lived in a part of California where there were plenty of open spaces to explore, and she preferred that her kids be outside exploring rather than inside on a screen. So the other kids got rollerblades and scooters and things that would keep them busy and active outside. Smart mother! I learned a lot from that experience.

So, I rarely get gifts for birthdays or Christmas that are a surprise to the mother (although that is fun to do once in a while, too). I also realized that it wasn't worth my time or money to buy something that the kids didn't want! Mothers are pretty smart about what their kids need and love! For example, I would never have thought of a pogo stick for Hazel. This mother also knew that physical exercise was one of the real needs for this voracious reader; at her mother's suggestion, a pogo stick it was! Here is the note she sent when I wrote to ask what she got for Christmas.

> Hi Grammie,
>
> I got an easel and five canvases from Santa and my mom gave me an antique version of little women that was tiny and probably 100 years old. and by the way I LOVED THE POGO STICK! my record on it is more than 260 jumps. I took it in to Boston and everyone made an awesome comment on it like: I haven't seen one of those in a long time. people were pretty amazed that I was that good at my Pogo stick after the second day!
>
> love hazel

When our kids were little, we became worried about the enormous "getting" mentality at Christmastime. We wondered how we could shift the emphasis at Christmas from getting to giving. We decided to make a big deal of having the kids save their money to buy gifts for their siblings. To ensure that *giving* those gifts didn't get mixed up with the wild frenzy of the Santa gifts on Christmas morning, we always had the siblings exchange their gifts on Christmas Eve. When the kids were little, they worked hard to earn a few dollars for the grand trip to the dollar store to buy their siblings' gifts. It was a riot watching them pick out all those "treasures" that they were going to present to their siblings on Christmas Eve. Call us crazy, but that tradition on the afternoon of Christmas Eve turned out to be the sweetest part of the Christmas season for Richard and me as we watched the kids' eyes light up as their sibling opened the gift they bought just for them! The hugs that followed the opening of each gift were priceless.

For birthdays, I know that many of you live close enough to your grandchildren to take them out to lunch on their birthdays and maybe even go shopping to buy something new. Since only one of our families has lived close enough to do that, I am thrilled when moms urge their kids to create an online wish list! Not all the families have bought into that, but when they do, it makes things so easy! Since most of them are not yet teenagers, they have had their moms help them with the list, or the mom at least checks them before they are posted on Amazon or Target.com or wherever. That way I know what the kids want as well as what their moms have approved. Since there are usually several items on their wish list, they can still be somewhat surprised at what I choose, but I know it's something they want.

For teenagers, I usually send gift cards or a small amount of money. It's impossible to guess what they want or need, but they always love money. We have a birthday calendar made every year for us by Shawni to remind us of the birthdays coming up each month. Also, we communicate with each other on a Yahoo group email (if you don't know how to do that, ask a child or a grandchild) that reminds all of Eyrealm about birthdays and anniversaries. We are usually traveling in January, so I have a big job to do before I leave, since we have ten birthdays in January. If there is no wish list, I send a check or gift card in an envelope with instructions not to open it until their birthday.

I don't expect thank-you notes, but I love getting them. A call or email is also nice. The mothers have trained their children well to acknowledge gifts, but I don't keep track. Recently, I got this nice note from a fifteen-year-old who has to earn the money for everything she needs:

> *Dear Grammie and Grandfather,*
>
>   *THANK YOU!! I loved reading your birthday cards and I miss you guys so so so much!!! I'm going to buy a hydro flask with the money gift you sent, which I have wanted for a very long time!!!*
>
>   *love,*
>
>   *Ana*

More important than any physical birthday gift, the thing we send to each member in the family through our family group messaging site is an email birthday message that includes memories, admiration, and a touch of adoration. Richard and I always send messages. He usually sends a poem that just falls out of his head. Mine is usually a fun memory or list of things I love about that person or appreciate about them. Not everyone sends a message to every person

More important than any physical birthday gift, the thing we send to each member in the family through our family group messaging site is an email birthday message.

every time, but several family members jump in on the chain and at least offer a happy birthday or anniversary wish with love.

One more gift-giving experience that we sort of fell into might be worth telling. A short time after we became empty nesters, we decided to downsize by selling the large old home where we had raised our children and move to a smaller place. Our grown children were a bit devastated by the idea of their childhood home being sold, but we softened the blow by informing them that we would be giving them all the furnishings in the home that we wouldn't be taking with us when we moved. The problem was that some of them wanted the same things.

So we decided to hold an auction. Richard put a numbered tag on all the items that we would be parting with and hired a professional auctioneer, complete with top hat and gavel and very fast-talking voice, and the stage was set for a fascinating family gathering. Most of our kids made it to the auction, and the two that lived too far away were bidding from their phones.

We gave each of them $40,000 in play money so that all had an equal amount and each could bid on the things he or she wanted. There were moments and surprises we will never forget. Some of the things we thought would draw high bids, like the old round kitchen table where we had eaten together for all those years, attracted little interest for bidding (it was too big and pretty much out of date). And other little things we thought no one wanted sent the bidding through the roof. A little old rickety bench that we had used as the "repenting bench" where two kids had to sit until they could resolve a fight or argument ended up selling for $17,000, the highest-bid item of the night except for the grand piano. When we asked Noah, who had the winning bid, why he had spent nearly half of his allotted money on that one little item, he replied "Are you kidding? I spent half of my life on that bench, and I want my kids to have the same opportunity."

Thoughts?

- Have you talked to your families with children about their preferences for gift giving? Do you acknowledge grandchildren when they send thank-you cards with a return call or text? (I don't always do this either.)
- What memories do you have about giving someone a gift you bought because you knew how much they would love it?
- Just for fun, reminisce about your favorite Christmas, Hanukkah, holiday, or birthday gifts as a child. Share your thoughts with a grandchild.

Ideas from Creative Grandmothers

Money issues are sensitive when dealing with more than one family and more than one set of in-laws. If you're just starting your grandchildren count, perhaps you can provide more expensive gifts or more time spent on gifts for birthdays, anniversaries, and Christmas or Hanukkah. For us who have many grandchildren, it has become necessary to simplify as our numbers have grown. Because every family has different opinions, parameters, and needs, deciding what is appropriate is an important thing to consider.

Here is a list of good ideas from other grandmothers about gift giving.

"Children in our church are baptized by immersion when they turn eight. It is a day they will never forget! It's a tradition for some families to give the baptized child gifts on their baptism day. Some receive a warm blanket to remind them about the warmth of the Holy Ghost that will now be with them when they are in danger or need to make a decision. Some get CTR [Choose the Right] rings. The best idea I've heard is from a friend whose gift isn't something the child gets to keep. On that day, she finds a quiet moment to give the child some money that is not to be kept but to be given away. She instructs the child to watch for a person or a family who really needs the money. Then she asks them to report to her within a month to tell the story about who that child helped along their way. She has some fantastic stories of the return on her investment."

"I have a daughter-in-law who adores her grandmother—one of the reasons being that this grandmother sends her grandkids a $20 bill in a birthday card every year. Without fail. Forever. She is so amazed that this grandmother without many resources makes this much of a sacrifice financially, and does it for each grandchild so faithfully, even though they may not need it. My daughter-in-law's sentiment about it has made an impression on me. The thing that means so much to her is her grandmother's devotion to the practice; and she translates it as her grandmother's devotion to her grandchildren."

One smart grandma says that she puts $25 in a savings account for her grandchildren each birthday.

"Our daughter-in-law comes from a family that doesn't have a lot of money. She has told me how much she appreciates the fact that we don't provide big expensive gifts that her parents feel a need to match. We've tried to be conservative when we know the other grandparents don't have the means that we do. But conversely, we have another daughter-in-law whose parents take the kids on cruises, big trips, etc., which we don't choose to do."

Some grandparents have plenty of money and love spoiling their grandchildren with it, especially when they only have a few grandchildren and love giving them what they always wished they had when they were a child. They pile the gifts and cash on their grandchildren. This is a particular problem in Asia, especially where children get a "Red Envelope" from not only parents but grandparents to celebrate the Chinese New Year, usually full of money. In the Muslim world, there is a celebration called Eid al-Fitr similar to Christmas that marks the end of Ramadan, a month of fasting. Kids of wealthy families are loaded with gifts of money! A wise grandfather said that his solution to that problem is to teach his grandchildren how to invest any money they received in the stock market—a great idea for families whose children have access to too much money! A gift for the future.

Matching Funds

By the time our grandchildren were old enough to want to have educational and broadening experiences that cost more money than they had or than their parents could afford, we were fortunate to be able to set up a small fund that has turned out to be a lot of fun. We told the grandchildren that if they would learn how to write a "grant proposal" (more informal than the real kind but still valuable as a learning experience), we would match the money that they could raise themselves if we accepted the proposal. They would have to earn or somehow raise half of the cost—and we would match it. It has turned out to be an exceptionally good way to teach them how to research the project, figure out what they would learn from it, and have some skin in the game when it came to gathering the funds for something they really wanted to do!

We have one granddaughter who is especially adept at writing grant proposals, and I'm including one of them to give you an idea of how it worked.

Hi Grammie and Grandfather-

Here's my proposal-for swim camp.

On June 19th-26th, I will be traveling with my swim team to Spokane for swim camp. I want to propose a $65 matched scholarship . . .

Here are some reasons why you should support me in going to swim camp:

1. Physical

We are going to be swimming 4 hours a day, and that doesn't include dry land workouts. This is

We would match the money that they could raise themselves if we accepted the proposal.

going to be HARD, even for me. I think that it's a really good way to have a rock solid week of swimming hardcore so I can stay in shape all through July and until we get back to Hawaii. I think it will be more advanced than BYU swim camp because I'll be with a coach who already knows me and how hard she can push me.

2. Social

I'm really looking forward to going with people I already know. We might not even come back to Sequim to visit so this would be my last time with them! :(They are a really nice group of girls and I have never been able to spend time with them outside of swim practice, so this is my chance.

3. Spokane

I'm really excited to see Spokane! I've never been there before, and even though the drive is 6 hours, I can't wait to get there. Its supposed to be really pretty. We are also staying in a MANSION-A huge house with a kitchen and bedrooms.

Please consider it!

Love you both!

Again i am SO SO SO EXCITED for summer!!

Last year, we were visiting this same granddaughter when she decided to upgrade her presentation in an attempt to get a matching grant, and at age fifteen, she did an amazingly comprehensive grant proposal for an AFY (Adventure for Youth) trip in the form of a PowerPoint presentation, complete with pictures of where she would be going. Needless to say, she got the grant!

Grandchildren will remember your contributions to their activities with love and appreciation if they have had to work for them by writing a grant proposal and earning half of the money on their own. These should always be projects with the prior approval of the parents.

Our fifteen-year-old grandson, who had never asked for a grant before, suddenly became interested in playing football. Here is his proposal:

> *Hi Grammie and Grandfather!*
>
> *This is my first year playing football and I am really loving the sport. I'm playing a wide receiver position and am working hard to learn all the routes and lineups and plays to be a good one. So far, this team has taught me a lot and helped me to gain strength physically and mentally and I'm excited to continue to learn and grow.*
>
> *For the fundraising, I need to come up with $300 to cover the cost of football gear, camp, team meals, and transportation. I don't have any sponsors yet, but I'm working hard to get the money that I need and that my team needs. Would you consider a grant that will match anything I can raise?*
>
> *Thanks for supporting me in everything I do. I can't wait to see you at Bear Lake this summer. Hopefully you'll be able to see me on the field this fall.*
>
> *Isaac*

These grants have become a way for us to get closer to our grandchildren as we see their needs and as they remember and appreciate our help. It has helped with entitlement issues since they have worked for what they want instead of having it handed to them on

These grants have become a way for us to get closer to our grandchildren as we see their needs and as they remember and appreciate our help.

a silver platter. They had "skin in the game" in having to raise half the money themselves. Some of you grandmothers who are unable to help have probably been proud of your grandchildren as they have done it completely on their own. That's even better!

Thoughts?

- Did you ever get financial help from your grandparents? (I certainly didn't. It was a different time when entitlement was not an issue.)
- How can you help your grandchildren with the money they need to participate in expensive activities like camps and even music lessons? Even if the parent can afford to help, we've found that it is so valuable for grandmothers or grandparents to offer matching funds when possible.

A Family Foundation to Help Kids Give Service

We are so very blessed to have been able to form a small foundation that provides a way to give aid financially to those in dire need. Our foundation is small, and the gift amounts are modest, but the amount of money is not as important as the desire to give, as in the powerful story of "The Widow's Mite" from the Bible. The real benefit is getting our kids and grandkids involved in thinking about needs and finding small ways to help those in need. If you don't have the capability to create a foundation, there are other ways to raise our grandchildren's abilities to give service. With that in mind, here is our story:

Twenty-five years ago, about the same time that we got worried about opening our kids' eyes to the needs of the world, Richard and I decided to start a foundation to help our kids become aware of the needs of those who live in poverty and cultivate within them a desire to serve and share. We had traveled extensively in impoverished areas of the world, as explained in Chapter 1, and it had opened our eyes to the vast needs of the poor. We wanted it to also open our children's eyes and felt that a modest family foundation would help us to do this.

We organized a mission statement for our "Eyrealm Foundation" and put all our children on the board of directors. They elected their oldest sister, Saren, to be the president. All requests for funding were sent to her, and she sent out emails to her siblings for input and approval. Richard and I contribute some of our speaking fees and make other donations to the fund, but we don't have a vote.

We challenged the kids when they were teenagers and young adults to find good causes that we could contribute small amounts to. As time passed, each of our children found causes to donate to after they developed a passion for and became personally involved in those causes.

Our son Tal and his wife Anita—who were a little older and had some savings when they got married—actually went on a one-year humanitarian honeymoon. They left their jobs in New York City and headed for Mozambique, where they worked with an incredible organization called Care for Life (*careforlife.org*), which is a powerful force for teaching self-reliance, for six months. Then they spent another several months in India, where they worked with Rising Start Outreach (*risingstaroutreach.org*), which does a remarkable job helping families affected with leprosy. Others of our kids also found favorite humanitarian groups or aid organizations and brought funding proposals to the Family Foundation. Josh has been to Ethiopia twice to help with a water project with an organization called Hope Arising (*hopearising.org*). Other kids' causes are mentioned elsewhere in the book.

More recently, we have elected a new Eyrealm Foundation board president: our daughter Saydi. After years at the helm, Saren turned the responsibility to her sister, who was extremely concerned about the refugee crisis in the world.

Saydi had friends who took their family to Greece and actually lived for two summers helping in a refugee camp there. They grew to love the refugees and sent us horrific stories of those good people's difficult lives as well as the sad conditions in the camp. Saydi requested that we donate Eyrealm funds for specific needs to help. Of course, we felt blessed to be able to help, especially when the money would be distributed by trusted friends. The vote *yes* was unanimous!

When our children were very young, we started having something called the "Children for Children Concert" in our neighborhood.

We are thrilled that our children have taken up the cause of helping families in need across the world. And maybe even happier that our grandchildren have gotten excited about it!

When our children were very young, we started having something called the "Children for Children Concert" in our neighborhood. All of our families, and now also their friends who have children old enough to organize and participate, have a concert every Christmas, completely organized by the kids and their friends. They ask all the other children in the neighborhood to participate by preparing a talent to present at a talent show at Christmas time. The talent can include a dance, a poem, a piano, violin, or flute solo, a dance, or even acrobatics.

When the audience is gathered and the talents have been performed, the kids who organized the event tell the story of the children they are raising funds for that year with a plea to the parents to donate to the cause.

This tradition has carried down to our kid's families. For example, our Boston grandkids and their friends recently organized a Children for Children concert that got enough notoriety that even the mayor of their Boston suburb attended. The kids prepared and distributed flyers that explained their event. There was also a note on the flyer indicating that if they reached their fundraising goal, the core group of boys who had helped organize the event would shave their heads! On the night of their concert, their home was overflowing with parents who were excited to pay for the excellent entertainment. They exceeded their fundraising goal, and the boys went to school the next day without hair!

The money raised at these concerts is matched by Eyrealm Foundation funds, so when kids promote them, they tell everyone that every dollar they donate will become two dollars that goes to the chosen cause or humanitarian group. Sometimes it was an orphanage in Bulgaria or Cambodia or for refugees in Greece.

Although our grandchildren still want "stuff," these events have definitely worn the edge off the sharp corners of entitlement.

We know that it is a privilege to be able to give funds where they are so desperately needed. We also know that other families find other ways to give. Any time our grandchildren are engaged in service and especially in giving back on their own initiative, it leads to a culture of empathy and service, which is the opposite of entitlement!

Of course, we don't have to go across the world or even across the United States to find ways to curtail an entitlement attitude through service. There are needs across the street! Saren's husband, Jared, is the bishop of his ward (a congregation in their neighborhood) in the center of a city that has enormous need. Jared helps the homeless, the down and out, and the desperate as Saren cares for the women and children in the ward. Their kids, ages twelve through seventeen, help with the kids and other needs of those families, whom they adore. There are service opportunities around every corner in their neck of the woods.

Service often takes the wind out of entitlement for us as well as our kids and grandkids! If you want to try doing the same, you can find opportunities for service anywhere, even right next door.

If you would like to see how this actually works in action, go to **71toes** *.com/concert-2015.*

Thoughts?

- Regardless of whether you have a family foundation to match funds, what could you do to encourage your grandchildren to raise funds for other children in need?
- Would your children support you in helping your grandchildren think of service projects that will not only be good for both parties but also help curb the culture of entitlement that our grandchildren live in?

Trust Funds, a Grandchildren's Education Fund, and FUN!

My angel mother was frugal enough to save enough money from her school job and piano lessons for many years to leave each of her fourteen grandchildren $5,000 to spend on something important to them. In 1995, that was enough to pay college tuition for a whole year at some institutions or a down payment on a small house! They each knew how hard Grandma Hazel worked to leave that money for them, and they valued it greatly and knew exactly what they would use it for.

Some grandparents, especially grandmothers who have been without a spouse for many years, or who have used all available funds for medical and mental health care, or for whatever other reason, may not have anything to contribute to their children and may not be able to leave much, if anything in their will.

On the other hand, some grandparents are able to put a lot of money into trust funds to be given to their children and grandchildren at certain ages and under certain circumstances. Others leave a lot of money in their wills that carry stipulations on how their children and grandchildren can access it. One potential problem with this, of course, is that the money may not come when their grandchildren need it the most, but it also could lead to, heaven forbid, the grandchildren waiting with bated breath for their grandparents' demise. No grandparent wants to be worth more dead than alive!

We decided many years ago that unless we had

It also could lead to, heaven forbid, the grandchildren waiting with bated breath for their grandparents' demise. No grandparent wants to be worth more dead than alive!

children or grandchildren with dire healthcare needs, we would let them know early and often that they were not going to inherit anything other than what was in a fund we had set up called The Grandchildren's Education Fund. This money will come only as matching funds for what they can raise themselves and will have a cap on it, since whatever is in the fund when we die will be

Instead of working and saving so we could leave money for an inheritance when we die, we would wisely use whatever money we could spare for their benefit while they are still young and we were alive.

divided by the number of grandchildren we have. Grandchildren who have already gotten all the formal education they will get by the time we die will leave the money in the fund for the younger grandchildren.

Richard and I thought that instead of working and saving so we could leave money for an inheritance when we die, we would wisely use whatever money we could spare for their benefit while they are still young and we were alive. So we began to use whatever extra funds we had or could accumulate to travel together and to buy a gathering place at our beloved Bear Lake. We set it up so that this gathering place is owned not by us but by an LLC, which in turn is owned by our kids but managed and controlled by us while we are alive and by them as the board of directors when we are gone.

The philosophy, in other words, was to have a way to help them through life insurance and an educational trust fund in the event of our death but to plan for a long life and to use our savings to do things together, draw us all together, and strengthen the bonds of our family.

I remember how influenced we were thirty years ago by a story we heard about the time we were trying to work out our money and inheritance strategy. The story was about a family of modest means who finally managed to scrape and save up a little nest egg. They had three options on how to spend it: (1) add a second bathroom to their little house, (2) put it away as a future inheritance for their kids, or (3) take their first real family vacation. The next part of the story went like this, "After a lot of thought and consideration and prayer, the couple finally decided to use the money for the thing that would last longest . . . ."

At this point, we assumed that meant that they opted for the new bathroom or possibly to build up their kids' inheritance. But the story ended with a revealing surprise: "They decided to take their first real family vacation because they felt that the memories and experiences together that it would create would last longer than a bathroom or than the savings."

That notion, along with the horror stories we continued to witness or hear of (about kids fighting over their inheritance or being lazy, knowing that it would come someday), framed our decisions. We would have a fallback in case we didn't live as long as we hoped, but we would plan to live long and to use what we had to build unity and memories and self-reliance *now*.

Thoughts?

- As a grandmother, if you do have extra funds, what are your plans for helping your children and grandchildren with the money you have been able to accumulate?
- Do you have a written will as well as plans that map out your desires for the money that you will share? How many families do you know that have serious conflicts and even family break-ups over money after the passing of their parents?

Notes

1. Eyre, Richard and Linda. *The Entitlement Trap: How to Rescue Your Child with a New Family System of Choosing, Earning, and Ownership.* New York: Avery, 2011.

CHAPTER 10

Times to Remember and the Joy of Reunions

To me, the phrase "times to remember" doesn't just mean looking back on our fond memories from the past. It means creating exciting times to remember now—in the present! Being a grandmother really is the dessert of life, and there is so much deliciousness to enjoy. As Erma Bombeck said:

"Remember all those women on the Titanic *who waved off the dessert cart."*

That makes me laugh. And think. We need to grab all the joy we can every day because we never know what tomorrow will bring!

"When you arise in the morning, think of what a precious privilege it is to be alive—to breathe, to think, to enjoy, to love—then make that day count!" —Steve Maraboli

I love the word *remember*! I have another rock on my desk that is engraved with that word.

Now, I've just said that "times to remember" means creating good memories in the present. But I also believe part of loving the present is holding onto the warmth of memories of the past. For a few minutes—right now—conjure up some of the good times in your life.

Think about your wedding, your honeymoon, and your first home. Mark the moments of joy as you experienced those first few years of your marriage and the important decisions that changed the course of your life together.

Think about the wonder (along with the anxiety) you experienced at the birth of your first baby. Our family loves a series on TV called *This Is Us*. The writing is extraordinary, as it captures the real life and current problems of just about every imaginable family dilemma. One of my favorite scenes is when one of the soon-to-be dads in the show is dealing with severe anxiety and worrying about failing as a dad. The planned (induced) birth of his first child is scheduled for the next day. He leaves the house in a frenzy and runs into a stranger who is a father of five and who understands the questions that flood the mind of a new father-to-be. Feeling the pain that he also felt at the birth of his first child, the stranger offers this advice:

> What they don't tell you is that babies come with the answers. They come out, they look up at you, and you look at them . . . [pause] . . . and they tell you who you are. You'll see. Tomorrow, you'll have all the answers you need.

I love that! I have always thought that babies teach you who *you* are and what you're made of, but they also teach you who *they* are and begin telling you that in the delivery room. Those precious babies and grandbabies emerge into the world as wise souls filled with wonder, and those moments of meeting them for the first time are some of my fondest memories. Never in our wildest dreams could we have imagined all the memories that infant in the delivery room would be creating in our hearts and minds by the time they were adults and beyond. I can't count the number of times I have said to our kids who are exasperated with the behavior of a child, *"They come who they are!"*

Conjure up memories by thinking back to the late-night talks with your husband when you were a young parent, remembering the funny things the kids did or said that day. Those stories are great memories and sometimes even funnier now. A great story from Noah and Kristi's memory books happened when their first child started kindergarten at a public school in Manhattan. They were alarmed when McKay, who is as innocent and freethinking as a child can be, came home after the first few days at school and said, "Today a girl at my table called me a 'loser.'"

Just when Kristi became alarmed, McKay said, "But I don't really think I lose things very often."

Remember how much time you spent worrying about things like a child who sucked his thumb so long that he created a big sore-looking bump on his knuckle? And now think how insignificant that was when you consider that the worry now is that he has quit his job and is starting a new business.

Remember your favorite family trips, which probably included a few disasters that, in hindsight, are hilarious. I have to admit that we once left a seven-year-old child at a gas station while we were on a trip. When we discovered he was gone (which was quite a while later), we frantically returned to find that the

Take some time to walk yourself down memory lane and remember those momentous moments of joy and sadness, because they changed the course of your future.

service station attendant had him waiting for us on a chair by the front door, drinking a Diet Coke and happy as could be.

But then there are the *really* hard times. You may have had to work through excruciating problems like a child going through a divorce, or a grandchild suffering a serious illness, or a child suffering with anxiety and depression, or an accident that altered a life, or a major financial setback.

Many of you may have lost your husbands through death or divorce. You may not want to remember some of those difficult days. But what you *do* need to remember is what you have learned from those trials in your life. The rewards of surviving with valor and honor with a big package of "lessons learned" will hold a precious place in your memory.

In addition to the memories you were challenged to write in Chapter 8, take some time to walk yourself down memory lane and remember those momentous moments of joy and sadness, because they changed the course of your future. Write a little about them. It will enrich your perspective, and it will someday mean a lot to your children and grandchildren.

I have taken my own advice and written about a great memory when Richard and I were first married, which was a landmark event in our lives, although we had no idea at the time what a difference this event, now almost fifty years ago, would make for our future family.

Our Story

Richard and I were married Logan, Utah, on July 30, 1969. He had grown up in Logan, graduated from Utah State University, and just earned a master's degree from BYU. I was just finishing my last year of college at USU when we decided to take the plunge and get married.

It took some mighty fancy persuasion on Richard's part to talk me into giving up my dreams of traveling all over Europe before I got married. I had determined that by the time I was twenty-eight, I would have traveled the world and would be ready to settle down. I was pretty sure that if I didn't see the world before I got married, I'd never see it! But that guy is a master negotiator, and he convinced me to marry him and start our lives in an exciting place called Boston, where he was to attend the Harvard Business School. I was twenty-two, and he was twenty-four.

On our wedding day, after a lovely wedding breakfast and a beautiful marriage ceremony, we traveled over the mountain about ninety minutes away to Montpelier, Idaho, where I had spent my childhood, for our wedding reception. The memories of the innocence of my youth and the old times in a rural community flood back as I remember that the refreshments at the wedding reception consisted of a chocolate brownie, a bit of fruit, and a cup of punch. My wedding colors were blue and purple. What a memory I have of standing in that reception line with my parents, Richard's mom, several of Richard's best friends, and seven of my best high school friends and college roommates, decked out in purple and blue satin and chiffon, greeting friends and family.

I had no idea where we were going for our honeymoon. After the reception, I changed into my "going-away outfit," and once in the car, Richard blindfolded me and drove around in circles for a while so I wouldn't know where we were going. We drove for over an hour before we came to a stop. He helped me out of the car, picked me up with a swish, and carried me a few yards before he put me down and unmasked me. On my right was a whole lot of sagebrush, and on my left (about fifty yards away) was the beach of Bear Lake. My first thought was, *Oh, great! We're camping!* But to my surprise (Richard is crazy about surprises), he said, "Welcome to our land!"

I was stunned! The only thing I could think to say was, "How can that be? We don't have *any* money!"

He smiled and said, "Your mom gave me your insurance policy, and I cashed it in for $1200 and bought this nice little piece of land. You won't need insurance now that you have me."

The "land" was about one hundred feet by one hundred feet. It did cross my mind that we could have used that $1200 for lots of other things, since we were destined to be starving students for the next two years, but I didn't mention it! I gave him a kiss and told him I loved it. It was, after all, only thirty miles from the place I had known and loved as a child and in the Bear Lake Valley, where my ancestors had struggled and scraped out a living as some of the first homesteaders in Bloomington, just across the lake.

And so began our sojourn at our now dearly beloved Bear Lake. Fast forward seven years when we accepted a volunteer leadership position in London for our church and moved there for three years with our four little children. We left my sister's husband, Bruce, with a few thousand dollars to build us a little A-frame house on that sagebrush-covered land while we were gone. When we returned, there was a cute bare-bones house (no interior walls and a ladder to get up to the second floor). Ever since, we have spent much of every summer there, fixing up and adding to that little humble vacation home and turning it into a bonding place and a getaway where family memories are made.

Just to move this along, fast forward another twenty years. After years of hard work, we had bought the lot next to us and built a tennis court. Another larger piece of land nearby also became available at a good price, so we grabbed it. As our family

Our children, who spent their summers there growing up, now cannot resist bringing their children back there each summer.

grew, we added a second home on that property, and then a third. We had realized that this place had the power to hold our family together, even as our children grew up and moved off into their own lives. It has become a gathering place with a value that we could never have imagined.

It is where our memories are. Our children, who spent their summers there growing up, now cannot resist bringing their children back there each summer. The beauty of it, for us, is that we have a grandkid magnet that pulls them all in from all over and gives us the chance to now create three-generation memories at our family reunions, to keep our kids coming back and introducing the place they love to their kids.

Thoughts on Reunions

I know not everyone loves family reunions! I went on the internet to find a quote about family reunions, and I found sarcastic things like "I love reunions! Maybe next year, we can give out samurai swords!" or "I shook my family tree, and a bunch of nuts fell out!" Sad. But maybe true in some cases. :) Other reunion thoughts were better, but a little cheesy, like "The love in our family flows strong and deep, leaving memories to treasure and keep." Or a little better: "Strong roots make strong branches." And funny: "Top Songs Played at Black Reunions."

Family reunions don't have to be big, planned, formal affairs and don't have to happen once a year.

We have been working on creating successful family reunions for many years. Every family is different, and there are many ways to do family reunions that are much simpler than ours, especially for those who have smaller families or who are dealing with troublesome family members.

Economic issues are often a challenge, and we have friends who do a terrific job of gathering their family at very inexpensive campsites. It's not what it costs but how it pulls you together that counts. As Charles Spurgeon put it, "It's not how much we have but how much we enjoy that makes us happy."

We know another family that has issues that make it awkward and financially difficult to organize a reunion longer than just a few hours. They agreed to read a book that would interest everyone and then meet on neutral ground at a quiet restaurant and spend a few hours catching up and discussing the book. That particular event was a great success; old wounds were not reopened, and everyone felt a bond that they hadn't experienced in a long time.

Planning a reunion is more difficult when there is a divorce in the family, but maybe that makes being together even more important. Different children can be in different financial situations, making it hard to be fair. There may be alienated family members and sadness for those who, for good reasons, can't come, but doing the best you can with the situation you have is what counts!

Family reunions don't have to be big, planned, formal affairs and don't have to happen once a year. You are having a kind of family reunion every week when your kids and grandkids join you for Sunday dinner. Whatever you do to encourage your family to get together, thank you for being a proactive grandmother! The future of your family depends on how you plan to keep them connected today.

My heart goes out to grandmas like my sister, who lost her husband twelve years ago. With seven adult children, she had to go on without him by her side to share the worries as well as the special occasions, joys, and sorrows that have occurred since he left. Yet she has managed to keep her family active and vibrant and enjoying robust family reunions, sometimes with one family at a time, sometimes with just the adults, and sometimes with everyone. Since most of her children live near her, there is an open invitation for everyone to join her for dinner every Friday night at an assigned restaurant. Because of these frequent "reunions," they are a team. They help each other, commiserate with each other, and support each other in new business ventures in remarkable ways. For her, this quote is perfect:

"Other things may change us, but we start and end with the family." —Anthony Brandt

As for us, when our kids started leaving home, getting married, and scattering all over the world, we realized how important it was to make deliberate efforts to keep everyone in touch and together. Lots of thought and finagling as well as evolution through the years has gone into the deep desire to get our kids together for a reunion once a year at Bear Lake. And it has worked!

It's pretty crowded when all fifty-one of us arrive, but for the most part, we love the mayhem! The actual reunion is only a scant four days—basically an extended weekend when those who work can get the time off—but many of the wives and kids stay for most of the month. Dads and moms who work come and go as their work demands. Some manage to work remotely so they can stay longer because, quite frankly, we just love being together!

The kids plan, budget, and save and anticipate being together all year. In the month before and the month after our reunion, we rent the little compound out to other families, covering some of our operating costs.

The Logistics

I don't want you to think that everything's rosy all the time at our reunions. I won't spend a lot of time on the "backstory," but there are always grandchildren who feel unsure of where they belong as the constellation of cousins moves around. Some teenagers have summer jobs, which leaves other younger teenagers without a friend hang out with. We have occasional eruptions among the younger kids, who start feeling more like siblings than friends after being together for a while. We have kids who suffer with anxiety, and a family or two are always in some kind of limbo, not knowing which direction their lives will go next. We have a single son who sometimes feels left out since everyone else has children. There are some issues we can help with, and there are other things that only time will fix.

We also have a danger of another kind. With so many people together in a relatively small space for a lengthy period of time, there is always the possibility of sharing germs. After having several years without any sickness at all, in 2017, twenty-four of our twenty-seven grandchildren threw up during our halcyon days together! It was a lovely bug that just kept on giving! The finale was Julie, who was so worried about their

> **We also have a danger of another kind. With so many people together in a relatively small space for a lengthy period of time, there is always the possibility of sharing germs.**

two-year-old throwing up on their long plane back to NYC. They arrived home with no mishaps, and then she threw up! :) Some years are like that! But most are pretty much germ-free, and we are able to limit the disasters to broken arms and stitches. But what memories we make!

I know that you, dear reader, may be on the opposite end of the spectrum for reunions or haven't thought much about it at all since your family is young. Reading through this might be a little like going to the circus. Or you may have had a disastrous experience with a reunion or maybe even quit having them because of a "nut" or two in the family. On the other hand, you may have a family similar to ours and are looking for ideas for your next reunion. So many people have requested details on how we do these events that I am including some details that you can pick and choose from or that may spur more relevant ideas for your own family in your own mind. If you hate reunions and don't plan to do one any time soon, feel free to skip this section and go to the end of the chapter. But you're going to miss seeing a lot of fun. :)

History

When we first started doing formal reunions, Richard and I thought that we needed to take all the responsibility ourselves. We laugh when we look back at those days when Richard basically wanted the reunion to consist of lots of food and some fun but mostly deep conversations about the world, including religion and politics. He actually wanted to assign topics to each of the kids. That went over like a lead balloon.

When the kids got married and started having their own families, they strongly suggested that the organizers for the reunion should not be the parents and that they should rotate the reunion chairmanship each year. Our oldest, Saren, was in charge with her spouse and their children the first year, and then we worked our way down the line. That way each family would only have to be the hosts and planners of the reunion every nine years.

Who Pays?

Who pays for what is always an issue and has changed over the years. Because we have a special fund for reunions, Richard and I pay for the food for our four-day official reunion. Everyone brings their own food for the days that they stay before and after the reunion. The moms put their heads together to decide who cooks on what nights before and after the official reunion ends.

Food

I have to mention that food is a big part of every reunion, and we are talking about *a lot* of food. For the actual days reunion days, everyone brings their own breakfast food, and each family is responsible for only one meal (for fifty-one) during the reunion. The mom or dad (whoever is doing the cooking) from each family lists what they need for their meal on a Google spreadsheet in advance of the reunion. Since the nearest grocery store to our location at the lake is an hour round trip, and many families are flying in and renting a car that will be packed to capacity for their stay, we tell them that if what they need for their meal can be bought at Costco, Richard and I will get the nonperishable and frozen food to the lake before everyone arrives. If their recipe includes special food that can only be ordered online or bought at a grocery store, they are responsible to buy it and get it there themselves. One of our sons-in-law, who lives locally, fills up his car with the perishable food after work and brings it up on the day of the reunion.

It is no small task to get everyone to decide on their meal and then send in the ingredients. There is a usually a deadline to get their food order in, or they will need to bring it themselves. Many of our kids are "foodies," and I must say we enjoy some pretty awesome food while we're together! Probably our all-time favorite is Japanese curry, Eli's specialty, and Jonah's famous "Jonah Burgers" that the kids look forward to every year. The kids also go crazy over chicken tikka masala, and the cooks come up with some pretty amazing gourmet dishes like watermelon salad. We are always looking for tasty recipes that are relatively easy and will feed a crowd. Many of our recipes are included in the Appendix. We simplify the drinks a lot by not buying juice or soft drinks. We stick to water. If people love Diet Coke or other "special" drinks, they bring it themselves!

If you are interested in more detail, Shawni creates great posts on her blog every year after the reunion. Some good reunion overviews of how we do it, with terrific photography, can be found by going to **71toes.com/reunions.**

An Example: Reunion 2017

Organization

The order of events for the reunion has changed through the years, but there are a few things that are now institutions! We always start with a dinner and an opening ceremony, in which the family in charge of the reunion that year announces the theme and the schedule for the reunion on a poster.

The Pothiers were the organizers that year. The theme was "Live Life to the MAX" in honor of their oldest son, Max, who wasn't able to be at the reunion since he was serving as a missionary in Taiwan.

Don't worry, though! He was there in cardboard! They had brought a cardboard cutout that they had used at Christmastime that showed all six feet, seven inches of him. In their introduction that first night, the Pothiers suggested that the way to "live life to the max" was to be balanced in the five facets of our lives: socially, emotionally, spiritually, physically, and mentally. Max stood behind the TV as the Pothiers showed the hilarious video they had created wherein each member of the family took a minute to explain in an engaging way how we would be experiencing each facet as a family during the reunion. As you can see from the poster below (created by the Pothiers' oldest daughter Elle) that they organized a fun activity for each day that corresponded with one of the five facets. (You may not be able to decipher it all, but you'll get the idea.)

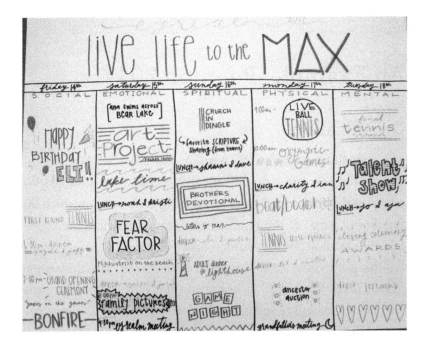

The unveiling of the T-shirts is always exciting. The T-shirts this year had "Live Life to the Max" across the top and five lines just below, representing the five facets of our lives.

Music and Social Bliss

As the sky darkened on the opening day of the reunion, we gathered in a big circle on the beach, where there was blazing bonfire, and we had the pleasure of hearing a small clip of a favorite song from each member of the family; the clips were gathered online by their fifteen-year-old, Grace. It was played through speakers so that everyone could hear. After a few measures, everyone tried to guess who sent that song. If no one got it right away, the one who sent it in stood up and told us why he or she chose that song. We've had music that went from pop to rock to country western to classical to *Hamilton*. Then we roasted marshmallows over the bonfire for s'mores and had a big raucous dance party on the beach to the music we'd just heard. It was a fun "social" event for the first day of the reunion.

Art, Fear, and Fun

The next morning, we gathered for the "emotional" experience of painting Bear Lake with real acrylic paints and 8x10 canvases! Adults helped the youngest ones just a little (mostly to keep them from painting each other). What everyone came up with was pretty incredible. Those paintings will hang in our kitchen at the lake for a long time!

That afternoon, we continued with a *very* emotional event called Fear Factor. Some of you will remember the old reality TV show *Fear Factor*, in which people were challenged to do outrageously fearful things for $50,000 prizes. You'll be glad to know that we modified this event considerably, since our prizes were from the dollar store. And our version of Fear Factor involved eating strange food, which does involve kids facing fears by eating things that take a lot of courage.

Eli, who lived in Japan for a couple of years, was the perfect person to introduce some very strange food to a long table loaded with kids, each thinking that they were going to be the winner! There was no compulsion to participate, and a prize was given to each child who dropped out after each round. A very small portion of something strange to eat was placed before each child every round, and then Eli gave the "go" signal to start eating. Funnily enough, many dropped out on the first round, which is usually something pretty innocuous, like drinking a few swallows of V8 juice or eating a small slice of lemon. (You know kids.) The crowd thinned pretty fast. Each round was something more exotic, which spanned from seaweed (which some loved) to clams out of the can to hard-boiled quail eggs to slimy squid tentacles.

This year, our gaggle of grandkids gathered around that long table at our outdoor pavilion with nervous anticipation of the love/hate relationship they have with this game. The first challenge before them was a small slice of red onion. Most survived the round, but several just couldn't do it. Adding to the anticipation, David announced that the second round would require a spoon for each contestant, and he promised in a loud voice that it was going to be "very, very slimy." Some extra time passed as the next challenge was being prepared, and the anxiety level rose visibly. To everyone's surprise, David and his team emerged from the kitchen with a tub filled with ice cream, smothered in chocolate sauce, caramel sauce, candy, sprinkles, and whipped cream! The expressions on the contestants' faces were priceless!

Deep Thoughts

The next day was Sunday, so it was perfect for our "spiritual" facet. It's always fun to go to church together in the tiny rural town of Dingle, Idaho. Yes, Dingle is the name of the town that we have grown to love, along with the great people there, through the past forty years. After a short twenty-minute ride on a dirt road, we mob that little place with an extra twenty kids or so in the Primary (a Sunday school class for kids from 3–12) and another eight or nine teenagers who attend Young Men and Young Women classes. Luckily, we always warn them when we're coming.

One of the highlights on the reunion Sunday is having the privilege of hearing the adult family members share thoughts about their lives and their faith and things they have learned during the year.

One of the highlights on the reunion Sunday is having the privilege of hearing the adult family members share thoughts about their lives and their faith and things they have learned during the year. We do this on a lovely lawn behind the church. Not everyone is expected to share, but we have several teenagers who join us, and we love hearing their thoughts.

Just Plain Fun Together

The next day, we worked on the "physical" facet of our lives. Everyone participated in fun "Eyrealm Olympics," which included some games from the Pothier family reunions. Teams are organized with a wide variety of ages, and it's great to see everyone working together to do their best. There is also an annual tennis tournament, and everyone loves watching the doubles matches at all skill levels. Richard is basically a tennis nut! He is a nationally ranked player in his age group, so he loves to watch the grandchildren's progress. There is a traveling trophy which shows tennis players with these words engraved on it: IT IS BETTER TO SERVE THAN TO RECEIVE. The winning team is etched on the back each year.

Of course, there were also water sports. We have a small sailboat and a ski boat, and the sailing and waterskiing alternate as priorities depending on whether the lake is windy or glassy.

The little kids love endless hours of playing in the sand, building sand castles, roads, rivers, and lakes; they somehow think if they dig deep enough, they might get to China! The teenagers are amazingly enamored with the little kids and love "hanging out." They also love watching Josh and Eli with their wonderful drones, hovering overhead as they video and document the activities. It's great to see groups of parents clustered together on the beach, just talking and enjoying sharing opinions, even though those opinions don't always match! Part of the fun!

Showing Off Talent

The final day, we did some "mental" activities, including a talent show by the kids, which is their favorite part. After years of practice, we finally have some serious talent on the violin, piano, and saxophone, and even acrobatics. Lots of the acts are hilarious skits and magic acts and dance routines that go on a bit, but it gives the kids a chance to show off individually and in groups.

Child Labor

What about cleaning up? I have to say that there is always some kind of scheme during the reunion to get the kids to help clean up. No cleaning ladies show up while we're there during July, and as you can guess, the clutter from fifty-one people can be pretty overwhelming! The kids are given assignments in "work groups." They are assigned certain days and nights to load the dishwasher, empty the dishwasher, wipe the countertops, vacuum, mop, and sweep the floor with points assigned to each task. The team with the most points at the end of the reunion gets a sleepover on the tennis court or a trip to the raspberry shake stand.

The grandkids have been trained by their parents to remind me to stop working. They are always telling me to sit down or pushing me gently aside while they take over at the sink. It's really hard for me, though, as all you grandmas know. When Eli and Julie were in charge of the reunion, they brought a bona fide pair of handcuffs and handcuffed me to a chair during meals and the cleanup afterward. Hummmph!

Reinforcement

The last activity of the reunion was reinforcement for what the kids had learned at Grammie Camp about their ancestors. Shawni divided everyone into teams, and she and David offered a big reward for the team who could answer the most questions about those who really made it possible for all of us to be there. Some of the questions were about Richard and me. The kids were amazed at some of the things about our lives that they never knew. It was fun for me to see that they actually remembered many things about their ancestors that they had learned in Grammie Camp that year. It was a perfect ending to a memorable reunion!

Special Events

Every year, it seems there is some special event that changes things up a bit, like a baby blessing or baptism of an eight-year-old in the lake. That means the in-law families that can come join us on Sunday for those special occasions, which makes a *really* big crowd, but we love it!

This year, our special occasion was our sixteen-year-old championship swimmer deciding to swim across the lake in the Bear Lake Monster Swim event. Ana represented Maui in the

All-Hawaii Select Swim Camp this year as the #6 best swimmer in the Islands in her age group. She decided to do the Bear Lake Monster Swim and swam seven miles in just over three hours. Her loyal dad, Jonah, who deserves a medal, followed her the whole seven miles on a paddle board.

The culmination of the reunion comes several months later, when Saydi collects photographs from our terrific collection of fabulous photographers and produces a yearly reunion book that is a wonderful collection of "times to remember." The thing that I love about the photographs is that even though the day might have been crazy and exhausting and a kid or two might have been being naughty or not feeling well, right at the moment of the photograph, everything was perfect!

If you want to see the fun with Shawni's photography for this reunion, go to 71toes.com/reunion-2017.

Afterthoughts

I hope you're not exhausted just reading all that, but remember that Richard and I don't have to do the planning or the execution! We get to go up to our little hideout on the hill late each night, "away from the madding crowds," and miss all the fights and throwing up before we return the next morning. We just enjoy and clean up around the edges! The older we get, the more we realize that the kids and grandkids are waxing while we are waning. The kids have warned us that there will have to be some changes as we get older. But for now, we are taking the opportunity to seize the day!

Our daughter-in-law Julie has about the same size extended family as ours. Her valiant parents have served three service missions for our church in Brazil over the past ten years and are often not even there for their family reunion. Their families take turns being in charge and reserving the place to meet. Each family brings their own food for

> The older we get, the more we realize that the kids and grandkids are waxing while we are waning.

their meals. They divide up the costs of the accommodations and supplies for the reunion, and each family pays their share according to how many kids they have. It works like a charm! Julie and Eli keep reminding us that as we get older, we may need to revert to that easier system!

I have to say that many extended families on both sides of our family get together only when special occasions arise. Other families carry on with regular reunions for generations. Our daughter-in-law Kristi's dad is number eight of a family of twelve siblings. The parents have passed on, but many of the siblings and their families still attend family reunions every other year. About a hundred direct descendants of his parents still come to catch up and bond with cousins.

Several of our friends (who are older and have lots of resources) have the simplest solution of all! Take everybody on a Disney Cruise, which they say is absolute heaven because there is something to engage every family member all the time, and the discussions at the dinner tables are wonderful without having to "haul in any food." But that does take some serious money! However, I have to agree with Jill Mansell:

> *"Money or no money, we're all searching for the same things, aren't we? It doesn't matter who you are or how much money you have. Love and happiness . . . that's what it's all about."*

Thoughts?

- Where are you in the process of planning to keep your family connected through the years? What have you done or what can you plan to do to get your family together regularly?
- If you still have children at home but others are gone, how important is it to remember to keep them engaged with each other?
- The challenge: Just do it! Get your children and grandchildren together. Whether it is just for a meal to talk and reminisce or if it's a full-blown reunion, it is a valuable component to maintaining lasting relationships.

In Conclusion

Twenty years after the birth of our first grandchild, I am stunned by what I have felt and what I have learned as a grandparent! I have realized that being a grandmother is one of the most exhilarating experiences of my life. Grandchildren have filled my life with wonder. As they began to grow in height and personality, I realized that even though the responsibility to raise these cherubs is no longer mine, I can make a meaningful difference in their lives.

No matter where you are in your journey as a grandmother, you can be a light that will glow in their lives forever. It's all about unconditional love, no matter what! We can be their champion.

The loving care you give your grandchildren as you work and play with them, correspond and believe in them, will last longer than you can now imagine. The important life lessons they learn from you will run not only through your grandchildren

I am stunned by what I have felt and what I have learned as a grandparent!

but will be passed on to your great-grandchildren and onward like a silver thread that never ends. They will remember your encouragement, your faith, your idiosyncrasies, and your goodness, and it will become part of their fiber as they grow and progress.

Ponder for a moment about the times you remember from your childhood when you were with your own grandmothers. What did you love about being with them, and what personality traits did you admire? What do you wish you had known then that you know now? What questions would you like to ask them if you could have lunch with them tomorrow?

Now ponder what you want your grandchildren to remember about *you*. Will they think you were gracious or grumpy? Fun-loving or fastidious? Cheerleader or chider? What are the times that they will remember with you? What have you taught them they will cherish? I like what H. Jackson Brown Jr. said:

"Live so that when your grandchildren think of fairness, caring, and integrity, they think of you."

As you and I finish our discussion of grandmothering together, the hope is that you might have found some ideas or, even better, thought of some of your own to hone your joyful opportunity to be a grandmother and to be a little more deliberate in loving and caring and enjoying these precious additions to your life. I know that I have been writing to a group of astonishing grandmothers who have probably done things that I've never thought of and who have already created great relationships with their grandchildren. The challenge, though, whether we live near or far, is that we can always do more. We can be more attentive, more interested, and more curious about what makes our grandchildren tick. We can spend more time thinking about them and, most of all, loving them. As Ghandi said, "The future depends on what you do today."

So have fun making a difference while having the time of your life!

In the end, one of the great purposes in life is to create great relationships. It's interesting to note that at funerals, there may be some references to the accomplishments of the person who died, but most of what is said about the deceased has to do with their warm and lasting relationships.

Robert Waldinger, the director of the Harvard Study of Adult Development (and a Zen priest) gave a TED talk entitled "What makes a good life? Lessons from the longest study on happiness." He was able to wrap up the longest study on happiness ever conducted as it followed 725 people from all walks of life for seventy-five years. The findings showed something that we could have told them without them having to go to all that trouble: "Joy in life is based on caring and loving relationships!"

As stated at the beginning, this book is more like a (long) letter to a friend than a book, so I can't close without commending you first for making it to the end and for also for being just what the world needs: a loving grandmother who is doing your part to change the world. Thanks especially to the dear friends who have made rich contributions to this labor of love and especially to my best friend: Richard. He has been a champion for me, and . . . and let's be honest, without him, I wouldn't have any grandchildren!

I can't close without commending you first for making it to the end and for also for being just what the world needs: a loving grandmother.

Here is precious bit of parting advice from someone I love.

"Go forward in life with a smile on your face, a sparkle in your eyes, and with great and strong purpose in your heart. The best things in life are the people in your life, the moments we live, and memories we made along the way." —Gordon B. Hinckley

Recipes for a Crowd

I thought it might be helpful to add an appendix to this book to address a problem we all face: "What can I feed them?" Let's face it: one big part of grandmothering is feeding people—and usually feeding a crowd (which is hard on us older grandmothers who don't cook much anymore).

These recipes are from great cooks, including our children (in-laws included) and friends as well as some from @r2sense, an Instagram feed from the daughters of the Boyer family, and Tess Wade, an expert at feeding huge crowds. Many of the recipes are from our family reunions. You will find several international recipes that we all love. It is not intended to be a cookbook, and there are only few recipes in each category.

Most recipes from cookbooks are intended to feed four, six, or eight people. I hope you will find it convenient to have the ingredients already measured for you to cook for larger groups.

These recipes are in two categories: (1) feeding a crowd of approximately 12–16 (depending on ages and appetites; double, triple, or quadruple as needed) and (2) feeding a *really big* crowd with about 60–80 servings! Many of us are headed in that direction, and many of you may already be there. (If needed, half or quarter those excellent recipes.)

The recipes occasionally suggest items from Costco or Trader Joe's. If you don't have access to those stores, you can substitute or improvise. :)

To make it easy to access these recipes when you don't have the book, I have created a blog at ***grandmotheringbook.com*** where you can access these recipes from any computer or mobile device. Down the road, I may even add a section called "Recipes for Two" there.

Since writing this book, so many new ideas have cropped up that I wish I could have included. The blog will include these ideas and others that *you* may want to add in the comment section. Thanks to the internet, we can stay connected beyond a bound book.

See you on the blog!

Feeding a Crowd

Most recipes serve about 12–16 people.

Breakfast | 290

Appetizers and Snacks | 296

Main Dishes | 300

Soups | 317

Salads and Breads | 322

Desserts | 328

Breakfast

Jonah's Granola

When we are all together at Bear Lake, our son Jonah makes several big batches of his masterful granola—and everyone loves it! It's by far the best granola we've ever had, and it makes all store-bought granola seem too oily or too sweet or just plain not that great. Whipping up a few batches of this before a family reunion is a great way to have a healthy and yummy breakfast on hand for everyone! This recipe makes about the equivalent of two big store-bought boxes of granola.

8 cups old-fashioned rolled oats (quick oats will do if that's all you've got)
1 teaspoon salt
1 teaspoon vanilla
3/4 cups chopped nuts (walnuts, pecans, almonds, macadamia nuts if you're Jonah and live in Hawaii, or whatever you've got)
1 cup wheat germ
3/4 cup ground flaxseed
2 cups flaked dry coconut
1 cup honey
1/2 cup coconut oil, melted (or canola oil)
1–2 cups raisins or Craisins (optional)

1. Mix 4 cups oats and all other ingredients except raisins or Craisins together in an electric mixer, or by hand in a big bowl.
2. Add remaining 4 cups oats 1/2 cup at a time. It might nearly overflow, but you can do it!
3. Spread the mixture out evenly over two cookie sheets.
4. Bake at 275 degrees F (135 degrees C) for 26 minutes. (If you don't have a convection oven, rotate the sheets halfway through.) It's done when everything's golden

and the edges are a bit brown. It'll be soft when you take it out of the oven, but after cooling, it'll become quite crispy.

5. When it's totally cooled, put it into a container, breaking up the big clumps as you scoop it off the cookie sheets.

6. Optional: Mix in 1–2 cups raisins or Craisins after cooking or upon serving.

Banana Pancakes

This recipe comes from our daughter Shawni. The pancakes are quick to make and a perfect use for overripe bananas. Plus they're delicious! Great for an easy but still special breakfast for a crowd.

2 extra-ripe bananas, mashed
1 1/3–1 1/2 cups milk (determines thickness of pancakes)
2 tablespoons melted butter
2 eggs
1 cup white flower
1 cup whole wheat flower
3 teaspoons baking powder
3 tablespoons sugar, honey, or molasses
1–2 cups chopped walnuts or pecans (optional—but really, really good)

1. Mix together all wet ingredients.

2. Add and mix in dry ingredients, folding in the walnuts at the end.

3. Turn on griddle or frying pan to medium-high heat. Use a 1/3-cup measuring cup to pour batter on a hot griddle or frying pan. Once bubbles come up on the raw side of the pancake, flip it over. Cook until both sides are golden brown.

4. Serve with maple syrup or fruit. Add a little whipped cream on top to make them extra special.

Quick Quiche

This recipe is great for a family breakfast or brunch, or a wedding or baby shower. I've provided a couple of variations, but you really can add a whole host of different ingredients to make it your own according to the tastes of your family!

4 1/2 cups milk
9 eggs
1 1/2 cups Bisquick
1 1/2 cubes (3/4 cup) melted butter
1 1/2 teaspoons salt
1/2 teaspoon pepper
1/2 teaspoon garlic powder (if you like garlic)
2–3 cups shredded cheese (swiss, mozzarella, cheddar—your choice)
5–6 chopped green onions (white part and green part) or 1 large sweet onion, chopped
3–5 chopped roma tomatoes

1. Mix milk, eggs, pancake mix, butter, salt, and pepper in a large blender. You can mix in a bowl and use a hand-held egg beater if you don't have a large blender jar.
2. Spread your choice of cheese and other ingredients in a greased 9x13-inch baking dish. Pour mixture from blender over the top.
3. Cook at 325 degrees F (163 degrees C) for about 1 hour and 15 minutes (until middle is pretty much set and top is slightly browned).

Variations

- For Italian style, use mozzarella cheese and add 10 leaves chopped fresh basil or 1 teaspoon dried basil or italian seasoning. You can also add 1/2 cup cooked chopped spinach (fresh or frozen) and/or 1 cup chopped mushrooms, if you like.

- For American style, use swiss or cheddar/monterey jack cheese and add 1–2 cups cubed ham, crumbled bacon, or sausage plus 1–2 cups chopped broccoli and/or 1 cup chopped mushrooms, if you like.

Delicious Overnight Steel-Cut Oatmeal

This breakfast is super easy for a large group of family members, because you just put it in the Crock-Pot the night before and voila! Nice, tasty, hot breakfast ready when you wake up.

2 cups dry steel-cut oats (don't try to use quick or old-fashioned rolled oats!)
8 cups water (or a bit less, if you like your oatmeal thicker)
1 cup sugar

Optional:

1 teaspoon cinnamon
Chopped walnuts/pecans
Fresh berries
Chopped apples
Raisins/Craisins
Banana slices
Coconut
Etc, etc!

1. Put the oats and water in the Crock-Pot before you go to bed. Set it to cook on low for 6 hours (if it doesn't have a timer, it can cook a little longer until you wake up, but it does get a bit mushier after 6 hours and many people prefer it slightly chewy).
2. In the morning, stir in the sugar, cinnamon, and other toppings. If you like, you can stir in chopped apples about 1/2 hour to 1 hour before serving so they can cook a bit.

3. Serve with a bit of milk or a dollop of vanilla yogurt. Add a little more sugar if you think it needs it.

Saydi's Christmas Morning Strata

This dish is a perfect make-ahead breakfast. We use the leftover ham from Christmas Eve dinner and have even thrown in the leftovers from the creamy scalloped potatoes just to make it even easier. Serves 10–12.

16–20 1-inch slices of supermarket french or italian bread
5 tablespoons butter
3 medium potatoes
4 medium shallots (or sweet onions)
3 medium garlic cloves, minced or pressed
2 teaspoons minced rosemary
1/2–1 cup diced ham
Salt and pepper to taste
3/4 cup white cooking wine
9 eggs
2 1/2 cups half and half
1 teaspoon kosher salt
3 tablespoons minced parsley
2 1/2 cups grated cheese (you can be fancy and use fontina or sharp cheddar or just the already-shredded Costco Mexican blend)

1. Toast bread in a single layer on a baking sheet in a 225-degree F (107-degree C) oven. This takes about 40 minutes (watch to not let them burn!) OR just leave slices out overnight to dry. When cooled, butter both sides.
2. Cut potatoes to bite-sized chunks and boil in salted water until just tender (4–5 minutes).
3. Heat 2 tablespoons butter in a skillet and cook potatoes until they begin to brown. Add shallots and cook,

stirring frequently until they are soft and translucent. Add rosemary and garlic and cook a few minutes more. Add ham. Transfer to a bowl. Season with salt and pepper.

4. Add wine to the skillet and cook until reduced to half. Mix in ham/potato-and-shallot mixture.

5. Whisk eggs and add half and half plus kosher salt and parsley.

6. Butter a 9x13-inch pan and assemble the strata by arranging three layers: bread, half the potato mixture, and cheese. Pour the egg/cream over top. Cover with plastic wrap, weigh the strata down with something heavy (a big bag of brown sugar; bags of dried beans), and refrigerate overnight.

7. To cook, heat oven to 325 degrees F (163 degrees C). Remove strata from fridge and bring close to room temperature. Bake for 60–70 minutes until it starts to get golden and puffed and bubbly.

8. Let sit for 5–10 minutes before serving.

Variation

You can make this with spinach and gruyère, and it's delicious. The big change is that you sauté a large onion (or 5 shallots) in butter and then add a box of chopped frozen spinach (or a 10-ounce bag of fresh spinach, chopped). Season with salt and pepper. Skip the rosemary and garlic. Add 8 ounces of gruyère cheese in place of fontina or cheddar.

Appetizers and Snacks

Cream Cheese Apple Dip

This recipe comes from our daughter Saydi, and it has become a family favorite in the fall. It's so easy and is so much better for you (and better tasting in my opinion) than caramel or other apple/fruit dips. Great for a family get-together when you need snacks!

1 8-ounce brick of cream cheese (or Neufchâtel low-fat cream cheese)
1/2 cup brown sugar
1/2 teaspoon cinnamon
1 teaspoon vanilla

1. Mix all ingredients together in an electric mixer until smooth.
2. Serve with slices of your favorite crisp apples.

Baked Cranberry Brie

Getting together around the holidays is such a joy with children and grandchildren. This easy appetizer is always a hit.

3 cups fresh cranberries (about 1 12-ounce bag)
1/2 cup packed brown sugar
1/2 cup water
1/8 teaspoon dry mustard
1/8 teaspoon allspice
1/8 teaspoon ground cloves
1/8 teaspoon ground ginger
1/8 teaspoon ground cardamom
1 8-inch or 2 4-inch rounds of brie
Baguette slices, toasted pita slices, crackers, and/or apple wedges for dipping

1. Put everything except the brie, bread, and apples into small pot. Stir together over medium heat until the cranberries have popped and the liquid has thickened a bit. Set aside (or refrigerate until you're about ready to serve the appetizer).
2. Skim the top white rind off the brie (leaving about a 1/4-inch border around the edges on the top).
3. Put brie on foil-covered baking sheet and add cranberry topping.
4. Bake at 350 degrees F (177 degrees C) for about 12–15 minutes until cheese is soft and warm. Serve with baguette slices or toasted pita slices and apple wedges.

Note: One 4-inch round serves about 8–10. Also, the topping keeps well in the fridge for another time.

Loosli Family Trail Mix

Our daughter Saren created this recipe after not being able to find a store-bought trail mix she liked. It has become not only a favorite for her family and our extended family but also a staple at all the Power of Moms retreats she puts on—it was served alongside fresh fruits and veggies during breaks and is always a big hit. It's much lower in fat and calories than many trail mixes but has a lot of protein. You can buy the individual ingredients packaged at most grocery stores, but it's cheapest and easiest if you can buy them at a good bulk food place.

1 cup raw unsalted sunflower seeds
1 cup raw unsalted pumpkin seeds
1 cup raw unsalted almonds (adjust to your taste—some people like to use the salted variety for one of the kinds of nuts/seeds)
1 cup Craisins (any flavor)
1 cup semisweet chocolate chips

1. Mix together all ingredients.
2. Eat handful by handful!

Cowboy Caviar

This recipe is wonderful with tortilla chips and is also really yummy as a topping for simple grilled chicken or fish, or you can just eat it by the spoonful! Feel free to adjust the amount of each ingredient according to taste, then gather the family and dig in!

1 12-ounce can of black beans
5 chopped tomatoes
1 bunch chopped cilantro
2 avocados, cubed
1/2 teaspoon garlic powder or 1 teaspoon crushed fresh garlic
1/4 teaspoon cumin
Juice from 2–3 limes
1 cup frozen corn
Salt, to taste
4 chopped green onions OR 1/2 sweet onion, chopped (optional)
1 cup finely chopped orange or yellow peppers (optional)
1 package Good Seasons Italian dressing mix (optional)

1. Mix all ingredients together.
2. Serve with tortilla chips.

Burrata with Balsamic Glaze

This recipe comes from a dear friend (@r2sense) with a huge family. After you buy all the ingredients, this takes about five minutes to prepare for a crowd! And yet it feels quite fancy—perfect for a special event! (Adjust amount to size of crowd.)

Burrata cheese balls
Balsamic glaze (at Trader Joe's or most grocery stores)
Basil, chopped
Pomegranate seeds

Pistachios
Sea salt
Crackers

1. Place cheese balls on a plate or serving platter.
2. Drizzle with balsamic glaze.
3. Scatter chopped basil, pomegranate seeds, pistachios, and sea salt on top.
4. Serve with crackers.

Greek Layer Dip

Here's another quick and delicious appetizer (from @r2sense) for a family gathering. (Adjust amount to size of crowd.)

2 packages veggie cream cheese
1 tub hummus
Diced cucumbers
Sliced green onions
Diced cherry tomatoes
Feta cheese
Pita chips

1. Spread cream cheese evenly on a platter.
2. Spread hummus on top.
3. Sprinkle cucumbers, green onions, cherry tomatoes, and feta cheese on top.
4. Serve with pita chips and/or baguette slices.

Main Dishes

Southwest Pizza

This is a quick, unique pizza that can easily feed a crowd. Adjust the ingredient amounts to the size and tastes of your crowd. Pre-made pizza dough can be purchased at most grocery stores, but if you'd rather make your own, the Easy Pizza Dough recipe is below.

Pizza dough for 4 large-sized pizzas
1 jar of your favorite thick salsa
Queso fresco crumbly Mexican cheese (or whatever cheese you want!)
2 cups corn (frozen or canned, whatever you've got)
2 cans black beans (drained)
1 bunch chopped cilantro
Optional additions: canned green chili peppers (mild or hot), grilled chicken, taco meat, sliced green or red peppers, etc.

1. Spray cookie sheet/baking tray generously with cooking spray.
2. Stretch out dough nice and thin into a circle/oval. (You can roll it out, but just stretching it out by hand works well for me.)
3. Spread on salsa, then top with cheese, beans, corn, cilantro, and whatever else you want.
4. Cook at 425 degrees F (218 degrees C) for about 12–15 minutes or until crust edges are golden and cheese is melted. You might need to use a paper towel to soak up extra liquid if your salsa/corn is quite runny.

Easy Pizza Dough

3 cups very warm water (Not hot. About 105 degrees F/40 degrees C.)
2 envelopes of yeast (4 1/2 teaspoons)
2 tablespoons sugar
4 tablespoons olive oil
3 teaspoons salt
8 cups of bread flour or all-purpose flour

1. Pour hot water into an electric mixer or large bowl.
2. Sprinkle with yeast and sugar, and stir slightly.
3. Add the oil, salt, and flour.
4. If using a mixer with a bread hook, mix on low for three or four minutes until it forms a soft ball or knead by hand on a floured surface until a soft ball forms.
5. Put the dough into a well-greased bowl, cover with a plastic wrap or a kitchen towel, and put in a warm place until the dough doubles (about 40–60 minutes).
6. Roll the dough out on a floured surface to the desired size. Cookie sheets or flat pan will work.
7. Cook according to the instructions above.

Italian Sausage Lasagna

Here's a family's favorite lasagna recipe. It's pretty quick to make (you use noodles that don't need to be boiled, and it's healthier than many other lasagna recipes, as it uses less cheese but still feels decadent). The sausage adds a lot of great flavor and makes this different than your average lasagna! Perfect for a hearty big-family dinner.

1 1/2 pounds italian-seasoned ground turkey or regular mild italian sausage (or you can slice up chicken italian sausage links)
1 onion, chopped
2 jars of your favorite tomato pasta sauce

1 24-ounce package low-fat, small-curd cottage cheese
2 eggs
1/2 cup grated parmesan cheese
1 teaspoon oregano
1 12-ounce box of oven-ready lasagna noodles
2 cups finely shredded mozzarella or italian blend cheese
Optional: thinly sliced zucchini coins from 3–4 small zucchini

1. In a large skillet, brown sausage with onion. Then add in 1 jar of tomato sauce.
2. While the meat is cooking, mix cottage cheese with eggs, parmesan cheese, and oregano in a mixing bowl.
3. Spread 1 cup of red sauce on the bottom of a 9x13-inch pan. Arrange oven-ready uncooked lasagna noodles on top of pasta sauce in the bottom of the pan. Spread half of the cottage cheese mixture over the noodles.
4. Sprinkle 1/2 cup of the shredded cheese on top of the cottage cheese layer. Spread half of the meat-and-sauce mixture on that (then a layer of sliced zucchini if you like). Put on another layer of lasagna noodles on top.
5. Repeat with the other half of the cottage cheese mixture, another 1/2 cup of shredded cheese, and the rest of the sauce and meat from the skillet (then another optional layer of sliced zucchini).
6. Do a final layer or noodles and spread the second jar of sauce on top of the noodles.
7. Finally, spread the last cup of shredded cheese on top.
8. Bake at 375 degrees F (190 degrees C) for 40 minutes, covered with foil. Take off foil and cook for about 15 more minutes.

Creamy Vegetable Orzo

This recipe is a hit among adults *and* kids! Some of our grandchildren even claimed that it is better than macaroni and cheese! It only takes about 30 minutes to make this recipe from beginning to end (it takes a bit longer if you add chicken). And you can use whatever vegetables you have on hand.

2 pounds orzo pasta
2 cups reserved pasta water or chicken broth
2–4 teaspoons olive oil
6 garlic cloves, finely minced
1 sweet onion, diced
4 medium chicken breasts, cut into chunks (optional)
Salt and pepper, to taste (optional, to season chicken)
2–3 large red bell peppers, cut into 1/2-inch pieces
16 ounces white button mushrooms, sliced
2 pounds asparagus, cut into 1-inch pieces
1 teaspoon dried thyme
16 ounces cream cheese, softened
1 cup freshly grated parmesan cheese
1 teaspoon salt (add more to taste once everything's assembled)
1 teaspoon pepper
Juice of 3 lemons
6 tablespoons chopped fresh flat-leaf parsley (optional)

1. Bring a large pot of salted water to a boil. Add the orzo and cook according to package directions until tender (but not overdone!).
2. When the orzo is ready, reserve 2 cups of the pasta water and then drain the orzo and set aside. (You can use chicken broth instead of pasta water if you forget to reserve it or if you just like the taste of broth better!)
3. While the orzo cooks, in a large nonstick skillet, heat the olive oil over medium heat. Put garlic and onion in the pan and sauté a little.

4. If you're using chicken, season the chicken with salt and pepper. Add the chicken to the hot oil and brown on all sides. When nicely browned (but not quite all the way cooked through), add the peppers, mushrooms, asparagus, and thyme.

5. If you're doing it without chicken, put the veggies in the skillet and sauté a bit, then add a tablespoon of water and cover to let veggies steam and soften—5–10 minutes depending on the hardness of the veggies used. Take lid off and allow veggies to brown a bit. Stir until most of the liquid has evaporated. Veggies shouldn't be totally done since they'll cook a bit more once you add in the cheeses.

6. While the veggies cook, cut cream cheese into chunks (about 6–8 chunks from each cube). When veggies are mostly done, add the cream cheese and the grated parmesan and stir so that the cream cheese melts and coats the chicken and vegetables.

7. Add the reserved pasta water or chicken broth and bring to a simmer. Add 1 teaspoon salt and 1 teaspoon pepper. Stir.

8. Add the orzo, lemon juice, and fresh parsley. Stir to combine and heat through.

9. Garnish with additional parmesan if you wish, and have some lemon slices available to squeeze over the top of individual portions if desired.

Chicken Tikka Masala

This is a huge family favorite for the Eyres, and we have it at almost every family reunion. It takes a bit of planning to do the marinade, but the actual cooking time is short, and it's a crowd pleaser! Even though the ingredients may look pretty spicy, even our little children love this recipe. This can be made up to one day in advance and reheated on the stove.

Main Ingredients

12 boneless skinless chicken breasts (serves about 18)

Marinade Ingredients

(If you double this recipe, double the chicken and sauce but don't double the marinade.)

2 cups plain yogurt
2 tablespoons lemon juice
4 teaspoons ground cumin
2 teaspoons ground cinnamon
2 teaspoons cayenne pepper
2 teaspoons black pepper
2 tablespoons minced fresh ginger (or 2 teaspoons ground ginger)
2 teaspoons salt

Sauce Ingredients

4 tablespoons butter
4 garlic cloves, minced
1 jalapeno pepper, thoroughly seeded and finely chopped (optional)
8 teaspoons ground cumin
8 teaspoons paprika
2 teaspoons salt
4 8-ounce cans tomato sauce
3 cups cream

Garnishes for serving

Fresh cilantro
Plain yogurt or sour cream
Rice

1. Combine all marinade ingredients, then pour over chicken and refrigerate in a plastic bag or reusable plastic container for at least an hour (or up to 8–10 hours).
2. Grill or cook chicken and discard marinade.

3. Melt the butter in a large skillet over medium heat. Sauté garlic and jalapeno for 1 minute. Add cumin, paprika, and salt.

4. Stir in tomato sauce and cream.

5. Simmer on low until sauce thickens (about 20 minutes).

6. Add the grilled chicken into the mix and simmer for 10 more minutes.

7. Garnish with fresh cilantro and a little plain yogurt or sour cream.

8. Serve over hot rice.

Honey Lime Enchiladas

This recipe is a family favorite from a church cookbook, and it's super easy, which is good when you're in a hurry or feeding a lot of people!

3/4 cup honey
10 tablespoons lime juice
2 tablespoons chili powder
6 large chicken breasts, cooked and shredded (even easier: use one bag of rotisserie chicken already cooked and shredded from Costco)
12–16 flour tortillas
5–6 cups shredded cheese (cheddar, monterey jack, or a Mexican blend)
2 12-ounce cans green enchilada sauce
Sour cream and/or other desired Mexican toppings (avocado, salsa, etc.)

1. In a bowl, mix up the honey, lime juice, and chili powder to make a marinade, and then combine it with the cooked chicken.

2. Let the chicken soak in the marinade in the fridge at least an hour and up to 8–10 hours.

3. Fill tortillas with shredded cheese and equal portions of the chicken mixture.

4. Spread a layer of green enchilada sauce in the bottom of 2 9x13-inch pans (sprayed with cooking spray).

5. Roll up those tortillas nice and tight and place them open-tortilla-flap down in the pan.

6. Spread another layer of enchilada sauce over the top.

7. Sprinkle the remaining cheese over the top.

8. Bake at 350 degrees F (177 degrees C) for 30 minutes.

9. Serve with sour cream or other desired toppings.

Fish Tacos

Our son Noah and his wife, Kristi, make this at almost every family reunion. Everyone raves! The fish is mild enough for kids, especially stacked in a yummy taco. If you're in a hurry, Shawni says you can buy tortilla-encrusted frozen tilapia from Costco instead of marinating the tilapia.

Main Ingredients

8–12 pieces of tilapia

Marinade Ingredients

4 garlic cloves
1 cup fresh parsley
1–2 lemons
1 cup olive oil
1/2–1 cup red wine vinegar
2 tablespoons dried oregano
1 teaspoon black pepper

Sauce Ingredients

1/2 cup plain yogurt
4 tablespoons lime juice
6 tablespoons chopped cilantro
3 garlic cloves, pressed

1 teaspoon cumin
2 tablespoons water

For Serving

Lime wedges
Cilantro
Salsa
Corn tortillas

1. Combine the marinade ingredients, cover fish in it, and marinate for 30 minutes.
2. Grill on high for 3–5 minutes on each side until fish flakes.
3. Combine sauce ingredients.
4. Serve with lime wedges, cilantro, salsa, and corn tortillas.

Grilled Pesto Chicken

This is incredibly simple and easy, but it yields gourmet-tasting tender chicken that we all scarf down! You can add this chicken to salads, pizzas, pasta, and so on—or just eat it as is with some vegetable and fruit sides!

8–12 chicken breasts
2 cups prepared pesto
1/4 cup olive oil
1/2 cup seasoned rice vinegar
1/2–1 teaspoon salt

1. Combine all ingredients in a plastic bag and put in the fridge to marinate for 2–10 hours.
2. Cook the chicken on a grill or in a skillet.

Lentil Tacos/Burritos

This is a great meatless option that is universally beloved among our children and grandchildren.

2 small onions
4 garlic cloves
4 tablespoons olive oil
1 1/3 cups dry lentils (green or black)
3 tablespoons taco seasoning
3 1/3 cups chicken broth
4 medium sweet potatoes
4 cups cherry tomatoes
1 big bunch cilantro
1 lime
2 teaspoons honey
4 avocados
3 cups feta cheese
1 1/3 cups of your favorite salsa
Corn tortillas, flour tortillas, or hard taco shells

1. Finely chop up onions and garlic.
2. Heat oil in a pot and cook onions and garlic for five minutes, stirring occasionally.
3. Add lentils and 2 tablespoons taco seasoning. Cook and stir for 1 minute.
4. Add chicken broth, bring to a boil, then reduce heat to low, cover, and simmer for about 30 minutes (or until lentils are tender).
5. While the lentils are cooking, chop up the sweet potatoes (leave the skin on) and mix them with a splash of olive oil and the remaining tablespoon of taco seasoning. Spread evenly on a baking sheet and roast in the oven at 400 degrees F (204 degrees C) for about 20 minutes or until they are slightly browned.
6. Meanwhile, cut cherry tomatoes in fourths and chop the cilantro. Combine these in a bowl and drizzle with juice from the lime and the honey. Mix to combine.
7. Open, pit, and slice up avocados and place in a separate bowl. Crumble feta cheese into another bowl.

8. When lentils are cooked, stir in the salsa.

9. To serve, pile lentil mix, sweet potatoes, tomato/cilantro mix, avocado, and cheese (as desired!) into a tortilla or taco shell.

Crock-Pot Coconut Chicken Curry

Here's a super easy recipe if you live near a Trader Joe's and have a large Crock-Pot. This recipe comes from some dear family friends who have even more grandchildren than we do!

8 frozen chicken breasts (or 16–18 chicken tenders)
4 bottles Trader Joe's yellow curry sauce
2 cans coconut cream (Shake before opening. Coco López is even better. Ask your grocer to help you find it.)
Stir-fry vegetables (of any variety—fresh or frozen)
Jasmine or basmati rice
Warm naan bread (available at Trader Joe's and Costco)
Optional: mangoes, cashews, and cilantro for topping

1. Put chicken in the Crock-Pot. Combine sauce and cream and pour over the top.

2. Cook on low for 6–8 hours, stirring occasionally.

3. During the last half hour, add the vegetables.

4. Serve with rice and bread. Top with mangoes, cashews, and cilantro if desired.

Easy Barbecued Pork Loins

So easy and delicious! Pork loins come in packages of two at Costco but are also available at most grocery stores.

4 pork tenderloins (each loin serves 4–6, and they are usually packaged with two loins shrink-wrapped in one package)
1 cup soy sauce
1 cup worchestershire sauce
4 garlic cloves, crushed or diced

1. Place pork loins in a plastic bag and pour sauces over the top. Add garlic.
2. Marinate in the fridge for a couple of hours or, even better, overnight.
3. Grill the pork at 350–400 degrees F (177–204 degrees C) for 20–30 minutes. Don't overcook! It should have just a tinge of pink in the middle.
4. Cut diagonally and cover in a warm oven (at about 200 degrees F/ 93 degrees C) until the crowd's all there!

Elegant and Super Easy Salmon Fillet

This is a recipe that is super easy, elegant, and delicious (as well as more expensive). It goes well with the pork loins above, which are a nice alternative for those who don't eat fish.

1 cup mayonnaise
2 tablespoons fresh lemon juice
1 tablespoon lemon pepper
1 large salmon fillet (about 3–4 pounds)

1. Mix mayo, lemon juice, and lemon pepper.
2. Spread equally over the salmon fillet.
3. Cook at 425 degrees F (218 degrees C) until the thickest part is still almost too rare (because it will continue cooking outside the oven).

Café Rio-Style Burritos/Salads

This recipe serves 15–20. Everyone seems to have their favorite recipe for this family pleaser. This is a combination of what our kids have found is easiest and healthiest. Maybe you'll find a little different twist! There are five parts: the meat, the salsa, the rice, the sauce, and the garnishes. Combine them all together into tortillas or just over beds of lettuce. You can also add beans, grilled vegetables, guacamole—whatever your family loves!

You may want to double the salsa recipe depending on your crowd's love of salsa.

The sauce is a simpler and lower-fat recipe from Saydi than the ones we have used in the past with mayo and sour cream. It is also a great low-calorie option for salads and sandwiches. According to Shawni, "It is so good it could make a piece of cardboard taste delicious."

Meat

2 pork sirloin tip roasts, about 2 1/2 pounds each (These are the low-fat, cheapest pork roasts. Costco sells these sqaure roasts in packages of 4.)
1 cup brown sugar
1 16-ounce jar of salsa
1/2 package of fajita seasoning (optional)

1. Combine all ingredients in slow cooker.
2. Cook on low for 7–9 hours.
3. Break apart/shred meat in sauce.

Salsa

4 fresh tomatoes, chopped
1 white onion, chopped
1/2 bunch cilantro, chopped
1/2 tablespoon lime juice
2 garlic cloves, minced
1 teaspoon salt
1 teaspoon pepper

1. Mix all ingredients in a food processor and pulse until desired consistency is achieved.

Lime Rice

2 tablespoons butter
1 yellow onion, chopped

4 cloves minced garlic
7 cups water
8 teaspoons chicken bouillon (7 cubes)
1/2 bunch cilantro, chopped
2 teaspoons cumin
1/4 cup lime juice
1/2 teaspoon salt
3 cups long-grain rice

1. Sauté butter, onion, and garlic for 5 minutes.
2. Bring all ingredients but rice to a boil in a large pot.
3. Add rice, cover, and simmer for 20 minutes.

Sauce (amounts depend on your crowd's preference)

1 avocado
1/2 cup plain greek yogurt
1/2 cup water (more or less as needed to adjust consistency)
1 bunch of cilantro leaves and stems
1 teaspoon salt
2 small cloves of garlic
Juice of 3 limes

1. Combine all ingredients in a blender an blend until smooth.

Garnishes (optional)

Cilantro
Lime wedges
Cheese
Black beans
Sour cream
Chips
Freshly cooked or regular tortillas
Guacamole or sliced avocado

Japanese Curry

Eli is our resident Japanese chef, and this is our favorite meal for adults and children alike, served at the reunion. The following are his own words:

> In Japan, curry is the comfort food of choice. While living there, I fell in love with Japanese curry, and I make it at least once a month for my family and once a year at our reunion. Every year, our crowd gets bigger. Cooking for fifty can be intimidating but quite rewarding, as everyone seems to love it.
>
> The easiest way to make Japanese curry is to buy the pre-packaged curry roux. You can purchase it in bulk on Amazon. Most US grocery stores now carry "golden curry," but it is usually in smaller portions than what you'll find online. My personal favorite brands are Kokumaro and Torokeru. They are sold at various spice levels. I prefer the spicy, but buy it according to your taste. I add milk and cheese to the spicy one, which ultimately makes it mild with a bit of a kick.
>
> Disregard the directions on the box and use the recipe below that I learned from a chef at a famous curry house in Japan.

This serves 12–16 people.

4 large russet potatoes
8–10 large carrots
6–8 cups of Japanese sushi rice or Botan or Calrose rice (This is much better than basmati, jasmine, or long-grain for this dish—trust me.)
2 large onions
4–6 chicken breasts (or more if you like lots of chicken)
10 cups water

2 8.4-ounce boxes of roux (golden curry or the recommended brands above)
2 cups milk
2 cups grated sharp cheddar cheese

1. Start a large pot of boiling water while cutting up the potatoes and carrots. Start cooking the rice either over the stove or in a rice cooker. Peel and cut the potatoes into cubes about the size of dice.

2. Cut the carrots into pieces about the same size as the potatoes. Put them in the water and boil until they start to soften.

3. While boiling, dice the onion and pan-fry the chicken breasts (with salt and pepper). Add the onion when the chicken is nearly cooked through. You can cube the chicken either before or after you cook it. For a big crowd, we barbecue the chicken and then cut into bite-size pieces.

4. Once the potatoes and carrots begin to soften, drain all of the water.

5. Measure 10 cups water and pour into the pot with the potatoes and carrots. Bring back to boil.

6. Once boiling, stir in the curry roux. It's important to keep stirring at this point so the roux dissolves and doesn't stick to the bottom of the pot. The sauce will thicken as the roux dissolves, and you'll smell the aroma of the curry.

7. Put chicken and onions into the pot so everything is now mixing together.

8. Add 2 cups milk to the mixture, and add the grated cheese. Let simmer while stirring occasionally.

9. Serve over the sticky rice. Depending on how much you like cheese, I like to sprinkle a little more cheese on top and let it melt into the curry. Enjoy your new favorite food!

Kids' Favorite Mac and Cheese

2 pounds macaroni
4 large eggs (whisked)
2 12-ounce cans of evaporated milk
1/4 cup milk
6 cups grated cheese (Mexican blend or cheddar)
4 teaspoons salt
1 teaspoon dry mustard (optional)

1. Cook macaroni according to package directions. Drain and return to the pot.
2. Add ingredients while stirring on low heat until the cheese is melted.
3. Serve immediately!

Easy and Delicious Crock-Pot Roast

Last but not least is this tried-and-true favorite family recipe for a pot roast you can put in the Crock-Pot in the morning and have it ready to serve when you get home. This will take two Crock-Pots to serve a crowd of 12–16. We haven't tried this in an Instant Pot pressure cooker yet, but it would probably work.

10 pounds chuck or cross-cut roast
4 cans cream of mushroom soup
2–3 packages of Lipton Onion Soup Mix

1. Place 5–6 pounds of roast in each Crock-Pot.
2. Pour 2 cans of cream of mushroom soup on top.
3. Sprinkle 1–1 1/2 packets of soup mix on top.
4. Cook on low for 8–10 hours until the meat falls apart. This will make a delicious, thick brown gravy. You can add potatoes and carrots to the pot for a complete meal.

Soups

Hearty Tortilla Soup

Once the chicken is cooked, this can be prepared in only about 15 minutes! It's really healthy and always a big pleaser. (You can put chicken in a Crock-Pot with the salsa and chili powder and let it cook all day, then shred the chicken and stir in all the other ingredients close to dinner time. Or you can skip the chicken—it's good with or without!)

2 cups of your favorite salsa—mild or medium—and best if chunky
1 28-ounce can crushed tomatoes
1 teaspoon granulated garlic or 1–2 fresh garlic cloves, crushed
1 large can (31 ounces) no-fat refried beans (or about 3 1/2 cups)
1 tablespoon chili powder
6 cups chicken broth (about 4 14.5-ounce cans of chicken broth, or use bouillon to make the broth)
4 cups frozen whole kernel corn
3–4 cups cooked shredded or cubed cooked chicken (3–4 chicken breasts)
Topping ideas: shredded cheese, sour cream or plain greek yogurt, chopped green onions, chopped cilantro, crumbled tortilla chips, lime

1. Over low heat, mix salsa, canned tomatoes, refried beans, garlic, and chili powder in a large soup pot until bean lumps are mostly integrated.
2. Stir in chicken broth slowly.
3. Fold in corn and chicken.
4. Bring to a boil, then reduce heat and simmer for 5–10 minutes, stirring occasionally.
5. Serve with toppings of your choice.

Curried Chicken and Apple Soup

If you and your guests like curry, you'll love this rich, flavorful soup. It's best if made on the day of your event.

2 teaspoons vegetable oil or olive oil
2 pounds boneless skinless chicken breasts (about 6 big breasts)
2 large onions, chopped
8–10 garlic cloves, crushed or chopped (or 1–2 tablespoons bottled crushed garlic)
2 medium bell peppers, of any color, chopped
3 tablespoons curry powder
2 tablespoons grated fresh ginger, or 1/2 tablespoon ground ginger
1/2 teaspoon black pepper
2 teaspoons salt
10 cups chicken broth
4 15-ounce cans diced tomatoes
4 apples, chopped in small chunks (Granny Smith or Fuji work well—the crisper, the better!)
1 1/2 cups rice
Optional garnishes: chopped cilantro, plain yogurt, sour cream

1. Sauté oil, chicken breasts, onions, garlic, peppers, curry powder, ginger, salt, and pepper down to the broth/ stock together in large soup pot until chicken isn't pink anymore and onion is tender.

2. Add the chicken broth, diced tomatoes, and rice. Bring to a boil, then reduce to a simmer. Simmer for about 20 minutes.

3. Add the apples and simmer about 8 more minutes or until apples are somewhat soft and rice is done.

4. If desired, serve with a garnish of chopped cilantro and a dollop of plain yogurt or sour cream. Great with warm, crusty bread!

Note: The rice will expand and take over this soup if added too early. Add rice during the last 30 minutes of simmering before serving. I learned this the hard way!

Crock-Pot White Bean and Chicken Chili

The slow cooker does pretty much all the work on this one! And adults and kids alike really love it.

5 frozen chicken breasts
2 16-ounce jars green salsa
4 15-ounce small white beans (undrained)
2 cups corn
2 teaspoons cumin

1. Place chicken in Crock-Pot and cover with salsa.
2. Cook on low 5–7 hours.
3. Shred the chicken with two forks.
4. Add beans, corn, and cumin, and leave in Crock-Pot until warmed through.

Black Bean Soup (aka Ghoul Goulash)

Our daughter Saren makes this super-easy soup every year for a traditional Halloween dinner. It's very quick and makes for a perfect savory meal on a spooky night . . . or any night of the year!

7 16-ounce cans of black beans
3 cups chicken broth or vegetable broth
3 small onions, chopped
3 teaspoons crushed or minced garlic
3 16-ounce jars chunky salsa
12 teaspoons lime juice or the juice of 6 limes (optional)
6 teaspoons ground cumin
3/4 teaspoons crushed red pepper (optional—adds heat)
Suggested toppings: plain yogurt or sour cream, chopped cilantro, shredded cheese, chopped red peppers, crumbled tortilla chips

1. Place three cans of beans with liquid from can as well as the broth in a blender. Blend until smooth.

2. Coat large saucepan or soup pot with cooking spray or a bit of olive oil. Heat over high heat and sauté onion until tender.

3. Add blended bean mixture, remaining unblended beans (with liquid), garlic, salsa, optional lime juice, cumin, and crushed red pepper (if desired). Mix together.

4. Reduce heat to simmer and cook for 25–30 minutes, stirring occasionally.

5. Serve garnished with toppings of choice.

Chicken Corn Chowder

1 chopped onion
2 garlic cloves, crushed
2 tablespoons olive oil
2 large cans chicken broth
1 cup milk or cream
2 packages cream cheese, softened
2 cans corn
2 cups or 1 16-ounce jar of salsa
1 can black beans (drained)
Avocado chunks
1 bunch cilantro, chopped
1 tablespoon chili powder
1 teaspoon cumin
3–4 cans of chicken (or you can boil and shred chicken, or use pulled-apart rotisserie chicken)
Optional toppings: sour cream, cheese, crushed chips

1. Sauté onion and garlic in olive oil for a couple of minutes.

2. Add broth, milk or cream, cream cheese, corn, salsa, beans, chili powder, cumin, and shredded chicken and

bring it all to a boil. Then reduce heat to low and simmer for 20 minutes.

3. Add the cilantro and chopped avocado at the very end of cooking.

4. You can add a dollop of sour cream, cheese, or crushed chips for serving.

Salads and Breads

Enormous salads are served at least once a day at our reunions. Saydi is the salad guru, but everyone has come up with great ideas. Here are three of our favorites.

Strawberry and Green Grape Salad with Arugula

This salad is easy, beautiful, and delicious. Use amounts to taste according to the number and preferences of your salad lovers.

Selection of lettuce
Arugula
Green grapes
Strawberries
Slivered almonds
1 tablespoon sugar (optional)
Apple chunks (optional)
Parmesan flakes
Salad dressing of choice

1. Depending on the size of your crowd, mix lettuces of your choice, including some arugula (which gives it a kick), in a large bowl.
2. Slice the strawberries and gently mix, along with the grapes, into the salad.
3. Top with slivered almonds (sautéed, if you like, with a tablespoon of sugar on low heat until golden and cooled) and large flakes of parmesan cheese on top.
4. Serve with a very light dressing of your choice. Our favorite dressing for salads with fruit is Brianna's Blush Wine.

Watermelon Salad with Halloumi Cheese and Green Beans

Saydi came up with this one, and we love it because watermelon goes a long way, it's different, and it's delicious!

1/2 watermelon
1/2 pound green beans (I like french beans here, but any will do)
1 package halloumi cheese (or feta—but halloumi is so good!)
Chopped fresh mint
Juice of 1/2 lemon
Olive oil
Pinch of salt

1. Cut watermelon into 1-inch chunks.
2. Blanch beans by flash cooking them in boiling water for 3 minutes and then immediately immersing them in a bowl of ice water.
3. Pan-fry halloumi until golden (it is a very firm cheese and keeps its shape), cool, and cut into bite-sized chunks.
4. Make dressing by squeezing the juice of 1/2 lemon and adding an equal amount of olive oil. Add a big pinch of salt, and mix well.
5. Stir all ingredients together gently, then add dressing to taste.

Napa Cabbage, Tomato, and Avocado Salad

This is a great way to get kids to eat cabbage. Everyone loves this salad. *Total preparation time: 15 minutes.*

2 teaspoons finely grated fresh lemon zest
2 tablespoons fresh lemon juice
2 teaspoons dijon mustard or whole-grain mustard
1 teaspoon salt

1/2 teaspoon black pepper
1/3 cup extra-virgin olive oil
2 1-pound Napa cabbages, or one really big head of Napa cabbage (or regular cabbage works fine too)
2–3 firm-ripe avocados
1 1/2 pounds cherry or grape tomatoes, halved (or you can use chopped roma tomatoes)

1. Whisk together lemon zest, juice, mustard, salt, pepper, and oil in a small bowl until smooth.
2. Tear off cabbage leaves, rinse and cut them down the middle of the ribs, then slice into half-inch sections (this helps make it easier to eat if the pieces of cabbage are somewhat small). You should have about 12 cups.
3. Quarter avocado lengthwise, then pit and peel. Cut into 1/2-inch pieces.
4. Toss cabbage leaves, avocado, and tomatoes in a large bowl with just enough dressing to coat (you likely won't need all the dressing).

Note: The cabbage in this salad holds up well enough to eat any leftovers the next day.

Pesto and Green Pea Salad

This is a good salad to have on hand since the ingredients (except for the lettuce) have a long shelf life.

Romaine lettuce (three or four heads, according to your salad lovers)
1 cup frozen petite peas
4–6 ounces feta cheese
4–6 ounces toasted sliced almonds
Chopped fresh mint (optional)

1. Finely chop the lettuce.
2. Toast the almonds, if desired, and put in the fridge to cool.

3. Add the frozen peas, which will keep the salad cold and crisp until you serve it.

4. Add the other ingredients and toss lightly.

Dressing

6 tablespoons pesto (Costco's pesto is excellent, but any brand is fine.)
3 tablespoons extra virgin olive oil
1 teaspoon rice vinegar
1/4 teaspoon salt

1. Shake all ingredients in a jar and dress salad according to taste. Keeps well in the fridge.

Everyday Flat Bread

This recipe comes from our daughter Shawni, whose daughters whip up this bread to accompany nearly every family dinner. It is so easy, and it can also be used for pizza crust. *Total preparation time: 15 minutes.*

2 packages yeast (2 1/2 teaspoons)
2 cups tap-hot water
1 teaspoon salt
2 teaspoons sugar
4 tablespoons oil
4 cups flour

1. Combine all ingredients, adding more flour if the dough is sticky (you may be able to add up to 3 more cups!)

2. Let the dough sit for 15–30 minutes while you work on the rest of dinner.

3. Spray a baking sheet with cooking spray, and then roll the dough out on top. You can score for breadsticks at whatever size you'd like.

4. Bake at 500 degrees F (260 degrees C) for 5–7 minutes.

5. Shawni's girls think this is best when spread, while hot, with a bit of butter and then sprinkled with garlic salt!

Never-Fail Sunday Rolls

This recipe makes 48 rolls—great for accompanying a big meal for a crowd! And this recipe is completely foolproof.

1/2 cup tap-hot water
2 packages (or 4 1/2 teaspoons) yeast
1 pinch sugar
1 cup butter
2 teaspoons salt
3/4 cup sugar
1 cup boiling water
4 eggs, beaten
1 cup warm milk
8 1/2 cups flour (best with bread flour)

1. Mix water, yeast, and a pinch of sugar in a bowl. Set aside until foamy.
2. Cream butter, salt, and 3/4 cup sugar. Add boiling water. Mix until dissolved.
3. Cool to 105–115 degrees F (40–46 degrees C). (If you don't have a thermometer, you can just wait a few minutes while it cools off and then carry on. The butter cools the boiling water pretty fast.)
4. Beat in yeast mixture and eggs. Beat in flour gradually along with the warm milk.
5. Knead for five minutes or until silky (dough will still be pretty sticky).
6. Let rise until doubled in size (approximately 1 1/2–2 hours).
7. Punch down and divide into four balls. Roll out into an approximately 14-inch circle.

8. Paint surface with melted butter, and cut up (in a slicing pie fashion) with a pizza cutter into 12 pieces.

9. Roll each piece from big end to small end (like a croissant) and place on greased cookie sheet with point tucked under.

10. Let rise, covered with a cloth, until doubled in size (again, approximately 1 1/2–2 hours).

11. Bake at 400 degrees F (204 degrees C) for 10–12 minutes.

Desserts

A you will see, we are partial to cake and cookies and are pretty much chocolate (and chocolate chip) nuts!

Chocolate Chip Pound Cake

It's perfect for a family celebration!

1 box yellow cake mix
1/2 cup sugar
1 package (3.9 ounces) instant chocolate pudding
3/4 cup vegetable oil
3/4 cup water
4 large eggs
1 8-ounce carton sour cream
1 cup semisweet chocolate chips

1. Combine and whisk together cake mix and sugar.
2. Add other ingredients except for chocolate chips and mix until smooth (but don't beat).
3. Stir in chocolate chips.
4. Pour into greased and floured bundt pan and bake at 350 degrees F (177 degrees C) for 1 hour (plus or minus 10 minutes depending on the oven).

Chocolate Chews

We love to whip up these no-bake cookies when we are gathered as a large group. They are quick and easy and so very delicious!

2 cups sugar
1/4–1/2 cup cocoa (depending on your preference of chocolatey-ness!)
1/2 cup milk
1 stick (1/2 cup) butter
1 teaspoon vanilla
4 cups oats

1. Combine sugar, cocoa, milk, and butter in a saucepan over medium heat, mixing as butter melts and all ingredients come together to a boil.

2. As soon as the mixture begins boiling, turn down heat to low and let simmer for exactly 4 minutes. The timing is really important—if you boil too long, you'll have really dry, crumbly cookies, and if you boil for not long enough, they'll turn into a goopy mess.

3. As soon as the 4 minutes are up, take the saucepan off all heat and add the vanilla and the oats. Mix together well.

4. Drop by heaping spoonfuls onto a baking sheet lined with wax paper or tinfoil.

5. Let cookies sit for about 30 minutes in the fridge, and then enjoy after they have completely set.

Bear Lake Brownie Cake

This is an Eyre all-time family favorite for a quick dessert that feeds a crowd. The amount of people this recipe serves depends entirely on how small the slices are cut . . . we recommend a big ol' slice for everyone. :)

Cake Ingredients

2 cups flour
2 cups sugar
4 tablespoons cocoa
1 cup water
1 cup butter
1 1/2 teaspoons baking soda
1 1/2 teaspoons vanilla
1/2 cup buttermilk (or milk plus 1/2 teaspoon vinegar)
2 eggs

Frosting Ingredients

1/2 cup butter
4 tablespoons cocoa
6 tablespoons milk
1 pound (about 4 cups) powdered sugar
1 cup chopped walnuts or pecans (optional)

1. Mix the flour and sugar and set aside.
2. Melt the cocoa, water, and butter in a saucepan.
3. Add the melted mixture to the flour/sugar mixture.
4. Add baking soda, vanilla, buttermilk, and eggs. Mix all well to combine.
5. Pour into a greased jelly roll cooking sheet. Cook at 375 degrees F (190 degrees C) for 20 minutes.
6. While the cake is cooking, prepare the frosting. First, melt the butter, cocoa, and milk in a saucepan.
7. Add the powdered sugar and nuts, and mix to combine.
8. Spread the frosting on the cake while it is still warm and cool. The cake freezes well and can be easily doubled if you have two sheet cake pans.

Healthy(er) Pumpkin Chocolate Chip Cookies

2 1/4 cups (1 15-ounce can) canned pumpkin
1/2 cup canola oil
1/2 cup applesauce
1 teaspoon vanilla
2 1/2 cups sugar
4 cups flour (you can use 3 cups white flour and 1 cup whole wheat flour, if desired)
2 teaspoons baking soda
2 teaspoons cinnamon
1 teaspoon allspice

1 1/2–2 cups semisweet chocolate chips (depends on how choco-
latey you want them to be!)
1 cup chopped walnuts or pecans (optional)

1. Mix together all the wet ingredients and the sugar.
2. Add the flour one cup at a time, mixing between each
   cup.
3. Add the baking soda and spices with the last cup of
   flour.
4. Fold in the chocolate chips.
5. Add a cup of chopped walnuts or pecans if you like.
6. Drop by spoonfuls onto a cookie sheet sprayed with
   nonstick spray.
7. Bake at 350 degrees F (177 degrees C) for 10–12 minutes—be sure not to overbake! Take cookies out when
   they're still a bit doughy looking.

Oatmeal Chocolate Chip Cookies with a Crunch

Of course every grandma needs another chocolate chip cookie
recipe. Saydi adopted this recipe from her mother-in-law and
makes it with Rice Krispies several times at the reunion. Last year,
she wond the Cookie Bake-off Contest with this recipe. Makes
about four dozen cookies. Double if necessary.

2 cups butter
2 cups sugar
4 eggs + 1 egg yolk
1 tablespoon vanilla
2 teaspoons salt
4 cups flour
2 teaspoons baking soda
2 teaspoon baking powder
4 cups oats

2 cups sweetened shredded coconut
2 cups semi-sweet chocolate chips
4 cups Rice Krispies

1. Cream butter and sugar until fluffy.
2. Add eggs and vanilla.
3. Add salt, flour, baking soda, and baking powder.
4. Add oats, coconut, and chocolate chips.
5. Add Rice Krispies and stir until just mixed.
6. Drop onto a cookie sheet by spoonfuls or with a cookie scoop.
7. Bake at 375 degrees F (190 degrees C) for 8–9 minutes, depending on the size. The cookies may look a bit undercooked, but that's how we like them.

Feeding a *Really Big* Crowd

These recipes are from Tess Wade, who is one of our co-grandparents (and an excellent cook!). She was in charge of feeding sixty to eighty young, single adults at regular big events in London for our church for eighteen months. These recipes are perfect for really large family reunions or gatherings of any kind. Several of these contain bulk ingredients from Costco. If you don't live near a Costco, you'll have to improvise. :) Lots of helping hands and/or a food processor are essential!

Chuck's Favorite Mac and Cheese

Serves 60–80.

4 large onions, chopped
1/4 cup chopped garlic
Olive oil
8 kilograms (17 pounds) whole wheat pasta (macaroni or your choice)
2 5-pound bags grated cheddar cheese (can be found at Costco)
8 16-ounce containers small-curd cottage cheese
2 32-ounce containers plain greek yogurt
2 cups grated parmesan cheese
1 12-ounce box cornflakes, crushed (about 12 cups)
2 cups melted butter

1. Sauté onions and garlic in oil and season.
2. Cook pasta.
3. Mix in cheddar and cottage cheeses, yogurt, and onion/garlic mix.
4. Mix parmesan, cornflakes, and butter in a separate bowl to create a crumble topping.
5. Place pasta mixture in six greased foil pans, top with crumble, and bake uncovered at 350 degrees F (177 degrees C) for 20–25 minutes.
6. Uncover and brown for 10 minutes.

Lentil Vegetable Soup

Serves 60–80.

8 16-ounce bags brown lentils
16 onions, finely chopped
1/2 cup crushed garlic
16 carrots, finely chopped
35 small white potatoes, scrubbed and chopped
8 15.5-ounce cans fire-roasted tomatoes

2 gallons vegetable broth
15 cups chopped spinach (2 large Costco bags)
Salt and pepper to taste

1. Rinse lentils and brown onions and garlic.
2. Combine all ingredients except spinach and salt and pepper to taste in large pot.
3. Cook on low for 2 hours.
4. Add spinach 5 minutes before serving.
5. Season to taste with salt and pepper.

Easy Pizza Dinner

Serves 60–80.

10 frozen Costco Italian pizzas (pre-cooked, rectangular)
2 bags Costco grated mozzarella cheese
2 large bags frozen peas

1. Add extra cheese to frozen pizzas and then cook according to instructions on package.
2. Cook peas in a small amount of water in a large saucepan.

Burrito Bowls

Serves 60–80.

15 cups dried rice, cooked
15 cups dried beans, cooked
15 cups chopped lettuce or steamed kale
10 cups cooked corn
10 avocadoes, chopped (optional)
Fresh salsa (see recipe below, or buy in bulk)
Tortilla chips

1. Layer all ingredients in individual bowls or plates, top with salsa, and serve with chips.

Fresh Salsa

Serves 60–80.

25 fresh tomatoes, chopped
4 cups chopped onion
6 jalapenos, seeded and minced
2 large bunches chopped cilantro/coriander
2 tablespoons lime juice
2 tablespoons salt
2 teaspoons pepper
1/3 cup minced garlic

1. Blend all ingredients in a food processor until desired consistency is achieved.

Quinoa and Sweet Potato Chili

Serves 60–80.

1/3 cup olive oil
6 onions, chopped
1/2 cup minced garlic
6 6-ounce cans tomato paste
1/3 cup chili powder
1/3 cup cumin
2 tablespoons oregano
12 15.5-ounce cans black beans, rinsed and drained (1.5 kilograms dry beans)
1.5 gallons vegetable stock
6 sweet potatoes, peeled and cut into bite-sized chunks
Salt and pepper to taste
6 cups quinoa
Avocado, cilantro for garnish (optional)

1. Heat oil in a large soup pot over medium heat. Add onions and cook until soft and brown. Add garlic and cook for about 2 minutes.

2. Add tomato paste and spices and cook for 2 minutes, stirring constantly.

3. Add beans, stock, and potatoes and season with salt and pepper. Cook for about 5 minutes, then add the quinoa.

4. Continue cooking for about 15–30 minutes, stirring frequently, until quinoa and potatoes are cooked and the chili has thickened.

5. Add a bit of water if the chili becomes too thick for your liking.

6. Top with avocado and chopped cilantro.

Jacket Potatoes

Serves 60–80.

3 bags Costco baking potatoes
2 bags broccoli
2 32-ounce (2-pound) containers of plain greek yogurt
1 bag grated cheese
Butter

1. Bake potatoes in batches as big as your oven can handle!

2. Meanwhile, steam broccoli until tender.

3. Set out toppings and allow everyone to add whatever they like to their potatoes!

Soul-Soothing Soup

Serves 50–60.

2/3 cup olive oil
6 diced onions
1/3 cup diced garlic
1 small jar jalapenos, seeded and diced
6 chopped sweet potatoes
6 28-ounce cans diced tomatoes with juice

Salt and pepper to taste
2 cups peanut butter
4 quarts vegetable broth
3 tablespoons mild chili powder
1 1/2 teaspoons cayenne pepper
6 14.5-ounce cans rinsed/drained chickpeas
2 large bags Costco spinach (about 15 cups)
2 32-ounce containers plain greek yogurt
2 bunches chopped coriander/cilantro

1. Sauté onions and garlic in oil until tender.
2. Add jalapenos, sweet potatoes, canned tomatoes, and salt and pepper and simmer for 5 minutes.
3. In a bowl, whisk peanut butter with three cups of broth until no lumps remain. Stir into ingredients prepared above with the rest of the broth and the spices.
4. Cover and simmer 30–40 minutes until sweet potatoes are tender.
5. Stir in chickpeas and spinach and simmer until spinach is just wilted.
6. Add a dollop of yogurt and garnish with cilantro.

Vegetarian Enchiladas

Serves 50–60.

Sauce Ingredients

3/4 cup olive oil
2 tablespoons cumin
1 1/2 cups flour
1 1/2 cups tomato paste
3 quarts vegetable broth
4 1/2 cups water
Salt and pepper to taste

Filling Ingredients

72 ounces grated cheese
6 15-ounce cans black beans, rinsed and drained
2 large bags Costco spinach (about 15 cups), steamed, drained thoroughly, and chopped
5 cups frozen corn
4 bunches chopped spring onions (divided)
2 tablespoons cumin
Salt and pepper to taste
96 4-inch corn tortillas or 64 8-inch flour tortillas

1. Heat oil, and then add cumin, flour, and tomato paste. Cook 1 minute, whisking.
2. Whisk in broth and water, bring to a boil, and simmer until slightly thickened (5–8 minutes). Salt and pepper to taste and set aside.
3. For filling, combine 2/3 of the cheese (saving 1/3 for topping) and all the beans, spinach, corn, the white portion of the spring onions (reserve green portion for garnish), cumin, and salt and pepper.
4. Preheat oven to 400 degrees F (204 degrees C) and lightly oil six 9x13–inch baking pans.
5. Stack one-third of the tortillas in a damp paper towel and warm in the microwave for 1 minute. Then repeat for the other two-thirds.
6. One by one, fill tortillas with about 1/3 cup filling, roll tightly, and arrange in baking dish, seam down.
7. Cover enchiladas with the sauce and top with remaining cheese.
8. Bake 20–25 minutes, until sauce is bubbly. Remove and let cool 5 minutes.
9. Top with remaining spring onions and serve.

Chicken Florentine Artichoke Bake

Serves 50–60.

48 ounces whole wheat fusilli or bowtie pasta
6 small onions, chopped
6 tablespoons butter
12 eggs
7 1/2 cups milk
2 tablespoons dried italian seasoning
1 1/2–2 teaspoons crushed red pepper (optional)
12 cups chopped cooked chicken
12 cups shredded cheese
2 32-ounce jars artichoke hearts, drained and quartered
2 large Costco bags spinach (about 15 cups), steamed and drained thoroughly
3 cups oil-packed sundried tomatoes, drained and chopped
3 cups grated parmesan cheese
3 cups soft breadcrumbs
1 tablespoon paprika
2/3 cup melted butter

1. Preheat oven to 350 degrees F (177 degrees C). Cook pasta and drain.
2. In a medium skillet, sauté onion in butter until tender, then set aside.
3. In bowl, whisk together eggs, milk, seasoning, salt, and red pepper. Stir in chicken, cheese, artichokes, spinach, tomatoes, 1 1/2 cups parmesan, cooked pasta, and onion.
4. Transfer to six 9x13-inch baking dishes and bake covered for 20 minutes.
5. In small bowl, combine remaining 1 1/2 cups parmesan cheese, breadcrumbs, paprika, and melted butter. Sprinkle over pasta.
6. Bake uncovered 10 minutes or until golden.

Oriental Chicken Salad

Serves 50–60.

Salad Ingredients

1 cup toasted sesame seeds
1 large bag Costco chicken breasts, boiled and broken up
1 cup slivered almonds
8 heads cabbage, shredded
16 green onions with tops, sliced
8 packages ramen noodles, broken up

Dressing Ingredients

1 cup sugar
3 tablespoons salt
1 1/2 cups vinegar
4 cups olive oil
4 teaspoons pepper

1. Evenly combine all salad ingredients in several bowls.
2. Whirl all dressing ingredients in blender.
3. Pour dressing over salad, and mix to combine.
4. Refrigerate overnight or for several hours before serving.

Everyday Meatloaf

Serves 50–60.

Meatloaf Ingredients

4 cups dry breadcrumbs
6 cups milk
9 pounds (4 kilograms) ground beef
12 beaten eggs
1 1/2 cups grated onion
2 tablespoons salt
1 teaspoon pepper
1 tablespoon sage

Sauce Ingredients

1 cup brown sugar
2 teaspoons nutmeg
2 cups ketchup
2 tablespoons dry mustard

Optional Sides

Steamed salad potatoes
Prepared frozen peas

1. Soak breadcrumbs in milk.
2. Add meat, eggs, onion, and seasonings; mix well.
3. Form into four greased aluminum pans (you can find these at Costco).
4. Combine all sauce ingredients well.
5. Cover meat with sauce and bake at 350 degrees F (177 degrees C) for 1 hour.
6. Serve with steamed salad potatoes and prepared frozen peas, as desired.

Cornbread

Serves 50–60. Goes well with the Lentil Vegetable Soup or Quinoa and Sweet Potato Chili.

4 cups butter
2 2/3 cups sugar
16 eggs, well beaten
8 cups buttermilk
4 teaspoons baking soda
8 cups flour
8 cups cornmeal
4 teaspoons salt

1. Melt the butter in a large saucepan.
2. Add sugar and mix well.

3. Add all other ingredients; mix well.
4. Bake in greased pans for 30 minutes at 375 degrees F (190 degrees C).

Easy Corn on the Cob for a Big Crowd

Here's a game changer for serving corn on the cob for a big family reunion or Labor Day barbecue. This is a great idea from @r2sense.

Ears of corn
Water for boiling

1. Shuck as many ears of corn as you need for your party and put them in a large, clean picnic cooler.
2. An hour or two hours before the party, boil enough water to cover the corn, pour it over the corn, and close the lid.
3. Drain the cooler when your guests arrive, and close the lid until ready to serve! Voila! You have perfectly cooked corn!

ACKNOWLEDGMENTS

With continued gratitude to my publisher, Christopher Robbins at Familius, who believes in family as much as I do; David Miles and Brooke Jorden, my brilliant designers; and Leah Welker and Sarah Echard, my terrific editors.

Undying thanks go my husband, Richard, who wisely advised me and heroically took care of me and himself during this challenging and time-consuming project. To the expert editing, advice, additions to the manuscript, and support of Charity Wright, Saydi Shumway, Shawni Pothier, Saren Loosli, Julie Eyre, Kristi Eyre, Anita Eyre, and Aja Eyre, which will always be treasured. Much gratitude goes to my best (and only) sister, Lenna, who helped me research the lives of our grandmothers. Thanks to our gifted photographer Eli for the cover picture (along with producing those adorable kids). And a great big shout out to my computer-genius son Josh, who always calmed my fears and fixed my technical difficulties!

The personal stories and ideas contributed by so many unique and wonderful friends have made this book so much broader and better. Those friends are Bobbi Snow, Bonnie Lloyd, Margaret Archibald, Sara Boyer, Jane Pugh, Jean Bentley, Marsha Richards, Eve Dayton, Margaret Broadbent, Vicki Smith, Polly Willardson, Lana Foy, Kathy Clayton, Athelia Wooley, Dagmar Roemer, Margaret Mackey, Carolyn Gardner, Elaine Dalton, Leslie Oswald, Karen Johnsen, Jan Zwick, Barbara Soulier, Tricia Stoker, Anne Stewart, and Julie Romney.

And with special gratitude to all the contributors to "Recipes for a Crowd" in the Appendix. Some are favorite family recipes and reunion recipes. Thanks to Saren and Shawni for recording great recipes on their blogs and for Saydi's fabulous recipes and expert advice. Thanks to other family members and friends who contributed. Kudos to contributors @r2sense and Tess Wade for sharing their excellent recipes for big crowds! Special love to Charity for editing and organizing the recipes.

This was a labor of love for my posterity and to you incredible grandmothers out there who are making a difference every day!

About the Author

Linda Eyre is a *New York Times* #1 bestselling author whose writing career has spanned four decades and whose books have sold in the millions. Linda and her husband, Richard, have appeared on virtually all major national talk shows, including *Oprah* and *Today*, and have seen their books translated into a dozen languages. They write a syndicated weekly newspaper column and currently spend most of their time traveling and speaking to audiences throughout the world on families, parenting, and life-balance (and trying to keep up with their thirty-one [and counting] grandchildren). The Eyres' vision statement is "Fortify families by celebrating commitment, popularizing parenting, bolstering balance, validating values, and glorifying grandparenthood."

About Familius

Visit Our Website: www.familius.com

Join Our Family

There are lots of ways to connect with us! Subscribe to our newsletters at www.familius.com to receive uplifting daily inspiration, essays from our Pater Familius, a free ebook every month, and the first word on special discounts and Familius news.

Get Bulk Discounts

If you feel a few friends and family might benefit from what you've read, let us know and we'll be happy to provide you with quantity discounts. Simply email us at orders@familius.com.

Connect

- Facebook: www.facebook.com/paterfamilius
- Twitter: @familiustalk, @paterfamilius1
- Pinterest: www.pinterest.com/familius
- Instagram: @familiustalk

The most important work you ever do will be within the walls of your own home.